Leadership in English Language Education

D0220286

Leadership in English Language Education: Theoretical Foundations and Practical Skills for Changing Times presents both theoretical approaches to leadership and practical skills leaders in English language education need to be effective. Practical skills are discussed in detail, providing readers with the opportunity to acquire new skills and apply them in their own contexts. The book is organized around three themes:

- The roles and characteristics of leaders
- Skills for leading
- ELT leadership in practice

Leadership theories and approaches from business and industry are applied to and conclusions are drawn for English language teaching in a variety of organizational contexts, including intensive English programs in English-speaking countries, TESOL departments in universities, ESL programs in community colleges, EFL departments in non-English-speaking countries, adult education programs, and commercial ELT centers and schools around the world. This is an essential resource for all administrators, teachers, academics, and teacher candidates in English language education.

MaryAnn Christison is a Professor in the Department of Linguistics and the Department of Teaching and Learning at the University of Utah. She teaches courses in the MA and PhD graduate programs and coordinates the ESL endorsement program. She was TESOL President 1997–1998 and serves on the Board of Trustees of The International Research Foundation (TIRF) for English Language Education.

Denise E. Murray is Emeritus Professor at Macquarie University, Australia, and San José State University, United States. She was Department Chair for nine years, director of a national center for six years, and TESOL President. Her research interests and teaching include leadership and management in ELT.

ESL & Applied Linguistics Professional Series
Eli Hinkel, Series Editor

Cultures, Contexts, and World Englishes
Kachru/Smith

International English in its Sociolinguistic Contexts
Towards a Socially Sensitive EIL Pedagogy
McKay/Bokhosrt-Heng

Leadership in English Language Education
Theoretical Foundations and Practical Skills for Changing Times
Christison/Murray, Eds.

Gesture
Second Language Acquisition and Classroom Research
McCafferty/Stam, Eds.

Idioms
Description, Comprehension, Acquisition, and Pedagogy
Liu

Building a Validity Argument for the Text of English as a Foreign Language™
Chappelle/Enright/Jamison, Eds.

Teaching Chinese, Japanese, and Korean Heritage Students
Curriculum Needs, Materials, and Assessments
Kondo-Brown/Brown, Eds.

Chicano-Anglo Conversations
Truth, Honesty, and Politeness
Youmans

English L2 Reading
Getting to the Bottom, Second Edition
Birch

Visit **www.Routledge.com/Education** for additional information on titles in the ESL & Applied Linguistics Professional Series

Leadership in English Language Education

Theoretical Foundations and Practical Skills for Changing Times

Edited by
MaryAnn Christison and
Denise E. Murray

Routledge
Taylor & Francis Group

NEW YORK AND LONDON

First published 2009
by Routledge
711 Third Ave, New York, NY 10017

Simultaneously published in the UK
by Routledge
2 Park Square, Milton Park, Abingdon, Oxon OX14 4RN

Routledge is an imprint of the Taylor & Francis Group, an informa business

Typeset in Perpetua and Gill Sans by Keystroke
Keystroke, 28 High Street, Tettenhall, Wolverhampton

Acknowledgement is made to the following for permission to reprint previously
published materials:

Geert Hofstede for tables from pages 107–8, 169–70, 244–5, 318 and 366 of
Culture's consequence (2nd ed.). Thousand Oaks, CA: Sage. Copyright 2001.
Adapted with permission of Geert Hofstede.

John Wiley & Sons, Inc for adaptation of pages 250–271 of *Leadership IQ*. by
Emmett C. Murphy. Copyright 1996. Reprinted with permission of John Wiley
& Sons, Inc

Robert Bruce (author), Russell Jeffrey (illustrator) and HarperCollins Publishers
for figure from page 169 of *Creating your strategic future*. Copyright 2000.
Adapted with permission of HarperCollins Publishers.

Library of Congress Cataloging in Publication Data
Leadership in English language education : theoretical foundations and
practical skills for changing times / edited by MaryAnn Christison, Denise E. Murray .
p. cm. – (ESL & applied linguistics professional series)
1. English language–Study and teaching. 2. English language–Study and
teaching–Foreign speakers. I. Christison, MaryAnn. II. Murray, Denise E.
LB1576.L3737 2008
428'.0071–dc22
2007046154

ISBN10: 0–805–86310–9 (hbk)
ISBN10: 0–805–86311–7 (pbk)

ISBN13: 978–0–805–86310–9 (hbk)
ISBN13: 978–0–805–86311–6 (pbk)

Contents

Notes on Contributors

Neil J. Anderson is a Humanities Professor of Linguistics and English Language at Brigham Young University, Provo, Utah, USA. He also serves as the Coordinator of the English Language Center. His research interests include ELT leadership, second language reading and language learning strategies. Professor Anderson served as TESOL President 2001–2002 and is also on the Board of Trustees for The International Research Foundation (TIRF) for English Language Education.

Kathleen M. Bailey received her PhD from UCLA. She is a Professor of Applied Linguistics at the Monterey Institute of International Studies. In 1998–1999 she was the president of TESOL.

MaryAnn Christison is a Professor in the Department of Linguistics and the Department of Teaching and Learning at the University of Utah. She teaches courses in the MA and PhD graduate programs and coordinates the ESL endorsement program. She was TESOL President 1997–1998 and serves on the Board of Trustees of The International Research Foundation (TIRF) for English Language Education.

Mark A. Clarke is Professor of Language, Literacy, and Culture, School of Education, University of Colorado Denver, where he teaches courses in the MA and PhD programs. His primary research interest is systems and systems change; he is a co-director of the research Lab of Learning and Activity, which is engaged in a large-scale, multi-level action research project on teacher professional development. He has lived and worked in Latin America and the Middle East. He has served as President of Colorado TESOL and Second Vice President of TESOL.

Andy Curtis is the Director of the English Language Teaching Unit and an Associate Professor in the Faculty of Education, both at the Chinese University of Hong Kong. He received his MA and his PhD from the University of York, UK.

Julian Edge is a Senior Lecturer in Education (TESOL) at the University of Manchester, U.K. His major professional and academic interest is in teachers' collaborative self-development and the language that facilitates it.

Kristen Lindahl is a Linguistics PhD student at the University of Utah, specializing in L2 Teacher Education. Having taught in public schools, Ms. Lindahl is currently the ELL specialist for a U.S. No Child Left Behind (NCLB) grant with the University.

Colin McNaught has many years experience in language center management, as a co-founder of the Australian College of English in Sydney and later with the National Centre for English Language Teaching and Research, Macquarie University. He was a director of the accreditation agency NEAS Ltd from 1992 to 2005.

Denise E. Murray is Emeritus Professor at Macquarie University, Australia and San José State University, United States. She was department Chair for nine years, director of a national center for six years, and TESOL President. Her research interests and teaching include leadership and management in ELT.

David Nunan is President and Dean of the Graduate School of Education of Anaheim University, CA. He has published over 100 books and articles in the areas of curriculum development, classroom research and teacher education. He is a Past President of TESOL and currently serves on the Board of Trustees of The International Research Foundation for English Language Education.

Juliet Padernal completed a Bachelor in Secondary Education (Biology/Mathematics) and the MA in English (TESL) at Silliman University, the Philippines, where she has been teaching for seventeen years and is currently the English language programs coordinator. She is a Leadership Fellow of the United Board for Christian Higher Education in Asia.

Fredricka L. Stoller is a Professor of English and teaches in the MA TESL and PhD in Applied Linguistics programs at Northern Arizona University. Her professional interests include content-based instruction, reading, disciplinary writing, and program administration.

Jaala A. Thibault received her Masters degree in TESOL from Monterey Institute of International Studies. She has taught English as a United States Peace Corps volunteer in both China (2002–2003) and Micronesia (2003–2004).

Preface

Interest in leadership in English language education is burgeoning with English language educators from many different contexts writing articles, offering workshops, developing certificate programs, and selecting leadership as a topic of research. This recent surge of interest in leadership is particularly exciting for us since we have been involved in leadership for several decades and are thrilled to see that more English language educators wish to give leadership a more purposeful and academic focus.

This volume entitled *Leadership in English Language Education: Theoretical Foundations and Practical Skills for Changing Times* is designed for a wide range of individuals interested in leadership in English language education. We want the volume to be useful for anyone interested in learning more about leadership. It is not only for individuals who are already in leadership positions, but also for those interested in holding leadership positions in the future, as well as for students who are studying in graduate and undergraduate programs to secure their professional degrees and certificates in English language education and wish to learn more about leadership for themselves and to consider it as a focus for research.

In addition to the wide range of interests in leadership that are represented in English language education, we also had to consider the many different contexts for leadership. English language teaching takes place in environments all over the world—with children, adolescents, and adults, with beginning to advanced level students, in public and private schools, in higher education, and in non-academic programs.

Creating a volume on leadership that had something for everyone, and still managed to be focused and useful, has been a challenge. We initiated the design for the contents of this volume by focusing on what all of the different individuals interested in leadership have in common, regardless of the contexts in which they work. What our research led us to conclude was that effective leadership is essential for the ultimate achievement of goals and objectives, no matter who the leader is or in what context the leader might work. In order to address the wide range of needs that our readership may represent, we have tried to answer the following questions in designing this book: What are the roles and characteristics of effective leaders? What are the essential skills for leading? What are some examples of effective leadership in practice? These questions ultimately became the organizational foci for each of the three parts to this volume.

In the Introduction to this book, we introduce theories of leadership, including transactional, transformational, Total Quality Management, situational, and values-based leadership, as well as reviewing the concept of complexity theory and leadership and other relevant research, particularly as the research relates to leadership skills. In addition, we offer a more complete definition of instructional leadership by identifying four roles that are crucial to leadership in educational contexts.

In Part I, "The Roles and Responsibilities of Leaders," we provide leaders and prospective leaders with the background and theoretical foundations necessary to create the sensitivity to and appropriate mindset for the development of leadership skills, focusing largely on the soft skills of leadership. We also focus on the different roles leaders assume and the characteristics of effective leaders. In Part II, "Skills for Leading," we offer six important chapters that focus on the creation of specific, technical skills necessary for effective leadership. In Part III, "ELT Leadership in Practice," we present three research and reflective chapters that demonstrate leadership in practice in the field of English language education in different contexts.

Part I begins with Chapter 1, in which Denise Murray talks about the ecology of leadership and explores two dissecting dimensions of leadership—the intercultural reality of the context in which we work and the changing nature of the work we do. In Chapter 2, MaryAnn Christison and Denise E. Murray present the concept of leadership IQ and suggest how teachers might develop their leadership IQ by working with eight workleader roles. In Chapter 3, MaryAnn Christison and Kristen Lindahl discuss leadership in U.S. public schools to include the concept of teachers as leaders. The concepts presented in this chapter provide valuable insights for leaders in all environments. Fredricka Stoller moves our thinking about leadership out of the box in Chapter 4 by helping us understand the importance of change and innovation in developing effective leadership skills. In Chapter 5, Denise E. Murray and MaryAnn Christison focus on the concept of emotional intelligence and its importance in the development of one's capacity as a leader. In Chapter 6, Andy Curtis discusses a non-traditional view of leadership, the concept of leading from the periphery. Part I concludes with Chapter 7, in which Neil Anderson presents the idea that leadership is not about position. Anderson moves our thinking about leadership away from the ideas associated with leaders being recognized because of position and focuses our attention on recognizing leaders by their behaviors.

Part II includes six chapters that focus on the development of specific technical skills for leaders. In Chapter 8, Denise E. Murray and MaryAnn Christison focus on models of organizational structure, such as functional, divisional, and matrix, and explore how leaders at all levels in an organization have responsibility for the maintenance, repair, and adaptation of the organization to its changing environment. Denise E. Murray and MaryAnn Christison focus Chapter 9 on strategic planning and offer specific activities for helping leaders develop the necessary skills to plan for the future. In Chapters 10 and 11, Colin McNaught teaches us about ensuring quality programs and managing performance of staff. Julian Edge and Mark A. Clarke offer leaders a toolkit for building effective leadership skills in Chapter 12. In Chapter 13, MaryAnn Christison and Denise

E. Murray talk about how to get individuals to work together in order to create effective teams.

In Part III, Chapter 14, Denise E. Murray and MaryAnn Christison present the results of their own research on the development of leadership IQ among English language educators in many different environments. In Chapter 15, Kathleen M. Bailey, David Nunan, and Jaala A. Thibault present their research on how leadership changes leaders. Finally, in Chapter 16, Juliet Padernal offers her personal experience with the concept of developing skills as a servant leader through cooperative development.

In order to make the book as accessible as possible to a wide range of readers (both familiar and unfamiliar with the content) and to make certain that the key concepts from each chapter are highlighted, the authors of each chapter have created tasks for the reader. The tasks appear in boxed text within the chapters. Chapters have a varying number of tasks, depending on the detail involved in the chapter and the goals the author has in mind for the specific content. The tasks provide the reader with an opportunity to check for understanding and to reflect on the information being presented. If the material is familiar to you and you feel confident in your abilities in this area, you may opt to simply read the task or skip it altogether. If the material is new to you and you need additional time to work with new concepts, the tasks are there to help you focus.

The book was designed by the editors. Although this is an edited volume, the editors themselves have written nine of the 16 chapters in the book—over half of the book. For the remainder of the chapters, the editors invited authors, colleagues, and leaders they admire to write specific chapters on topics on which they are known to have expertise. We believe this approach has created a cohesive and unique edited volume, much as if the entire book had been written by a single author, but with the benefit of many different views and perspectives. It has been such a pleasure working on this volume. Leadership is very near and dear to the work we do as English language professionals, and it is heartening to see the subject receive the serious academic focus in the field of English language education that it deserves.

Acknowledgments

We would like to acknowledge and thank our acquisitions editor at Lawrence Erlbaum/ Education Routledge/Taylor & Francis, Naomi Silverman, for having faith in the concept we presented to her and for agreeing to publish the work. We appreciate Eli Hinkel for agreeing to include this volume in her *ESL & Applied Linguistics Professional Series*. We would also like to thank Mary Hillemeier, Editorial Assistant, for her invaluable work on the manuscript. A special recognition and thanks go to the wonderful authors in this volume. We thank you for responding to our requests for chapters, for meeting deadlines, and for your patience with our editing and suggested changes in your amazing work. This volume would not be possible without your expertise and support. Last, but not least, we would like to thank and acknowledge our families, particularly, Bill Murray and Buzz Palmer, for their continued support of our academic work even when our commitments have meant less free time and more personal travel and family trips with laptop computers. We appreciate your love, good humor, and unwavering support.

MaryAnn Christison
University of Utah

Denise E. Murray
Macquarie University

Introduction

MaryAnn Christison and Denise E. Murray

Leadership or Management?

The terms leadership and management are often used interchangeably, as though they are synonyms. Other scholars have set them up as dichotomies, as the following quotations indicate:

> Leaders do the right thing; managers do things right. (Drucker, 1974)
>
> Leaders master the context; managers surrender to it. (Bennis, 2003)
>
> Managers cope with complexity; leaders cope with change. (Kotter, 1990)

However, "Organizational effectiveness . . . is dependent upon both capable leadership and sound management" (McCaffery, 2004, p. 58). The two concepts are complementary, with differences between them defined by the characteristics of what each represents. For example, leaders set visions, motivate staff, mold teams, and empower people, while managers budget, staff, administer, and create systems and structures. McCaffery provides the differences in perceptions of managers and leaders in the United Kingdom and lists the different challenges faced by the two roles; Kotter devotes his entire book to differentiating between the two roles. Leaders in educational environments, especially those who administer programs and head departments or centers, are expected to both lead and manage.

In this volume, we will be focusing on leadership, on the qualities and activities of those in leadership roles and those who lead without being in a formal positional role of management or leadership. However, throughout the volume, we will be working on the assumption that in English language education, most people with leadership responsibilities will also need to manage the affairs of their department, center, or section.

Leaders and Theories of Leadership

There have been many different theories of leadership and many individual theorists that have influenced our thinking about leadership in the field of English language education. In writing and selecting the chapters for this volume, we have drawn broadly on ideas represented in theories prominent in politics, business, and education. These theories include transactional, transformational, instructional, personal, servant, situational, change, and instructional leadership, leadership IQ,[1] and total quality management. Although not all of these theories are reviewed in this work, we want to acknowledge their influence in the development of our own ideas about leadership. The theorists include Kenneth Blanchard, James Burns, Stephen Covey, Edward Deming, Peter Drucker, Robert Greenleaf, Kenneth Leithwood, Paul Hersey, Randy Pohlman and his colleagues, Robert Manzano, Emmett Murphy, among others. They have provided us with a foundation and with reference points for thinking about our own roles as leaders.

Transactional and Transformational Leadership

Perhaps the two most prominent theories of leadership that have been given the most attention in the field of English language education are transactional and transformational leadership. We present these two theories of leadership together even though they are very different in their approach. Both theories stem from the work of James Burns (1978). Although Burns' original ideas stemmed from his work in politics, his ideas are equally applicable to education. According to Bass and Avolio (1994), there are three forms of transactional leadership. In the first form of transactional leadership the focus is on maintaining the status quo. This involves setting standards and waiting for major problems to occur before responding. In the second form of transactional leadership, leaders actually pay attention to issues and monitor behavior, but they do not believe in taking risks or in demonstrating personal initiative. In the final form of transactional leadership, there are rewards and recognition for accomplishments. The leader also clarifies desired outcomes, provides suggestions, and gives feedback and praise. All three forms of transactional leadership place an emphasis on maintenance of the status quo to varying degrees. While there is more involvement in the management process with the third form of transactional leadership, the focus is still on how to maintain the status quo. It is easy to see these forms of leadership in the administration of English language and teaching programs in establishing standards, monitoring behavior, determining how to meet desired outcomes, and interacting with personnel in order to give effective feedback.

In transformational leadership, individuals are transformed in some way, and they produce results beyond their expectations (Bass, 1985; Bass and Avolio, 1994; Burns, 1978). This form of leadership is favored over any of the three forms of transactional leadership. Bass states that there are four factors that characterize the behavior of transformational leaders. These factors are: (1) individual consideration (i.e., giving personal attention to individuals, particularly the individuals who may not be getting much attention or who may be overlooked); (2) intellectual stimulation (i.e., helping individuals to think of old problems in new ways); (3) inspirational motivation (i.e., communicating high performance expectations to individuals); and (4) idealized influence (i.e., modeling behavior that is exemplary). Leithwood (Leithwood et al.,

1999) extended this model into education, noting that the four characteristics of transformational leaders are essential qualities of school principals as well. We have noticed these four qualities of leaders and the influence of the ideas from transformational leadership in many different administrators and leaders in English language education throughout the world, from the Americas to Europe and from the Middle East to Asia. We see leaders offering personal attention to staff and faculty, modeling the behaviors they want to see in others, providing intellectual stimulation, and inspiring others.

Covey (1990, p. 254) identifies the characteristics of each type of leadership as described in Table 0.1. A large body of research literature provides evidence that transformational leadership is more effective than transactional leadership because it

Table 0.1 Transformational vs. Transactional Leadership

Transformational Leadership	Transactional Leadership
Builds on man's [sic] need for meaning	Builds on man's [sic] need to get a job done and to make a living
Is preoccupied with purposes and values, morals, and ethics	Is preoccupied with power and position, politics, and perks
Transcends daily affairs	
Is oriented toward meeting long-term goals without compromising human values and principles	Is mired in daily affairs
	Is short-term and hard data-oriented
Separates causes and symptoms and works at prevention	Confuses causes and symptoms and concerns itself more with treatment than prevention
Values profit as the basis of growth	Focuses on tactical issues
Is proactive, catalytic, and patient	Relies on human relations to lubricate human interactions
Focuses more on missions and strategies for achieving them	Follows and fulfills role expectations by striving to work effectively within current systems
Makes full use of human resources	
Identifies and develops new talent	Supports structures and systems that reinforce the bottom-line, maximize efficiency, and guarantee short-term profits
Recognizes and rewards significant contributions	
Designs and redesigns jobs to make them meaningful and challenging	
Releases human potential	
Models love	
Leads out in new directions	
Aligns internal structures and systems to reinforce overarching values and goals	

"broadens and elevates the interests of followers, generating awareness and acceptance among the followers of the purposes and mission of the group and/or the organization" (Den Hartog et al., 1999, p. 223) and "can ultimately transform organizations" (ibid., p. 224).

Servant-Leadership

Servant-leadership is a term that is associated with the work of Robert Greenleaf (1970, 1977). Greenleaf believed that in order to be an effective leader, one must have a keen desire to help other people. His perspective is in contrast to the transformational model of leadership that focuses on oversight and control. In order to be an effective servant-leader, the leader must be at the center of an organization and must have contact with all individuals within the organization and with all aspects of the organization. An effective servant-leader is focused on helping and nurturing those within the organization. The idea of servant-leadership has become an important component of the thinking of many leadership theorists (Covey, 1990; Spillane et al., 2001). In Chapter 16 Juliet Padernal talks specifically about her personal experiences in developing servant-leadership skills through a cooperative development project in her workplace.

Instructional Leadership

In their book, *Changing Leadership for Changing Times*, Leithwood, Jantzi, and Steinback (1999), state that the term *instructional leadership* is one of the most frequently mentioned educational leadership concepts in North America; yet it is not well defined. In an attempt to provide some clarification on this concept, Smith and Andrews (1989) identify four roles of instructional leaders. These roles are: (1) resource provider; (2) instructional resource; (3) communicator; and (4) visible presence. Resource providers see that teachers have the materials and facilities necessary to do their jobs. As an instructional resource, they support the instructional needs of teachers by modeling desired behaviors, participating in programs and classes, and consistently giving priority to instructional concerns. As a communicator, the instructional leader is able to articulate clearly important goals to teachers, parents, students, and the community. As a visible presence, an instructional leader is highly accessible to students, staff, and teachers.

Other researchers, such as Blase and Blase (1999) and Glickman, Gordan, and Ross-Gordon (1995) have proposed other qualities for instructional leaders as well as a list of general functions of instructional leaders. One might consider that instructional leadership is an extension of Burns' transformational leadership in that the focus is on developing skill as a leader as demonstrated through certain behaviors.

Total Quality Management

Total Quality Management (TQM) (Deming, 1986) is associated with the framework that was used in post-World War II Japan to help restore Japan's manufacturing base (see also Chapter 10 for further information on TQM). It has also been used successfully in such businesses as Xerox in order to improve on the quality of their products and services (Sosik & Dionne, 1997). Central to TQM are 14 principles that define behaviors of effective leaders. In order to make these principles more manageable and useful to practitioners, Waldman (1993) organized the 14 principles into five basic factors: change agency, teamwork, continuous improvement, trust building, and eradication of short-term goals. Change agency has to do with behaviors that leaders exhibit to bring about change. Teamwork has to with how leaders work to establish teams and work with them. An effective leader must always invite continuous improvement into an organization and keep improvement the focus of all employees. Trust building refers to the fact that leaders are responsible for building a climate of trust, a "win–win" environment (Covey, 1991). According to Covey, leaders must exhibit integrity, honesty, and openness in order to develop such a climate. The final factor, the eradication of short-term goals, refers to the elimination of goals based on quotas (Deming, 1986). Deming believes that it is important to focus on long-term goals and to keep one's perspective regarding where you want to be in the future.

Situational Leadership

In situational leadership (Blanchard & Hersey, 1996), the leader adapts his/her leadership behavior to the "maturity" of the followers and their ability to perform specific tasks. Four leadership styles are presented relative to how willingness intersects with ability. Followers may be unwilling and unable to perform a task. In this case, the leader directs the followers' actions without much concern for personal relationships. When followers are unable but willing to perform a task, the leader interacts with the followers in a friendly manner but still provides specific direction. When followers are able but unwilling to perform a task, the leader works to persuade followers to engage in the task. When followers are able and willing to perform the task, the leader leaves the execution of the task to the followers with little or no interference. An effective leader is skilled in all four styles and can adjust his/her behavior accordingly.

Values-Based Leadership

A number of theorists have included the values a leader holds as an important factor in effective leadership. Covey (1990), for example, focuses on the character of the leader, in particular the leader's commitment to continuous growth, both internal and external. For him, transformational leadership is value-centered, while transactional leadership is event-centered. Bennis and Nanus (1997) and Bennis (2003) identify four specific characteristics of effective leadership. Leaders must be able to communicate effectively with others and engage them in a shared vision. Second, they must be able to communicate a sense of purpose, a positive sense of self, and self-confidence. Third, leaders must live by a strong moral code and believe in the higher good. Finally, they must be able to adapt to the pressures of change. Research conducted by Pohlman (Pohlman &

Gardiner, 2000) and his associates at the Wayne Huizenga Graduate School of Business has found that leaders of learning, innovative, proactive organizations consider eight value drivers in their leadership, management and decision-making: external cultural values, organizational cultural values, individual employee values, customer values, supplier values, third-party values, owner values, and competitor values. They contrast this perspective with the short-term profit perspective prevalent in many businesses. These theorists and researchers all agree that a focus on learning and values of staff, customers, and suppliers creates value-added programs, products, and services, which in turn lead to effective (and profitable) organizations.

Complexity Theory and Leadership

> Often the emergent nature of change as experienced by other members of the organization is overlooked. Change, instead, is treated as continuous, step-like, or even chaotic but with a definable scope and focus. The experienced sense of change—that the whole is bigger than the sum of the parts and than the patterns observed and felt are unexpected—is not captured.
>
> (Lissack, 1999, p. 12)

Most of the management science literature is based on Newtonian physics, that is, a linear, systematic world where parts add up to wholes and where change can be predicted and controlled. Newtonian physics provides effective explanations of closed systems, but not of open systems. We have found that insights from the new science indicate that organizations are in fact open systems and therefore the laws of Newtonian physics and the traditional ways we think about organizational behavior do not explain how organizations and the people who *are* in those organizations act (see, for example, Wheatley, 1999).

The new science identifies the following as characteristic of open systems. Open systems are:

- *non-linear, dynamic.* There is no cause–effect relationship. The pebble that results in an avalanche is often used to illustrate this characteristic. We don't know which pebble will be the one to start the avalanche. However, it is not actually that particular pebble that causes the avalanche; many millions of pebbles do.
- *chaotic, unpredictable, and sensitive to initial conditions.* Chaos is the point of complete randomness that complex nonlinear systems enter into irregularly and unpredictably. One small change in the initial condition can cause major changes throughout the system. Often the effect of a butterfly flapping its wings in one place and its effect on weather continents away is used to illustrate this characteristic.
- *fractal, not random, but recursive.* Fractals are basic patterning, which is not always observed, that form the organizing principle of a system. Ferns and trees, for example, have a simple branching pattern as their basic organizing principle. Such underlying patterns produce an infinite variety of trees and ferns.

- *adaptive and self-organizing*. Open systems don't respond passively to events; they turn what happens to their advantage. Evolution is an excellent example of this principle.
- *emergent*. Behavior emerges from interactions of components of the system and so we can't understand the whole by only examining its parts.

As a result of these characteristics of open systems such as organizations, and educational organizations in particular, "stability is only a chance, temporary phase. Planning innovative change then becomes impossible. Instead 'changeability' must be built into the organization" (Stacey, 1996). So, in English language education, we cannot control the variables, but we can be aware of unexpected consequences, understand the context in which we work, and also understand how staff might view change and its effects.

Leadership Skills

Over the past couple of decades, researchers and practitioners in a variety of fields have acknowledged the importance of the human element in the workplace (see Norman, 1993, for an early elaborated discussion of the role of humans in the machine age). They have shown the need for "soft skills" as well as "hard skills" for effective job performance. Soft skills, in the field of accounting, for example, have included communication skills, team work, and problem-solving, while hard skills include technical accounting practices such as business law, auditing, and assurance services or financial management.[2] National and international surveys of Chief Financial Officers (CFOs) have been conducted with varying results concerning the soft skills most desired by CFOs. One such study found CFOs rated the interpersonal skills of positive attitude and team skills as most important (Robert Half Finance, 2001).

In some settings, soft skills are referred to as generic skills or employability skills (Gibb, 2004; for example, Turner, 2002). Soft skills have become so important in accounting that universities advertise their teaching programs, highlighting the attention they pay to developing soft skills in their graduates. Software companies have developed programs for assessing soft skills in accounting and companies hiring accountants include soft skills as criteria in recruitment.

Within the ELT field, generic skills or employability skills are often stated as essential competencies for language learners, but little attention has been paid to their place in the ELT workforce, whether for teachers or manager leaders. Humes (2000), who studied the discourse of educational management, distinguished between what he called rational and emotional skills, the former referring to the language usually identified with economic rationalists, while the latter refers to the humanistic and developmental language more usually associated with education. For many educators, there is a tension between these two aspects, with some claiming that there is no place in education for the "rational." We take the position that both the soft skills and the technical skills are essential for effective leadership.

The Structure of the Book

The basic outline for this book originated with work that we, the editors, began almost
a decade ago while we were both serving in leadership positions within the same
professional organization and were also involved in leadership roles within our respective universities. At that time, both of us felt that it would have been useful to have had
all of the information that we have tried to put into this volume, available to us *before*
we assumed our roles in leadership and, at least, during our tenure in these roles. When
we discovered some important piece of information, we often commented on the fact
that it should be required reading for any person even considering a leadership role.
However, very few educators receive formal training in leadership development before
they take on leadership roles. Most of us are left to our own devices to acquire the
information and skills to help us be successful in our roles as leaders. Traditionally in
English language education, it has been the "school of hard knocks" that has helped us
acquire the information. We do not believe it should be this way. We can also learn from
research and from the leadership experiences of others; we need a growing body of
scholarship on educational leadership. With this impetus in mind, we began the initial
planning of this book.

   One of us (Denise) had taken courses in management/leadership in an attempt to
better understand her role as a leader. While these courses were based on work in the
world of business, she found them valuable and of relevance to leading in English
language education. So, the first step we took was to find out what research was available
to us on leadership. Since there has been little research done in education, we turned
our attention to the work that had been done in the business world. In this Introduction,
we provide an overview of research on leadership and leadership models that we have
found a valuable basis for our own thinking and work. This introduction is meant to
provide essential background for our thinking about leadership as an academic discipline, worthy of research and scholarly attention.

   Our next step was to begin planning for the content of the book. We began our
planning for this volume centered around the roles and responsibilities of leaders. From
our own experiences as leaders, both of us realized that effective leadership was about
developing both a knowledge base and the requisite skills. In this volume, therefore, we
focus Part I on the knowledge base for leadership, understanding the roles and responsibilities of leaders, and Part II on developing the skills for leading. We have also added
Part III, providing three specific examples of leadership skills in practice.

Notes

1   Leadership IQ will be dealt with extensively in Chapter 3.
2   This dichotomy between soft and hard skills can be found in many professional fields such
    as IT. We use accounting purely as illustrative.

References

Bass, B.M. (1985). *Leadership and performance beyond expectations*. New York: Free Press.

Bass, B.M. & Avolio, B.J. (1994). *Improving organizational effectiveness through transformational leadership*. Thousand Oaks, CA: Sage.

Bennis, W. (2003). *On becoming a leader*. New York: Basic Books.

Bennis, W., & Nanus, B. (1997). *Leaders: The strategies for taking charge* (2nd edn). New York: HarperBusiness.

Blase, J., & Blase, J. (1999). Principals' instructional leadership and teacher development: Teachers' perspectives. *Educational Administration Quarterly*, 35(3), 349–380.

Blanchard, K.H., & Hersey, P. (1996). Great ideas revisited. *Training and Development, 50*(1), 42–47.

Burns, J.M. (1978). *Leadership*. New York: Harper & Row.

Covey, S.R. (1990). *Principle-centered leadership*. Provo, UT: IPCL.

Covey, S.R. (1991). The taproot of trust. *Executive Excellence, 8*(12), 3–4.

Deming, W.E. (1986). *Out of the crisis*. Cambridge, MA: Massachusetts Institute of Technology.

Den Hartog, D., House, R.J., Hanges, P.J., & Ruiz-Quintanilla, S.A. (1999). Culture specific and cross-culturally generalizable implicit leadership theories: Are attributes of charismatic/transformational leadership universally endorsed? *Leadership Quarterly, 10*(2), 219–256.

Drucker, P. (1974). *Management tasks, responsibilities, practices*. London: Heinemann.

Gibb, J. (2004). *Generic skill in vocational education and training: Research readings*. Retrieved January 22, 2007, from http://www.ncver.edu.au/research/proj/nr 2200.pdf

Glickman, C.D., Gordan, S.P. & Ross-Gordan, J.M. (1995). *Supervision of instruction: A developmental approach*. 3rd edn. Boston: Allyn & Bacon.

Greenleaf, R.K. (1970). *The servant as leader*. Indianapolis: Robert K. Greenleaf Center for Servant-Leadership.

Greenleaf, R.K. (1977). *Servant leadership: A journey into the nature of legitimate power and greatness*. New York: Paulist Press.

Humes, W. (2000). The discourses of educational management. *Journal of Educational Enquiry, 1*(1), 35–53.

Kotter, J.P. (1990). *A force for change: How leadership differs from management*. New York: Free Press.

Leithwood, K., Jantzi, D., & Steinbach, R. (1999). *Changing leadership for changing times*. Philadelphia, PA: Open University Press.

Lissack, M.R. (1999). Complexity and management: It is more than jargon. In M.R. Lissack & H.P. Gunz (Eds.), *Managing complexity in organizations* (pp. 11–28). Westport, CT: Quorum Books.

McCaffery, P. (2004). *The higher education manager's handbook*. London: RoutledgeFalmer.

Norman, D.A. (1993). *Things that make us smart: Defending human attributes in the age of the machine*. Reading, MA: Addison-Wesley.

Pohlman, R.A., & Gardiner, G.S. (2000). *Value driven management*. New York: American Management Association.

Robert Half Finance. (2001). A new bottom line for next generation accountants. Retrieved January 22, 2007, from http://www.roberthalffinance.com/PressRoom?LOBName=RH&releaseID=96

Smith, W.F., & Andrews, R.L. (1989). *Instructional leadership: How principals make a difference*. Alexandria, VA: Association for Supervision and Curriculum Development.

Sosik, J.J. & Dionne, S.D. (1997). Leadership styles and Deming's behavior factors. *Journal of Business and Psychology, 11*(4), 447–462.

Spillane, J.P., Halverson, R., & Diamond, J.B. (2001). Investigating school leadership practice: A distributed perspective. *Educational Researcher, 30*(3), 23–28.

Stacey, R. (1996). *Complexity and creativity in organizations.* San Francisco: Berrett-Koehler.

Turner, D. (2002). Employability skills development in the United Kingdom. Retrieved January 21, 2007, from http://www.ncver.edu.au/research/proj/nr1004.pdf

Waldman, M. (1993). A theoretical consideration of leadership and TQM. *Leadership Quarterly, 4*(1), 65–79.

Wheatley, M.J. (1999). *Leadership and the new science: Discovering order in a chaotic world.* San Francisco: Berrett-Koehler.

Part I

The Roles and Responsibilities of Leaders

Introduction

Part I of this volume focuses on the roles and responsibilities of leaders. It contains seven chapters written by five different authors. In Chapter 1, Denise E. Murray discusses the ecology of leadership in ELT. The field of English language education is practiced in countries across the globe and any individual organization may have staff from a variety of different cultural backgrounds. Murray has invoked the metaphor of ecology to help us examine the context of our leadership in English language education so that we can better understand the contexts in which we do our work and how our work changes as a result of context.

In Chapter 2, MaryAnn Christison and Denise E. Murray present a model for leadership development known as Leadership IQ, a model that focuses the reader on eight specific roles associated with effective leadership. The authors also provide readers with an opportunity to determine their own specific leadership IQ by taking a questionnaire that is directly tied to the model of leadership IQ model they present.

In Chapter 3, MaryAnn Christison and Kristen Lindahl discuss leadership in U.S. public school settings. They focus on presenting the results from a meta-analysis conducted on school leadership and on the characteristics of effective leadership that the model presents. In addition, they discuss sustainable leadership—how to maintain effective leadership over time when school leaders constantly change. They tie sustainable leadership to the development of teachers as leaders. The concept of teachers as leaders has become not so much an innovation in education, but a necessity for effectively improving and sustaining current school leadership.

In Chapter 4, Fredricka L. Stoller focuses on an important role for leaders, that of the innovator. She discusses innovation as a hallmark of effective leadership. She does this by distinguishing change from innovation, making the point that innovation typically results from deliberate efforts to bring about improvements. She discusses the complex nature of innovations, the symbiotic relationship between top-down and bottom-up innovations, impetuses for innovation, characteristics of more easily adopted innovations, and the cycles of the innovation diffusion process. In addition, she offers leaders 12 guiding principles to inspire innovation in English language education.

Demonstrating emotionally intelligent behavior is an important role for leaders. In Chapter 5, Denise E. Murray and MaryAnn Christison discuss why the concept of Emotional Intelligence (EI) is important for effective leadership in the volatile, unpredictable world of English language education. The authors believe that EI is a key competence for successful leadership; indeed, they believe it is key for star performance for all personnel. In this chapter, Murray and Christison provide an overview of EI and explain how to develop it and how to plan for the professional development of staff.

Chapter 6 considers leadership in another way. In order to help the reader understand the different roles a leader can play, Andy Curtis revisits the well-established leadership positional metaphor of "leading from the front" by suggesting that this position may not necessarily be the most effective position for a leader in English language education. In his chapter Curtis considers an alternative role for leaders, the role of leading from the periphery. He devotes this chapter to exploring this metaphor and helping readers to see the value in this alternative positioning of leaders.

In addition to thinking about the skills associated with formal positions of leadership, we have addressed the skills that are essential for English language professionals in order to be successful and contributing members in the workplace, regardless of whether they hold formal positions of leadership or not. In the final chapter in Part I of this volume, Chapter 7, Neil J. Anderson explores the concept of leading from behind. The chapter is meant to encourage all English language professionals to think about leadership and focus the reader's attention away from leadership as defined by one's title or position and towards leadership as defined by one's behaviors.

Chapter 1

The Ecology of Leadership in English Language Education

Denise E. Murray

Introduction

The leadership theories discussed in the Introduction, apart from situational leadership, are all based on a sense that leadership is universal. Situational leadership, on the other hand, acknowledges that different people respond to different leadership styles. Just as leaders need to adapt to the variation among their staff, so too do leaders need to respond to the context of their organization. This is undoubtedly as true, if not more so, for the field of English language education, which is practiced in countries across the globe and where any individual organization may have staff from a variety of different cultural backgrounds. I have invoked the metaphor of ecology to help us examine the context of our leadership in English language education.

Ecology has been used as a metaphor to describe the situation of language maintenance and death and to describe the work of language teaching. Tying ecology to language was first suggested by Einar Haugen (1972) who defined language ecology as the study of interactions between any given language and its environment. Haugen states that linguistics should be more than descriptive; it should be concerned with the status of languages, functions, and attitudes and with a "typology of ecological classification, which will tell us something about where the language stands and where it is going in comparison with other languages of the world" (ibid., p. 337). Mühlhäusler has applied this concept to language teaching:

> When speaking of linguistic ecologies we focus on the number of languages, user groups, social practices and so forth that sustain this language ecology over longer periods of time. Language teaching involves the introduction of a new language into an existing language ecology.
>
> (1994, p. 123)

Murray (2001) has used it to describe the practice of English language teaching, discussing how, in introducing a new language into an existing ecology, the relationship between culture and language needs to be deconstructed.

It is a useful metaphor because, as defined in the *Australian Learners Dictionary*, it refers to "the study of how living things work and live together in the earth's environment"

(Candlin & Blair, 1997). Its etymology is from the Greek "icos" meaning "home," so it is the study of the system that supports and sustains the home. I use it here to evoke an image of leadership in English language teaching that is context-sensitive. The position I take in this chapter is that, while global issues impact on language and teaching programs and their management, all leadership is local in that it needs to be responsive to and support and sustain the environment (home) in which the leadership occurs. I will therefore focus on two aspects of the context that we need to study in order to determine how leaders work with others to create a sustainable organization—the challenge of constant change in our environment and the intercultural[1] nature of our work of English language education.

The Changing Context of English Language Education

> This is an era marked by rapid and spastic change. The problems of organizations are increasingly complex. There are too many ironies, polarities, dichotomies, dualities, ambivalences, paradoxes, confusions, contradictions, contraries and messes for any organization to deal with.
>
> (Bennis & Nanus, 1997, p. 8)

Their view reflects the work in chaos/systems theory such as that discussed in the introduction (Wheatley, 1999), which describes human organizations such as language and teaching programs as open, not closed, systems. Bennis and Nanus note the tremendous changes not only in the environment in which organizations operate, but also in "our view of what leadership is and who can exercise it" (1997, p. 3). They list three aspects of the environment that impact on organizations today: commitment, complexity, and credibility. In the early 1980s in the United States, many workers were not working to their full potential, which led managers to downsize, reducing work-forces by half or more. The remaining workers often had increased workloads, but did not object for fear they too would be fired. But, like the workers before them, they too are not committed to their workplace. Bennis and Nanus argue that this failure in commitment is because "leaders have failed to instill a vision, meaning, and trust in their followers" (ibid., p. 7).[2] Their second contextual condition, complexity, is often spoken of as constant change by other researchers. In this constantly changing, complex environment, traditional linear approaches to controlling the environment no longer work, an issue discussed in more detail below. Their third point is the almost uncontrolled desire for accountability, often led by media enquiries and scrutiny. This trend has led to uncertainty—of what workers are expected to do, of how they will be measured and of what will happen if they are found wanting.

In the educational arena, we have seen our context change in these same three ways. Many teachers feel that, with the casualization of their work (at least in Western countries), they have no desire to commit to an organization that is not committed to them. Even the lifelong employment of Japan Inc. has evaporated. Teachers' work has become more and more complex. Theories of language learning keep changing, text-book production brings new materials out each year, online learning has been imposed on many teachers, teachers are often expected to juggle instruction with counseling and curriculum development and marketing and many more activities. And teachers are being asked to become more accountable for their work. In some states in America, for example, merit pay is the norm and merit may include how well students perform on standardized tests. Walker (1999) notes that the English language education industry has become customer service-oriented and identifies one way of measuring an organization's accountability to its customers—a customer service questionnaire. He also cautions that questionnaires (and other measurement tools) found reliable in other industries may not be valid and reliable in English language education largely because of the cultural definitions of what constitutes customer service.

Bennis and Nanus (1997) describe four strategies leaders need to employ in order to lead in this new environment:

1   attention through vision
2   meaning through communication
3   trust through positioning
4   the development of self.

Leaders as Learners

A key element of their strategies is that effective organizations and leaders focus on learning. Murphy's empirical research (1996) demonstrates that leadership can be defined and measured as a form of intelligence, but it is an intelligence that is only activated through experiences, and then only if the person learns from those experiences (see Chapter 2 for an in-depth discussion of Murphy's theory). So then, leadership is essentially learning. To focus on the learning organization, Bennis and Nanus note that

> Leaders can provide the proper setting for innovative learning by designing open organizations in which participation and anticipation work together to extend the time horizons of decision-making, broaden their perspective, allow the sharing of assumptions and values and facilitate the development and use of new approaches.
> (1997, p. 198)

While Bennis and Nanus' research has identified activities that lead to effective leadership, Covey (1990) and other researchers (for example, Goleman, 1998), show that for effective leadership, leaders need to focus not on learning new skills, but on changing habits, developing virtues, learning basic disciplines, keeping promises, being faithful to vows, exercising courage, or being genuinely considerate of the feelings and convictions of others (adapted from Covey, 1990, p. xiv), a leadership style Covey has identified with transformational leadership, compared with a more transactional style, as discussed in the Introduction. Parry (1996), who also makes a distinction between transactional and transformational leadership, takes a slightly different approach from Bennis and Nanus, while still agreeing that leadership is about change and can be learned. He identifies mechanisms for establishing an organizational culture through visionary leadership, organizational structures that support that vision, and leaders who are considerate, stimulating, reward staff and provide effective role models for staff. There exists a long tradition of research into transformational leadership (see, for example, Bass, 1996), sometimes also referred to as charismatic or visionary leadership and its characteristics cluster around notions of articulating a realistic vision of the future, sharing that vision, stimulating staff intellectually, and caring for individual differences among staff.

Emotional Intelligence

Parry and Covey both refer to the importance of consideration for others, a concept taken up by other researchers. The work of Goleman (see Chapter 5 for an in-depth discussion of Goleman's theory and research) has drawn attention to the interpersonal dimension of leadership, what others have called interpersonal acumen or relational competence (Dickson et al., 2003). While the latter refer to the leader's ability to determine and understand underlying intentions in other people's behavior, Goleman goes further, by also focusing on the leader's ability to understand himself or herself. To understand other's intentions also requires understanding cultural differences. Therefore, implicit in the notion of emotional intelligence is intercultural competence. The two components of emotional competence are personal competence and social competence. The former, which determines how we manage ourselves, includes self-awareness, self-regulation and motivation; the latter, which determines how we handle relationships, includes empathy and social skills.

The Intercultural Space of English Language Teaching

In order to lead with emotional intelligence, create a vision for the organization, and position one's organization for change, leaders also need to understand the cultural context in which they work. The nature of English language teaching is, by definition, intercultural, whether it is a teacher and learners from the same cultural and linguistic background learning English or a multilingual teacher teaching learners from a variety of different linguistic and cultural backgrounds. The latter clearly involves the negotiation of meaning around the different cultures and languages in the classroom; the former also requires an understanding of the cultures in which the target language is used.

Additionally, our colleagues are often from a variety of different cultural backgrounds. Expatriates learn to work with local staff; immigrant teachers learn to work with longer-term residents. But, what do we mean by culture? Certainly not the culture as content view, where culture is the arts, music and other high culture features or the everyday activities such as fiestas, food and famous people. Rather, the position taken in this chapter is that culture is "the process by which people make sense of their lives, a process always involved in struggles over meaning and representation" (Pennycook, 1995, p. 47).

To teach language from such a view of culture requires viewing culture as dynamic, changing, and negotiated through interaction. Murray (2001), borrowing Liddicoat and Crozet's (2000) notion of "intercultural space" to describe the environment for English language teaching, proposes several strategies for creating such a space for language learners:

- explicit instruction in linguistic codes and text types for success;
- explicit instruction in the arbitrariness of and power attributed to different codes and text types;
- presentation of authentic culturally-specific language;
- focusing on intercultural communication rather than multicultural education;
- explicit instruction in the relationship between the culture of the first and second languages;
- learning how to relate to otherness.

This view of culture and these strategies equally apply to leaders in English language education. Because leadership is a cultural phenomenon, we would expect that cultural values of a society would be found in values ascribed to effective leadership. While there is no published research on the intercultural dimension of leadership in English language education, there is now a growing body of published research on effective leadership across cultures, much stemming from the seminal work of Hofstede (1990). Hofstede identified four dimensions of culture, based on extensive survey research within IBM internationally over 40 countries:

1   individualism–collectivism
2   masculinity–femininity
3   uncertainty avoidance
4   power (distance).

In later work, he has also identified a fifth dimension—future orientation.

Hofstede's work has been criticized on several grounds, such as being based on self-reported data (survey), being within one company (which might have its own cultural norm), and treating nations as appropriate units for cultural comparison (and thereby ignoring within-country variation). More recent work of the Global Leadership and Organizational Behavior Effectiveness (GLOBE) project, in which 60 countries are being studied to identify both universal and culturally-contingent leadership attributes and behaviors, is uncovering additional characteristics, or redefining some, and separating some of the concepts embedded in Hofstede's dimensions. However, Hofstede's framework is a useful tool for examining how culture may influence leadership, which

I will examine here, while also drawing on the published work from other research such as GLOBE. For Hofstede, culture is the "collective programming of the mind" (2001, p. 3), which includes shared values and "habitus," a system of permanent and transferable tendencies (ibid., p. 4). This definition contrasts with that of Pennycook since it takes culture as static and uncontested. Much of the management literature on the influence of culture on leadership behavior and workers' perceptions of effective leadership is based on Hofstede's definition.

From the survey data, Hofstede has been able to identify how nations rate on different combinations of the dimensions. So, for example, Australia is slightly more masculine, highly individualistic, has lower power distance and uncertainty avoidance compared with Thailand. By graphing nations on two dimensions, Hofstede is able to develop clusters of nations with similar characteristics. So, for example, for the dimensions of power distance and uncertainty avoidance, Australia clusters with New Zealand, Norway, the U.S., Canada, South Africa and the Netherlands, while Thailand clusters with Pakistan, Taiwan, Iran, and Ecuador. On the dimensions of power distance and individualism/collectivism, Australia clusters with the same group without South Africa and Norway, but including Great Britain. Thailand clusters with a large group of nations that have high power distance and are collectivist. If Hofstede's five dimensions provide a framework for characterizing national groups, what effect do these dimensions have for leadership? Hofstede identifies workplace behaviors for each of the dimensions, behaviors that affect the relationship between leaders and their staff.

Individualism–Collectivism Dimension

This dimension refers to the extent to which the individuals are embedded in their group. Collectivist societies have strong in-group and out-group memberships. Individualist societies have loosely knit social groupings and individuals are expected to take care of themselves. Table 1.1, which identifies some of the characteristics of the collectivist–individualist dimension in the workplace, is adapted from Hofstede (2001, pp. 244–245).

Individualist characteristics such as independence contribute to effective leadership in some cultures, but not others. Collectivists identify with their leaders and exhibit loyalty to their leader, as well as to the organization.

Table 1.1 Collectivist/Individualist Societies' Workplace Behavior

Low Individualist Societies	High Individualist Societies
Employees act in the interest of their in-group, not necessarily of themselves	Employees are supposed to act as "economic men"
Employer–employee relationship is basically moral, like a family link	Employer–employee relationship is that of a business deal in a "labor market"
Employee commitment to the organization is high	Employee commitment to the organization is low

Table 1.1 continued

Low Individualist Societies	High Individualist Societies
Treating friends better than others is normal and ethical	Treating friends better than others is nepotism and unethical
Belief in collective decisions	Belief in individual decisions
Innovations occur within existing networks	Innovations occur outside existing networks
Relationships with colleagues are cooperative for the in-group, but hostile towards the out-group	Relationships with colleagues do not depend on group identity
Personal relations more important than task organization	Task and organization are more important than personal relations
Rewards and incentives are more effective if given to in-groups	Rewards and incentives are more effective if given to individuals

Source: Adapted from Hofstede (2001).

Task 1.1

Consider the country and organization in which you work. Where does it fit along Hofstede's collectivist–individualist continuum?

Masculinity–Femininity Dimension

This dimension refers to values around warmth of social relationships and caring for the weak (feminism) compared with assertiveness and materialism (masculinity). Table 1.2, which identifies some of the characteristics of the masculine/feminine dimension, is adapted from Hofstede (2001, p. 318).

Table 1.2 Masculine–Feminine Societies' Workplace Behavior

Low Masculine Societies	High Masculine Societies
Work in order to live	Live in order to work
Managers are employees like others	Managers are culture heroes
Managers are expected to use intuition, deal with feelings, and seek consensus	Managers are expected to be decisive, firm, assertive, aggressive, competitive, just
More women are in management	Fewer women are in management
Managers hold modest career aspirations	Managers hold ambitious career aspirations

Table 1.2 continued

Low Masculine Societies	High Masculine Societies
Resolution of conflicts is through problem solving, compromise, and negotiation	Resolution of conflicts is through denying them or fighting until the best "man" wins
Preference is for smaller companies and fewer work hours	Preference is for larger companies and more pay
Successful managers are seen as having both male and female characteristics	Successful managers are seen as having solely male characteristics
Women leaders adapt their careers to their families' needs	Women leaders adapt their families to their career needs

Source: Adapted from Hofstede (2001).

While Hofstede claims that masculine cultures prefer leaders who are decisive and assertive, while feminine cultures prefer leaders who are intuitive and compromisers, other research does not necessarily support this view. A study comparing American (masculine culture) and Danish (feminine culture) workers from both cultures considered individualistic leaders as more effective and feminine leaders as more collegial (Helgstrand & Stulmacher, 1999). Because this dimension contains many different topics, the Global Leadership and Organizational Behavior Effectiveness (GLOBE) project has examined some of the sub-components separately—gender egalitarianism, assertiveness, performance orientation, and humane orientation. These studies have found that cultures with gender egalitarianism supported transformational leadership qualities such as enthusiasm, self-sacrifice, delegation and collectivism (House et al., in press). Aspects of assertiveness, such as direct conversational style, showing of emotion, and so on have also been shown to vary across cultures and so leaders are judged for effectiveness on the basis of how close they come to the cultural norm.

Task 1.2

Consider the country and organization in which you work. Where does it fit along Hofstede's masculine–feminine continuum?

Uncertainty Avoidance Dimension

Uncertainty avoidance refers to how comfortable people feel with ambiguity and an unpredictable future. Societies that avoid uncertainty believe in absolute truths and the establishment of formal rules. Table 1.3, which identifies some of the characteristics of the uncertainty avoidance dimension is adapted from Hofstede (2001, pp. 169–170).

Table 1.3 Uncertainty Avoidance Societies' Workplace Behavior

Low Uncertainty Avoidance	High Uncertainty Avoidance
Skepticism toward technological solutions	Strong appeal of technological solutions
Innovators feel independent of rules	Innovators feel constrained by rules
Top managers are involved in strategy	Top managers are involved in operations
Transformational leader role preferred	Leader expected to exhibit hierarchical control role
Relationship oriented	Task oriented
Power of superiors depends on position and relationships	Power of superiors depends on control of uncertainties
Tolerance for ambiguity in structures and procedures	Highly formalized conception of management
Belief in generalists and common sense	Belief in specialists and expertise

Source: Adapted from Hofstede (2001).

Research that examined small business leaders in Germany (with high uncertainty avoidance) and Ireland (with low uncertainty avoidance) showed that detailed planning was favored by German leaders, but not by Irish leaders, who considered it did not give them sufficient flexibility to change with the changing needs of their customers (Rauch et al., 2000).

Task 1.3

Consider the country and organization in which you work. Where does it fit along Hofstede's uncertainty avoidance continuum?

Power Distance Dimension

This dimension refers to the extent to which people accept that power is distributed unequally. While all leadership is associated in some ways with power and status, societies fall along a continuum with egalitarian at one end and hierarchical at the other. Hofstede identifies the following as some of the behaviors of societies along the power distance dimension. Table 1.4 is adapted from Hofstede (2001, pp. 107–108).

Research indicates that in societies with low power distance, the major factor of transformational leadership behavior is participation in decision-making, whereas in societies with high power distance, directive behavior is more effective. As Ashkanasy and Falkus (in press) note for Australia, which is highly egalitarian, leaders must be

Table 1.4 Power Distance Societies' Workplace Behavior

Low Power Distance	High Power Distance
Flat organization pyramids	Tall organization pyramids
Centralized decision-making	Decentralized decision-making
Managers rely on personal experience and on subordinates	Managers rely on formal rules
Consultative leadership leads to satisfaction, performance, and productivity	Authoritative leadership and close supervision lead to satisfaction, performance, and productivity
Privileges and status symbols for managers are frowned on	Privileges and status symbols for managers are expected and popular
Innovations need good champions	Innovations need good support from the hierarchy
Openness with information, also to nonsuperiors	Information constrained by hierarchy
Subordinates are expected to be consulted and are influenced by bargaining and reasoning	Subordinates are expected to be told and are influenced by formal authority and sanctions

Source: Adapted from Hofstede (2001).

"visionary and inspirational but still be seen as 'one of the boys'" (quoted in Ashkanasy et al., 2002, p. 35). For societies with high power distance, on the other hand, workers prefer leaders who use rules and procedures and they seek management approval before attempting anything new. However, no matter what power distance, "an outstanding leader is expected to be encouraging, motivational, dynamic and have foresight. . . . [and leaders] are expected not to be noncooperative, ruthless, and dictatorial" (Dickson et al., 2003, p. 738).

Task 1.4

Consider the country and organization in which you work. Where does it fit along Hofstede's power distance continuum?

Future Orientation Dimension

This dimension refers to long-term versus short-term orientation to life. This dimension was not found in Hofstede's original IBM study, a result he attributes to Western bias in the writers of his survey. This dimension was developed in work by a Hong Kong scholar, working from Confucian values, rather than from Western ones. On this dimension, "East Asian countries scored highest, Western countries on the low side, and some Third

Table 1.5 Short- and Long-Term-Oriented Societies' Workplace Behavior

Low Long-Term Orientation	High Long-Term Orientation
Focus on short-term results, the bottom line	Focus on building relationships and market position
Family and business sphere are separated	Vertical coordination, horizontal coordination, control, adaptiveness
Meritocracy: economic and social life are ordered by abilities	People should live more equally
Traditions are sacrosanct, with rigid rules about good and evil	Good and evil depend on circumstances and so traditions are adaptable to changed circumstances
Leisure time is important	Leisure time is not important

Source: Adapted from Hofstede (2001).

World countries lowest" (Hofstede, 2001, p. 351). Table 1.5, which identifies characteristics of the short-term/long-term dimension, is adapted from Hofstede (2001, p. 366).

Managers and leaders in long-term-oriented cultures such as Chinese are not expected to get instant results and so are given time and resources to build the relationships necessary to develop strong market positions. In contrast, short-term-oriented cultures are quick to take up (but also abandon) new ideas (Hofstede, 2001). The horizontal connections or personal networks are vital in such societies. While collectivist-oriented societies also value such networks, in cultures that are long-term oriented, these networks have lifetime influence and so must not be discarded for immediate gain.

Task 1.5

Consider the country and organization in which you work. Where does it fit along Hofstede's future orientation continuum?

Transformational Leadership in English Language Education

Given that change is inevitable in the twenty-first century and in our field, and that we work in a complex intercultural space, what strategies might we adopt as leaders? I suggest here that transformational leadership provides a framework to help direct our future, while realizing that within this framework, some cultures will prefer more participative leadership styles and others more directive. If transformational leadership has been identified as being and as being perceived as being more effective than transactional or *laissez-faire* leadership, do the attributes of transformational leadership hold across cultures? The most comprehensive studies to date have been those conducted as part of the GLOBE research program. Their work has also identified clusters of nations sharing certain characteristics: Eastern Europe, Nordic Europe, Germanic Europe, Latin Europe, Anglo, Sub-Saharan Africa, Confucian Asia, Southern Asia, Middle East, Latin America. A number of articles have been published to date and several books are currently in press, all presenting aspects of this research. Some studies demonstrate that the transformational/transactional leadership continuum holds across diverse cultures and that transformational leadership is deemed more effective across many cultures (Bass, 1997). Their studies show that collectivist values of group work fit better with transformational leadership. Jung and Avolio (1999) found that collectivists were more creative with a transformational leader, while individualists were more creative with a transactional leader. Collectivism also related positively to charismatic leadership, which in turn lead to job satisfaction and leader effectiveness. A universal that was not expected is that of charismatic leadership (Dorfman et al., 1997). Several researchers investigated what aspects of charismatic leadership were indeed universal, finding that the following characteristics were universally endorsed as contributing to outstanding leadership: motive arouser, foresight, encouraging, communicative, trustworthy, dynamic, positive, confidence builder, and motivational (Den Hartog et al., 1999, p. 250).

Goleman (1998) also shows that leadership is more than skills, more than cognitive abilities and expertise. Building on the work on multiple intelligences of Howard Gardner (1985), he and others have researched highly effective workers and leaders in private and public companies and organizations, in many countries across North and South America, Asia, and Europe, in 15 global companies, both public and private sector. This research shows that "for star performance in all jobs, in every field, emotional competence is twice as important as purely cognitive abilities. For success at the highest levels, in leadership positions, emotional competence accounts for virtually the entire advantage" (Goleman, 1998, p. 34). Goleman's work has demonstrated that while the various components of emotional intelligence are important for effective leadership, different jobs require different balance among those components, as do different societies. For example, in low power distance cultures, awareness of one's own interactive skills is more important for effectiveness; whereas in high power distance cultures, awareness of one's own controlling skills is more important. See Chapter 5 for extended discussion on the role of emotional intelligence in leadership.

We can therefore conclude that, while many of Hofstede's dimensions identify differences in leadership across cultural groups, to lead in a context that is unstable, changing, and unpredictable and in which staff may feel a lack of commitment because of this ever-changing workplace in which they are held accountable, requires a learning leader. Whether preferring a more directive or a more participative transformational style, all staff expect their leaders to be transcultural, creative leaders who can

> learn to (1) transcend their childhood acculturation and respect very different cultures; (2) build cross-cultural partnerships of mutual trust, respect, and

obligation; (3) engage in cross-cultural creative problem solving to resolve conflicts; and (4) help construct third cultures in various operations.

(Graen & Hui, 1999, quoted in Dickson et al. 2003, p. 758)

Such competencies in their turn require development of the intercultural space referred to earlier, a space that requires relational competence, the ability to manage relationships effectively and appropriately across a variety of contexts (Clark & Matze, 1999).

Acknowledgments

Some of the ideas presented here were first presented at the 6th Annual DOS Conference in Sydney in 2002 and subsequently incorporated in Linguistics 942, Strategic Planning, Management and Leadership, a unit in the Doctorate in Applied Linguistics at Macquarie University. An earlier version of this chapter was presented at the TESOL Symposium in Bangkok, Thailand, January 2005.

Notes

1   I specifically use the term "intercultural," even though much of the literature on leadership uses "cross-cultural." The latter has connotations of conflict that needs to be managed, whereas the former connotes interaction and therefore perhaps understanding through negotiated discourse.
2   The management literature uses a number of terms to refer to staff working for a leader. Followers and subordinates are the most common. Both terms have connotations at odds with a more egalitarian view of leadership, implying hierarchical management structures as they do. Except where directly quoting from other sources, I will use the term staff in preference to follower or subordinate.

References

Ashkanasy, N.M., & Falkus, S. The Australian enigma. In J. Chhokar, F. Brodbeck & R.J. House (Eds.), Culture and Leadership across the world: The GLOBE book of in-depth studies of 25 societies (pp. 299–334). Mahwah, NJ: Lawrence Erlbaum and Associates.

Ashkanasy, N.M., Trevor-Roberts, E., & Earnshaw, L. (2002). The Anglo cluster: Legacy of the British Empire. Journal of World Business, 37, 28–39.

Bass, B.M. (1996). A new paradigm of leadership: An inquiry into transformational leadership. Alexandria, VA: U.S. Army Research Institute for the Behavioral and Social Sciences.

Bass, B.M. (1997). Does the transactional-transformational paradigm transcend organizational and national boundaries? American Psychologist, 52(2), 130–139.

Bennis, W., & Nanus, B. (1997). Leaders: The strategies for taking charge (2nd edn.). New York: HarperBusiness.

Candlin, C.N., & Blair, D. (Eds.) (1997). Australian learners dictionary. Sydney, Australia: NCELTR.

Clark, B.D., & Matze, M.G. (1999). A core of global leadership: Relational competence. In W.H. Mobley (Ed.), Advances in global leadership (Vol. 1, pp. 127–161). Stamford, CT: JAI Press.

Covey, S.R. (1990). *Principle-centered leadership*. Provo, UT: IPCL.

Den Hartog, D., House, R.J., Hanges, P.J., & Ruiz-Quintanilla, S.A. (1999). Culture specific and cross-culturally generalizable implicit leadership theories: Are attributes of charismatic/transformational leadership universally endorsed? *Leadership Quarterly, 10*(2), 219–256.

Dickson, M.W., Den Hartog, D.N., & Mitchelson, J.K. (2003). Research on leadership in a cross-cultural context: Making progress, and raising new questions. *Leadership Quarterly, 14*, 729–768.

Dorfman, P.W., Howell, J.P., Hibino, S., Lee, J.K., Tate, U., & Bautista, A. (1997). Leadership in Western and Asian countries: Commonalities and differences in effective leadership processes across cultures. *Leadership Quarterly, 8*(3), 233–274.

Gardner, H. (1985). *The theory of multiple intelligences*. New York: Basic Books.

Goleman, D. (1998). *Working with emotional intelligence*. London: Bloomsbury.

Graen, G.B., & Hui, C. (1999). Transcultural global leadership in the twenty-first century: Challenges and implications for development. In W.H. Mobley (Ed.), *Advances in global leadership* (Vol. 1, pp. 9–26). Stamford, CT: JAI Press.

Haugen, E. (1972). *The ecology of language: Essays by Einar Haugen*. Stanford, CA: Stanford University Press.

Helgstrand, K.K., & Stulmacher, A.F. (1999). National culture: An influence on leader evaluations? *Journal of Organizational Analysis, 7*, 153–168.

Hofstede, G. (1990). *Culture's consequences: International differences in work-related values*. Newbury Park, CA: Sage.

Hofstede, G. (2001). *Culture's consequences* (2nd edn). Thousand Oaks, CA: Sage.

House, R.J., Hanges, P.J., Javidan, M., Dorfman, P.W., & Gupta, V. (Eds.) (2004). *Culture, leadership, and organizations: The GLOBE study of 62 societies*, Vol. 1. Thousand Oaks, CA: Sage.

Jung, D.I., & Avolio, B.J. (1999). Effects of leadership style and followers' cultural orientation on performance in group and individual task conditions. *Academy of Management Journal, 42*(2), 208–218.

Liddicoat, A.J., & Crozet, C. (Eds.). (2000). *Teaching languages, teaching cultures*. Melbourne: Applied Linguistics Association of Australia and Language Australia.

Mühlhäusler, P. (1994). Language teaching = linguistic imperialism? *Australian Review of Applied Linguistics, 17*, 121–130.

Murphy, E.C. (1996). *Leadership IQ*. New York: John Wiley and Sons, Ltd.

Murray, D.E. (2001). The ecology of language education. Paper presented at the ATESOL Conference, Sydney, Australia.

Parry, K. (1996). *Transformational leadership: Developing an enterprising management culture*. Melbourne: Pitman Publishing.

Pennycook, A. (1995). English in the world/the world in English. In J. Tollefson (Ed.), *Power and inequality in language education* (pp. 34–58). Cambridge: Cambridge University Press.

Rauch, C., Frese, M., & Sonnentag, S. (2000). Cultural differences in planning/success relationships: A comparison of small enterprises in Ireland, West Germany, and East Germany. *Journal of Small Business Management, 38*, 28–41.

Walker, J. (1999). Perspectives on service in ELT operations. *ELT Management, 27*(March), 16–20.

Wheatley, M.J. (1999). *Leadership and the new science: Discovering order in a chaotic world*. (2nd edn). San Francisco: Berrett-Koehler.

Chapter 2

A Model for Leadership in English Language Teaching
An Introduction to Leadership IQ

MaryAnn Christison and Denise E. Murray

Introduction

In Chapter 1, Murray helps us understand the *ecology* of leadership, the study of how leaders help individuals and organizations work together by exploring two intersecting dimensions of leadership in English language teaching: the fact that change is inevitable and that English language teaching occurs in varied cultural contexts that create varied cultural experiences and expectations for the individuals involved. In order to respond to these intersecting dimensions, Murray builds on the concept of transformational leadership in English language teaching. Transformational leadership, sometimes known as charismatic or visionary leadership, is a description of leadership that is open and responsive to the needs of both the organizational system and the individuals within the organization. The key element in transformational leadership is that effective leaders focus on learning. In other words, leadership is committed to learning and learning about leadership.

Chapter 2 introduces the reader to a body of empirical research (Murphy, 1996) that focuses on learning more about the nature of leadership. This research demonstrates that leadership can be defined and measured as a form of intelligence, and Murphy claims that this intelligence can be activated through specific activities that lead to effective leadership. In this chapter, we will explore Murphy's notion of Leadership IQ, the principles that govern effective leadership, and the development of leadership roles that help leaders learn new skills that support transformational leadership.

Intelligent Leadership

For a number of years, we have been interested in developing our own leadership skills. While reviewing and researching applicable leadership materials from both business and education, we discovered Emmett C. Murphy's book entitled *Leadership IQ* (1996). Murphy's firm, E.C. Murphy Ltd., has dedicated over 25 years to the scientific study of the nature of leadership. In 1991, his firm launched a comprehensive empirical study to identify the characteristics and talents of leaders. Murphy believes that "virtually every other system of our society and economy has gone through rigorous empirical analysis" while the study of leadership has remained at a primitive level. The research provided his firm with a number of important insights about leadership that we found valuable to our own work.

One of the most important insights is that "leadership can be defined and measured as a form of intelligence" (Murphy, 1996, p. 2). When we look at intelligence through the lens of one of the most popular views of intelligence in educational settings, namely, Gardner's multiple intelligences theory, we see intelligence as dynamic. In other words, intelligence is something humans possess that can be developed over time. Some personalities seem to be more naturally suited to leadership, but all leaders can improve as a result of study and effort. No amount of natural ability can supplant comprehensive and in-depth study.

The second insight has to do with the work that leaders do. Organizations often put people into one of two categories—people who lead and people who work. However, when Murphy studied successful leaders in workplace environments, he found that every leader works and every worker leads. Murphy analyzed more than 18,000 contemporary leaders to find 1,029 individuals who emerged as authentic leaders (Murphy, 1997, p. 3) and who were considered to be highly effective. These individuals were known as *workleaders*, a term that binds both work and leadership in such a way as to represent what Murphy believes to be the "true nature of effective leadership" (ibid., p. 3).

The third insight has to do with the behavior of *workleaders*. They know how to say the right thing to the right people at the right time in order to get the right work done well, on time, and within budget. They serve as models for everyone with whom they interact. Contrary to traditional notions about leaders, they are made, not born. Anyone can learn to be a *workleader*.

Murphy's fourth insight arose as the research uncovered the fact that *workleaders* rely on specific tools to fulfill eight specific roles (ibid., p. 4). In every case, *workleaders* knew how to do the following eight things: (1) select the right people; (2) connect people to the right cause; (3) solve problems as they arise; (4) evaluate progress towards goals; (5) negotiate resolutions to conflicts; (6) heal wounds inflicted by change; (7) protect the work culture from the perils of crisis; and (8) synergize all stakeholders in a way that enables them to achieve improvement together.

The fifth insight may be the most valuable. When *workleaders* master the first seven roles, they achieve what Murphy call a *synergistic kick*. Collectively, the roles ignite a chain reaction so that the "state of achievement [is] far beyond what individuals, teams, and organizations ever dreamed was possible" (ibid., p. 5).

The sixth insight has to do with *Work Imaging*. *Work Imaging* is a process of obtaining a clear picture of what *workleaders* do every day in order to perform an accurate self-assessment and also to assess the work of their associates with the ultimate goal of helping others refocus their responsibilities and efforts.

Research on Leadership IQ

In the research, Murphy (1996) and his colleagues identified 1,029 people who demonstrated leadership excellence and were considered by both their peers and superiors to have a high leadership IQ. Murphy's task was to determine the behaviors that set these leaders apart from others (see the fourth insight above). They used a variety of assessment tools "ranging from psychological inventories and customer satisfaction assessments, to work productivity and performance measures" (ibid., p. 12). The results of their research showed that effective leaders follow certain principles and carry out specific roles. With the results in mind from the assessments, Murphy and his colleagues created the "Leadership IQ Development Guide," a development tool that can be used by anyone to boost leadership skills.

Leadership Principles

Effective leaders follow seven guiding principles that provide the basis for fulfilling the eight roles of a workleader.

Principle 1: Be an achiever. Highly effective workplace leaders believe that "self-reliance and personal achievement" (ibid., p. 14) are the most important prerequisites for success. Success as a leader is not about who you know or a function of whom you can buy or manipulate. The participants in Murphy's study were asked to rank the factors as to their importance in contributing to success as a leader (Table 2.1).

The ranking of success factors on the left represents the results of the workleader rankings. Notice that individual competence and experience were rated #1 and #2 by workleaders while luck was rated #10. Clearly workleaders believe that hard work and individual initiative contribute to effectiveness as leaders and that the title you have, who you know, and just pure luck have little to do with achieving success. In contrast

Table 2.1 Success Factor Rankings

Workleader Ranking	Average Leader Ranking
1. Individual competence	1. Support from the organization
2. Experience	2. Support from the boss
3. Respect of customers	3. Formal education
4. Respect of colleagues	4. Luck
5. Support of loved ones	5. Other
6. Formal education	6. Respect of customers
7. Support from the organization	7. Individual competence
8. Support from the boss	8. Experience in the front lines of service
9. Other	9. Support of loved ones
10. Luck	10. Respect of colleagues

to workleader rankings, average leaders ranked these factors much lower and ranked individual competence #7 as opposed to the workleader ranking of #1.

Principle 2. Be pragmatic. In order to be pragmatic you need to think like a scientist. Pragmatism involves being able to ask questions, keep an open mind, and find solutions to very practical problems. Workleaders who are pragmatic have learned to experiment and to withhold judgments.

Principle 3. Practice strategic humility. Effective workleaders don't let pride get in the way of effective leadership. They don't take credit for other people's work, and they readily admit it when they are wrong. They also know how to and when to ask for help.

Principle 4. Focus on the customer. Workleaders place other people at the center of their concern. Their main concern is the quality of service they are providing. They advocate for customers and work to focus their energies or the company or organization on service. Within English language education, many have rejected using the business model whereby students (and others) are considered customers (see Chapter 8 for a detailed discussion). However, such an orientation helps leaders focus on the needs of those whom we serve, rather than on the staff who provide the services. Within English language education customers can be a diverse range of people, from governments to individual students. Service also includes a wide range of services, products and programs, such as the processes used to register students, arrange contracts, and the instructional program. The chapter on ensuring quality (Chapter 10) describes in more detail the types of activities within English language education that need to be considered when ensuring quality services, products and programs that meet customer needs.

Principle 5. Be committed. Workleaders are committed to "creating a prosperous future" (Murphy, 1996, p. 23) with their peers. In other words, in order to create a prosperous future, they must be committed to facing and overcoming adversity and to building optimism. If you are committed, it is possible to overcome failures, anger, loss, and disappointment.

Principle 6. Learn to be an optimist. Not all workleaders are natural optimists; they have learned to be optimists because optimists enjoy greater success in life. Learning how to be an optimist means coping with disappointment and adversity in order to succeed in spite of the odds. Many well-known journalists and popular fiction writers (e.g., J.K. Rowling, author of the Harry Potter series and Stephen King, popular writer of fiction) tell stories of the numerous times their manuscripts were turned down by publishing houses. If they had given up and become discouraged (i.e., if they had not remained optimistic), their works would never have been published. One never knows when success might be just around the corner.

Principle 7. Accept responsibility. Workleaders accept responsibility for everything in their lives—the decisions they make, the outcomes of those decisions, and the inter-actions with other people. By accepting responsibility for everything in our lives we begin to realize that it is possible to see our personal dreams fulfilled. As Murphy puts it, "seize control of your destiny or someone else will" (ibid., p. 25).

Workleader Roles

Murphy defines eight roles that effective workleaders use to help them improve their understanding of the Guiding Principles. These roles appear in Table 2.2. As workleaders master these eight roles, they develop a more precise understanding of these principles. Some 125 average to low average leaders were selected to participate in an assessment and self-development process that focused on workleader roles. As a result of this process, all workleaders improved their performances and 73 joined the ranks of the benchmark workleader group within 12–18 months. We believe that the results of this study speak to the importance of leadership development and are also consistent with the idea of intelligent leadership.

For a detailed account of workleader roles, readers should consult Murphy's work directly (Murphy, 1996). Our aim here is to provide only a summary of the types of skills that leaders need and the types of roles leaders assume in English language programs.

Table 2.2 Workleader Roles

The Selector
The Connector
The Problem Solver
The Evaluator
The Negotiator
The Healer
The Protector
The Synergizer

The Selector

The role of the Selector is to put the right person in the right job. Attracting the instructors and staff that have the right fit is important in developing and maintaining strong English language and teaching programs. Selection includes choice of team members or particular staff for specific activities. However, just as important as hiring or selecting the best people is knowing when to deselect. The same skills used to select are also used in de-selection or separation. Because selection and de-selection deal with personnel issues, they can be uncomfortable processes. In addition, selection and de-selection are difficult processes to master, but leaders who develop tools and know the steps to follow can be more successful in applying these processes. When English language program leaders have confidence in their own ability to make the right choices, they let go of control, encourage faculty and staff to take responsibility, and allow themselves to develop confidence in other people working in the program.

In order to develop skills in the role of the Selector, leaders need the appropriate tools to do the job. According to Murphy's research, these tools are: (1) using appropriate questioning strategies that prompt others to speak spontaneously and get others to do the talking; and (2) relying on the four steps to selection. The order for the steps in the selection process is: (1) to establish a context for action; (2) conduct formal assessment; (3) diagnose and evaluate results; and (4) take action. These same steps are also used in deselection or separation, but they are used in a different order. These same tools are used for hiring, reselection, debriefing, and separation. The focus for all four actions remains on the process for getting the information necessary to make effective decisions.

The Connector

Connectors work to build relationships. One important tool that we have found useful is Murphy's Connection Ladder. We have used this tool to assist us in assessing team and colleague receptivity or communication aptitudes so that we understand how we can develop a plan to improve on relationships. A summary of the Connection Ladder appears in Table 2.3.

Table 2.3 The Connection Ladder

Level of Commitment	Description
1. Contempt	Characterized by distraction and anger and a defiance for goals and performance criteria
2. Hostility	Passive aggressive behavior is often used to undermine confidence in other members and leadership
3. Avoidance	Being preoccupied, ignoring others, and not responding to other's comments and questions
4. Indifference	Passive in reaching out to others or in responding and withholds opinion
5. Contact	Shows common courtesy and acknowledges the other person's presence
6. Awareness	Recognizes the other person and adjusts behavior to the other's presence
7. Involvement	Actively listens and responds and puts distractions aside when interacting with others
8. Empathy	Tries to walk in the other person's shoes and tries to understand the other person's needs
9. Empowerment	Interested in both giving and receiving information, generating options, reinforcing the other person's strengths
10. Commitment	A focus on mutual understanding, trust, and effective collaboration is the most important value

---

Task 2.1

Assess each person in the workplace with whom you interact regularly. Where does each person fit on the Connection Ladder?

The Problem Solver

Workleaders who are skilled Problem Solvers focus on getting results and do not consider any problem unsolvable. They ask five important questions of each problem and follow this process faithfully in order to help them transform problems into solutions.

1 What did we do?
2 How much time and money did it take?
3 What problems got in the way?
4 How much time and money were consumed by the problems encountered?
5 Based on what happened, what should we do?

The Evaluator

Workleaders with a high leadership IQ approach evaluation from a positive standpoint and think of it as an opportunity for improvement. In order to be a successful Evaluator, workleaders must demonstrate not only competence, but also come from the knowledge that improvement can and should be achieved by harnessing the potential of all workers more fully. In order to achieve success with evaluation, workleaders follow five principles.

Principle 1 Purpose: The evaluation must be done with the clients, students, or customers in mind.

Principle 2 Responsibility: Each person is responsible because only individuals can improve individual behavior.

Principle 3 Involvement: Every person on the team or in the organization should be involved in evaluation. Workleaders must figure out how to make that happen.

Principle 4 Guidance: Workleaders are responsible for providing guidance and for helping others so that everyone understands the need for improved performance.

Principle 5 Service: Workleaders focus on the people they serve and learn how to effectively give recognition for service. They also learn to recognize when to make changes in personnel so that everyone can be more productive, that is, they undertake the role of selector.

The Negotiator

Negotiators focus on achieving consensus and on finding a better way to focus on the people they serve, whether it be a customer, client, or student. Workleaders who are skilled negotiators are able to combine the strengths and visions of each person involved in the negotiating process so that what is achieved is something that no one individual could have achieved alone. They use two important tools in the negotiation process— the customer needs analyzer and the consensus negotiating guide. An in-depth discussion of both these tools is provided in Murphy's work.

The Healer

For most people it takes only a moment to think of exceptional leaders who have demonstrated an awareness of human suffering and tried to appeal to the importance of compassion in human interactions. Murphy's research shows that attendance on the job, wellness among associates, and productivity are increased under workleaders who focus their energies on the healing process. Workleaders know how to diagnose "the symptoms of organizational disease" (Murphy, 1996, p. 170) early on and take steps to remedy the situation. Workleaders use important tools to diagnose the need for healing and to find effective solutions that allow them to take action.

The Protector

When crises threaten people and/or the organization, workleaders believe they can respond to these difficult circumstances and turn them into opportunities. Leaders with high leadership IQs learn how to anticipate the risk and then assess it. In order to assess the risk, they use a Risk Assessment Guide to identify: (1) the type of risk; (2) whom or what the risk affects; (3) the level of the risk; and (4) the duration of the risk. Workleaders also develop a plan to learn from the risk. They also use the Conflict Management Guide to determine a course of action.

The Synergizer

The principle behind synergy is that the whole is greater than the sum of its parts. The key is in finding out how to help all associates work to the best of their abilities. The Synergizer process focuses on diagnosing the various choices for change (see Murphy, 1997, pp. 226–228) and on a seven-step guide for self-improvement. By using these tools, workleaders help the organization generate one synergistic kick after another. When workleaders are able to master the eight roles, they can achieve what Murphy calls *a synergistic kick* by starting a chain reaction where the one plus seven roles no longer equals eight but creates a "state of achievement far beyond what individuals, teams, and organizations ever dreamed possible." Synergy represents the ultimate goal toward which all workleaders strive.

The Leadership IQ Assessment for English Language Program Administrators

In order to help English language program leaders and administrators develop their Leadership IQ, we developed the Management and Leadership IQ Assessment for ELT. In this questionnaire you will be given an opportunity to develop your understanding of the importance of each of the workleader roles discussed in this chapter. This instrument appears in Appendix 2.1 (pp. 36–43) and is an adaptation of Murphy's Leadership IQ Assessment. The focus of the specific scenarios in Management and Leadership IQ Assessment for ELT is on education events and problems that administrators experience working in English language and teaching programs.

Task 2.2

Respond to the assessment in Appendix 2.1, check your answers, and give yourself a score. If you miss some questions and don't understand why, read the explanations in Appendix 2.2. If you want further information, consult Murphy.

References

Murphy, E.C. (1996). *Leadership IQ: A Personal Development Process Based on a Scientific Study of a New Generation of Leaders*. Hoboken, NY: John Wiley & Sons, Inc.

Scherer, M. (2004). What do leaders do? *Educational Leadership*, 6(7):7.

Appendix 2.1

Management and Leadership Questionnaire For ELT*

Directions: Circle the answer for the action you **would most likely perform** in the situation. If you have a position of leadership, think about how you act in that role. If you are not in a leadership role, think of how you expect you would act. Each situation is in an educational setting. The questions use faculty to refer to people whose major responsibility is teaching; staff for people whose major responsibility is clerical; administrator for people whose major responsibility is management.

The first two questions refer to the same scenario: One of your staff who has always been effective in her job shows negative signs such as tiredness, loss of a sense of humor, general malaise.

1. It's best to:

   a. Discuss the situation with her as soon as you notice the changes.
   b. Discuss the situation with her as soon as possible after you witness a specific incident.
   c. Wait and only discuss it with her after you have several specific examples or other staff mention the signs, too.

2. When you discuss these changes in your staff, it's best to:

   a. Discuss these signs only as they relate to her performance of her job.
   b. Discuss these signs as they might affect all aspects of her life.
   c. Avoid discussing the causes of the problem, focusing instead on how she can change.

3. You are the administrator of an academic department. You hear that a faculty member in your department has major personal problems. She comes to you for advice. Your best response is:

   a. Listen to her problems and offer advice based on your own knowledge and experience.
   b. Listen to her problems and tell her several places where she might get help (e.g., the counseling center).
   c. Tell her you can't really help her because she needs help from a professional and you are not a professional counsellor.

4. One of your staff comes to you and complains that another staff member (Sue) is being rude to students, but asks you to keep the complaint confidential. She doesn't want you to do anything about it, just wants to inform you. Your best response is:

   a. Tell her that since this affects students, she has put you in a very awkward position by requesting that you not act, and that you will have to talk with Sue.

b. Tell her that you won't do anything, but nor will you hold this against Sue.

c. Tell her you'll talk to the two of them together and try to get to the bottom of the issue.

5. You're the administrator of an academic department. You are in your office, which is off the main department office. One day, the department secretary is the only other person in the office. She is working at her computer on the department web page. You notice there are several students waiting to ask her questions. Your best response is:

a. "Why are you working on that web page when there are students waiting? If you have tasks to do that interfere with serving students, tell me at once."

b. "Who told you to work on the web page? If it's another faculty member, tell me immediately they ask you to do something. Other people can't run what goes on in the office."

c. "Can you work on that web page later? There are a number of students who need help. When the student assistant comes back from lunch, let her deal with the front office and let's talk about the web page then."

The next two questions are about the same scenario. Two faculty members have a conflict that is affecting the entire department.

6. You decide to ask the two of them to come together to your office to try to resolve the conflict. Your most effective approach is:

a. To control the discussion and insist that each faculty member provide specific information about their differences.

b. Not to intervene unless they get out of control.

c. To draw specific information from both faculty, but also give them opportunity to discuss freely between themselves.

7. In the meeting with the two faculty members you are initially unable to help them reach consensus. Your best course of action is to:

a. Adjourn the meeting for a couple of days.

b. Adjourn the meeting and decide on what to do yourself.

c. Keep the meeting going until they reach consensus.

8. You have just been hired as the director of an intensive English program. One of the instructors, Carlos, has been teaching in the program for over 15 years. In reading the personnel files, you notice that he had always received excellent student evaluations until the last two quarters. In your first meeting with all the faculty you notice that he seems withdrawn and unenthusiastic. You arrange to have lunch with each instructor to get to know them better. After some general conversation with Carlos, you say:

a. "You've clearly been an excellent instructor here for many years, so your last two semester student evaluations really seem odd. But, I don't want to talk about them first—let's talk about you. How do you feel about the program? About the students and your job?"

b. "You've clearly been an excellent instructor here for many years, so your last two semester student evaluations really seem odd. Let's go over all the students' comments and find out what's going wrong with your teaching."

c. "You've clearly been an excellent instructor here for many years, so your last two semester student evaluations really seem odd. When I see a sudden change like this, I get very worried. Perhaps it's time for you to think about a change. As you know, I do have to ensure the whole program provides excellent instruction for all our students."

9. You are the director of a very successful privately owned intensive English program. You have decided you must terminate Laura, one of the instructors. Students and other instructors have complained to you often that she is rude, doesn't come to class prepared, rarely returns homework on time (if at all), and is often late. Student evaluations are consistently negative. You have counseled her on several occasions, trying to help her "get her act together," but nothing has worked. You call her into your office to terminate her and say:

a. "Laura, I've asked you in to discuss your separation from our program. We've discussed your evaluations and performance many times over the past year and there's been no improvement. So, it would be best for all of us if we went our separate ways. You'll need to go to the director of administration to arrange for your final check, turning in of keys and so on. She's expecting you."

b. "Laura, I've asked you in to discuss your separation from our program. We've discussed your evaluations and performance many times over the past year and there's been no improvement. I'm still not sure what the problem is. I think we've agreed on goals for you to improve your teaching; but you just haven't been able to reach those goals we established."

c. "Laura, I've worked really hard to be fair to you over the past year, but you just don't seem to have listened to me. I wonder if there is a more fundamental problem you just haven't acknowledged. Students still think you're rude and faculty and students still don't think you're doing your job. I just don't think you can continue being an instructor here."

The next two questions relate to the same scenario. Your institution's President is embarking on a major, large-scale change—moving from a quarter system to a semester system. This will give you as the intensive English program director, the opportunity to make a change you have been wanting to do for many years—have six 8-week language programs each year. This, of course, has many implications for curriculum, staffing and so on.

10. The best way for you to behave as director is to:

a. Take action as soon as the general direction of six 8-week programs is established and fine-tune as you go.

    b.   Do an adequate needs analysis and then mobilize for action.

    c.   Do a thorough needs analysis and then don't take any action until everyone on the faculty supports all the changes.

11. You have a contingent of people who are unwilling to participate in making this change happen. Your best approach is to:

    a.   Work hard to get them all on board because they might derail the process later.

    b.   Isolate them from the faculty who are willing to spearhead the change, not renewing contracts for some of them if possible.

    c.   Invite them to participate, but don't use a lot of effort to get them to participate; instead, focus on the faculty who are excited about this change.

12. When addressing productivity problems with your staff, the best way to start is by asking:

    a.   How do you feel?

    b.   What are you doing?

    c.   Where's the problem?

13. To ensure high levels of teamwork and productivity, the main issue to address is:

    a.   The way work is organized.

    b.   Performance incentives.

    c.   Team and interpersonal skills training for everyone.

14. One of your program directors comes to you and tells you that the department secretary is really messing up. She's making errors in scheduling, in giving information to students, and in purchasing. The director is really worried that the department will lose students if this continues. You say, "I hear you." The director angrily reminds you that he's heard this before and demands that you do something about it. Your best response is to say:

    a.   "I understand that you're angry. Your job is to coordinate your program and tell me if you have problems. You've done that, so now it's my problem, not yours. Let me do my job and you do yours, okay?"

    b.   "I understand that you're angry. I'll speak with her and take care of it as soon as you leave."

    c.   "Look, this is my problem and I'll deal with it my way. I won't do it on your or any one else's schedule. I'll do what I think is right when I think it's appropriate. That might mean I won't take actions based on what you've told me."

15. If you make a mistake, it's best to:

    a.   Admit your mistake before trying to find a solution.

    b.   Move on to something else without admitting your mistake.

    c.   Admit your mistake and try to remedy it immediately.

16. When one of your faculty or staff is having a serious problem with another person in the department, the first thing to do is to:

    a. Bring them together to discuss their conflict.
    b. Talk with each person individually so you can assess the issues for yourself.
    c. Stay out of it and let them work out their problem themselves.

17. You are a college President, responsible for contract negotiations with the faculty association/union. There are still some outstanding disagreements over pay, benefits, etc. But, the major concern for the faculty is the rumor that the district is about to amalgamate with another district. Faculty are concerned that if this happens, there will be layoffs, regardless of any contract. You say to the faculty negotiating team:

    a. "I can understand the faculty's concerns here. What I hear you say is that they can't see the point in agreeing to a three-year contract when they don't know whether there will even be the same district next year. Do I understand this right?"
    b. "Well, the faculty just seem to be missing the point. They really don't have an option. The board of trustees will do whatever they want, regardless of what faculty want. So, the best I can offer is for you to have an acceptable contract for as long as the current situation exists."
    c. "OK, if you need some promises, let me see what I can do. I'm certainly willing to do whatever I can so the faculty feel comfortable."

18. One of the office staff has major personal problems. The best way to ensure his usual high level of performance in the office is to:

    a. Give him a few days off to sort out his problems, but remind him that the purpose is for him to get back to his usual high level of performance.
    b. Let him sort out his problems in his own time but try to give him structure and a sense of control while he's at work.
    c. Give him as much time off as he needs to reach closure to his problems.

19. The most defensible/unbiased performance evaluation is:

    a. A very general form with lots of specific notes from the evaluator.
    b. A very specific form with few written notes from the evaluator.
    c. No form at all, with extensive written notes from the evaluator.

20. You have had a number of complaints about one of your staff, so you decide to set some specific goals for her and evaluate them every three months, instead of the usual annual performance evaluation required by your institution. Your best approach is to:

    a. Arrange a meeting with her after the first three months, explain the review process and give her the results of your first quarter evaluation.
    b. Arrange two meetings with her. In the first, explain the review process and review with her the draft of goals she is to work towards in the first quarter.
    c. Meet with her and ask her how and when she would like to be reviewed.

The next three questions relate to the same scenario. You have been appointed chair of a new campus committee that is to undertake a restructuring of campus departments and programs. Over the years, departments and programs have grown up willy-nilly. The new Principal has decided a review of the current situation and recommendations for change are her top priority. She is particularly interested in developing greater opportunities for interdisciplinary programs and theme-based learning. She has assigned four faculty and two staff to your redesign team. Their attitudes range from enthusiastic to outright rejection of the whole idea. So, before the committee meets together, you decide to talk with each person individually to "get them on board."

21. The first person you talk with, Deanna, is highly competent in her own field and very enthusiastic, seeing this as an opportunity to make significant changes that she has long advocated. She tells you she knows she can contribute because she has already worked with a couple of other departments to develop interdisciplinary units.

    a. You thank her for her input and say how pleased you are to have someone so enthusiastic on the team. But, you remind her that she must work as a team and not be tempted to work for her own individual agenda.

    b. You thank her for her input and tell her you'll be getting back to her about her actual role on the committee after you've talked to everyone else.

    c. You thank her for her input and enthusiasm. You tell her that you look forward to her playing a major role on the committee.

22. The second person you speak with, Mike, is moderately enthusiastic. He is known to be dependable, but not a risk taker. He tells you he's worried that they'll end up antagonising other faculty. But he says he's pleased Deanna is on the committee because he knows she's already tried some of the ideas.

    a. You tell him you don't think he need worry about antagonising the rest of the faculty because you and the Principal have everything under control and it's a good committee. You tell him Deanna feels like you do, so why doesn't he talk with her before the full committee meets.

    b. You tell him you understand his concern, but are pleased he wants to be on the committee. You tell him that you're sure with him and Deanna as core people on the committee, the recommendations will be excellent.

    c. You thank him for his concern, but tell him that you'll all just have to live with the consequences—this is something the Principal really wants, even if it's not feasible.

23. The last person you speak with, Kim, is antagonistic. She thinks it's an impossible task and that it's typical of new Principals, always just wanting to do things because they're different, without concern for faculty or students.

    a. You tell her she has the right to feel that way, but you're sure the committee can come up with a creative redesign. So, if she doesn't want to be part of it, she should say so and resign from the committee.

    b. You tell her you value her opinion and that it's important to build a team that can work well together. So, you ask her to think about all the potential problems and prepare a list that you can use later with the whole committee. You tell her that it's important for the committee to address all the real issues that might affect acceptance of their recommendations.

c.   You ask her what she would do if she were chair of the committee, telling her it's not good enough just to criticize. You all have a task you have to get done, whether you like it or not.

24. You have to present the annual performance evaluation to one of your staff. What is the most effective way to ensure she takes your suggestions seriously and attends to the evaluation process?

a.   You and the staff member together fill out the evaluation form rating her performance.

b.   You fill out the evaluation form alone and then go over it with her.

c.   You have her fill out the evaluation form rating her own performance.

25. Your Dean of Continuing Education has just come back from a trip to Utopia, where he met with local leaders and found that the leaders would like more of their citizens to come to the US to study, but their English skills are not sufficient to pass the TOEFL. Your Dean asks you to arrange a special intensive program for their students. He's keen to have the students come to the university because Utopia is very rich and this could bring additional funds to the university. You take the proposal to your faculty, who say the program is already overextended (not enough staff support, not enough faculty offices, etc.) and why should they pander to some rich country.

a.   You tell the Dean the faculty are not interested and so you won't pursue this any further.

b.   You thank the Dean for his confidence in your program and tell him you know you could develop a quality program for these students. However, you need his assurance that you'd be granted additional resources, not just to run that program, but to support all the important work you do.

c.   You tell the Dean that it would be better if the university just admitted those students from Utopia who passed the TOEFL so Utopia would be sure of their success at the university.

You have advertised for several new teachers for your language program. You have selected a short list of five to interview. The next questions ask how you will arrange the interview.

26. The best seating arrangement is

a.   in an office or conference room, with the interviewers facing the applicant

b.   in an office or conference room with the interviewers and applicant sitting side by side

c.   over lunch at a local, relaxed and casual restaurant

27. To gather the most useful information from each applicant,

    a.   create a list of core questions to ask each candidate and use the same structure approach for each candidate

    b.   ask questions so the candidate will tell you their work history

    c.   use a loose format, allowing each applicant to focus on his or her strengths.

Note: Adapted from Murphy (1996).

Appendix 2.2

Answers and Discussion of Management and Leadership Questionnaire for ELT*

Question	Appropriate Response	Role	Discussion
1	B	Healer	It's important always to intervene as soon as you identify a workplace behavior or attitude
2	A	Healer	that is inappropriate. The malaise or personal problems are only relevant to the workplace
3	B	Healer	if they affect her work. If you wait too long to respond (question 1 c.) you may have put her and her colleagues at risk. While you may be sympathetic about her problems, how they affect her out-of-work life is not relevant to the workplace. When discussing her work performance it is important to find the causes of the problems to be able to help her deal with them. If the causes are personal, as in question 3, then she needs to be referred for professional help. As workleader, you need to focus on your work role and that of your colleagues. This can be seriously undermined if workleaders move to counselor or friend, especially without such training.
4	A	Protector	It is important for workleaders to act quickly if the workplace is at risk; however, they should never act on hearsay and should validate complaints for themselves.
5	C	Problem Solver	The most important issue here is the customer and so an effective workleader would solve the immediate problem by asking her to attend to the customers. An effective workleader also ensures that the secretary takes responsibility for talking with him/her later.
6	C	Protector	In both these questions, the effective workleader assumes the role of protector.

Question	Appropriate Response	Role	Discussion
7	A	Protector	For question 6, the effective workleader wants to check for him/herself what the issues are, hence the effective workleader draws information from each person. Additionally, the effective workleader makes the two people in conflict take responsibility for their own actions by also giving them opportunities to discuss among themselves. In this way, the workleader protects the organization from risk of the conflict escalating. For question 7, rather than let the meeting escalate the conflict, the workleader adjourns. But it's also important that the workleader only postpones the meeting, ensuring the conflicting employees realize a consensus must be reached for the sake of the organization's business.
8	A	Selector	According to Murphy's research, the most effective workleaders choose a. He cites the example of a new manager who asked just such questions of a long time, successful employee and in so doing found out just how valuable that person's contribution to the company had been, but that he was burned out after working such long hours for so many years. Their joint solution was for the employee to remain in the company, but in a new position that provided new, not-too-demanding challenges.
9	A	Selector	While a. may seem a harsh response, Laura has already been given warnings and so to re-open the performance as though it's a performance review, rather than a separation is ineffective. Once you have made the decision to separate an employee, it needs to be done as efficiently as possible. It's important to show Laura that her lack of improvement means her performance is not acceptable and separation is the only option.

continued

Question	Appropriate Response	Role	Discussion
10	B	Synergizer	To manage change, it's important for work-leaders to establish the context for the change.
11	C	Synergizer	They need to assess how the change impacts the organization and its ability to deliver services and products. Part of this assessment is assessing the organization's capacity for change. This assessment provides the work-leader with data so the plan for change is based on data, not emotion or the whim of the leader. For question 11, the workleader mobilizes the support for those who are ready for the change. By focusing on those who are ready for the change, the workleader builds on the positive energy of these colleagues.
12	B	Problem Solver	As in question 5, the effective workleader focuses on the business. In order to solve the problem, he/she needs to understand what the employee is doing. The data that are then discovered become the basis for action.
13	A	Problem Solver	Like question 12, the focus for question 13 is the work. To solve the problem, the effective leader needs data.
14	A	Protector	In this scenario, the workleader defines his/her own responsibility for the work of the department secretary, at the same time reminding the program director to focus on his work. Options b. and c. do not acknowledge the work and responsibilities of the program director.
15	C	Healer	To heal, the workleader needs to practice strategic humility. But apology or admission is not sufficient. The workleader needs to remedy the mistake since he/she has, in his/her admission, recognized that the mistake caused harm to the organization. If the mistake alienated an employee, the workleader needs to re-connect with that person.

Question	Appropriate Response	Role	Discussion
16	B	Protector	As with questions 6 and 7, the workleader needs data in order to act.
17	A	Negotiator	An important aspect of negotiation is to re-phrase others' comments to ensure that your understanding is the same as theirs. Options b. and c. do not provide an opportunity for understanding. B creates a win–lose situation, while c. makes a promise that the workleader probably could not keep.
18	A	Healer	As with questions 1, 2 and 3 above, the focus needs to be on the work of the organization. Choice a reminds the employee that his work performance is critical to his employment, but that you as workleader understand his need to find solutions to his personal problems.
19	B	Evaluator	Performance appraisals need to be tied to specific goals and objectives that are tied to the mission of the organization. A specific form provides a concrete system for objective recording of observations. Using lots of notes usually leads to subjective choices and language.
20	B	Evaluator	As with question 19, it's important for the workleader to provide specific goals for employees to accomplish. It is inappropriate to hold staff accountable for criteria they are not informed of.
21	C	Connector	In order to build teams, it's necessary to link your group together for a common cause. For
22	B	Connector	Deanna, the more appropriate strategy is to reinforce her positive attributes and behavior
23	B	Connector	So, you would most likely choose c. as your response. Both a. and b. remind her that you are in charge; your thanks for her input then seems superficial. It's important to capture her goodwill and enthusiasm and ensure that she's a positive force on the team.

continued

Question	Appropriate Response	Role	Discussion
			For Mike, while you need to express an understanding of his anxiety, you want him to strengthen your team. Thus, you want him and Deanna to present a fairly united, positive contribution, but not become a subgroup within the committee; hence you don't recommend he talk with Deanna before the meeting. It's important to ensure the team is a whole group, not made up of smaller splinter groups. You need to be sure that you don't make promises you can't keep (that everything's under control). Nor do you want to convey that this committee's work will just be done to appease the boss (answer c.). This will only feed into his anxiety. The most appropriate response, therefore, is b.
			With Kim, you want to reach out a hand of cooperation, giving her responsibilities; but you need to be sure you frame those responsibilities very carefully so they provide positive input to the team (answer b.). Answer c. does not help get her on board; rather it reinforces her negative attitudes, giving her permission to continue being antagonistic. If you ask her to leave the team, you have missed the opportunity, hard as it will be, to get her cooperation in the project. She will instead, continue to be antagonistic and possibly undermine the committee's work.
24	A	Evaluator	By jointly completing the form, the workleader guides and coaches the employee to self-appraise. It also helps the employee focus on the aspects of his/her performance.
25	B	Negotiator	Options a. and c. cut off any discussion. By choosing option b., the workleader acknowledges the opportunity the Dean is providing, while at the same time stating the department's needs to take up that opportunity.

Question	Appropriate Response	Role	Discussion
26	B	Selector	To select the best people, workleaders pro-
			vide opportunities for potential employees to
27	B	Selector	relate as much as possible about their previous
			experiences and responses to different work
			situations. Interviews therefore should not be
			intimidating, but they should be formal. While
			it may be superficially fair to each candidate to
			have core questions (27 a.) and use the same
			structure for each candidate, such a rigid struc-
			ture often means the interviewers do not learn
			as much about the candidate, whether positive
			or negative. However, in many countries
			and institutions, there are legal requirements
			to conduct interviews with each candidate
			in exactly the same manner. It is therefore
			important to have at least one question that
			is sufficiently open-ended for candidates to
			reveal their work behavior. This can often be
			achieved through asking a question that asks
			the candidate how they responded to
			a particular work event.

Note: *Adapted from Murphy (1996).

Chapter 3

Leadership in Public School Environments

MaryAnn Christison and Kristen Lindahl

Introduction

Some time ago, we read an ad in a large metropolitan newspaper listing the job requirements for a superintendent of a large urban school District (*The Washington Post*, January 27, 2004, p. A16). The job ad read something like the following:

> The next superintendent should be someone who has worked with a difficult and entrenched bureaucracy, someone who has developed and monitored a multi-million dollar budget, someone who knows how to deal with a demanding community, minority language parents and an aggressive press corps, someone who has a mission for the district, leadership skills, management expertise, and political smarts, someone who can develop effective partnerships with linguistic minority communities, someone who can inspire teachers and improve teacher quality, and someone who is committed first and foremost to children and to their advancement and education.

Margaret M. Scherer, Editor-in-Chief of *Educational Leadership*, stated, "Thank goodness, school leaders—like all educators—are an optimistic bunch" (2004, p. 7). We ask so much of our public school leaders. If we weren't an optimistic bunch, no one would ever apply for leadership positions in public education. We have cited a U.S.-based newspaper above and our experiences in public education have been in the U.S., but we believe the situation in the U.S. is typical of the requirements of leaders in public schools elsewhere in the world. As citizens, we want our public school leaders to accomplish the impossible and expect them to do so.

The challenges for public school leaders are enormous. In this chapter we will focus on the challenge of leadership as it relates to student achievement and academic success. We will review 21 responsibilities of individual leaders that are tied to student achievement. Then, we will review seven principles for sustainable leadership, leadership that goes beyond the characteristics of one school leader. Finally, we will look at individual teachers as leaders and the importance of fostering teacher leadership as a part of sustainable leadership in public school settings. We will investigate answers to the following questions: Is there a relationship between school leadership and student academic success? How do we nurture the qualities of effective leadership in such difficult circumstances? What are some ways to sustain productive change? How can we distribute leadership throughout the school community?

School Leadership and Academic Success

There are approximately 53.6 million students attending 94,000 K-12 schools (National Center for Educational Statistics, 2002) in the United States. These public school children, their parents, and the public in general hope that the 12–13 years of public school education that children receive will prepare them to succeed in the modern world. Just what factors contribute to student success in the modern world and just how schools go about preparing students to experience success motivate an on-going debate in education and spawns movements, such as the U.S.-based 2001 No Child Left Behind (NCLB) in the United States, that try to suggest that the answer to ensuring this success rests with implementing an aggressive standardization agenda.

In truth, the answer to questions about the relationship between what students learn in the public school classrooms and how well prepared they are for work in our modern world is a complex one that goes far beyond such movements. The standards movement places responsibility on classroom teachers—on their knowledge base and on their ability to implement core curricula. While teacher knowledge is critical in ensuring student success, it is not the only factor that should be considered in determining school effectiveness in preparing public school students for success in the modern world. Our interest in public school leadership leads us to consider the relationship between school leadership and student academic success as a major factor in determining success.

There is emerging evidence in the literature on public school leadership in the United States and Canada to suggest that there is a relationship between school leadership and academic success of students. In a Spencer Foundation-funded study on change that occurred over three decades in eight U.S. and Canadian high schools, more than 200 teachers and administrators were interviewed (Hargreaves & Goodson, 2004). This study found that a key force leading to long-term change, was leadership sustainability (Hargreaves & Fink, 2004). Marzano (2005) suggests that school effectiveness increases or decreases a student's chances of success and that what leads to school effectiveness in large part is its leaders. Leadership is considered to be vital to the successful functioning of many aspects of a school, such as whether the school has a clearly stated mission (Bamburg & Andrews, 1990) or a clearly-articulated organizational framework for the overall curriculum and instruction (Oakes, 1989; Eberts & Stone, 1988). What leaders do in schools ultimately influences the success that students have.

Characteristics of Effective Leaders in Public School Settings

Background

Marzano, Waters, and McNulty (2006) reviewed 69 studies in their meta-analysis on general characteristics of school leaders. They looked for specific behaviors related to school leadership that are associated with student achievement. Although each of the characteristics identified by Marzano and his team "have been addressed in the theoretical literature for decades," their work is critical because this is the first time in the history of leadership research in the United States that we can point to a set of competencies for school leaders that are research based. In the next section of this chapter, we will review each of these characteristics and discuss the specific behaviors of leaders associated with each characteristic.

The 21 Characteristics of Effective School Leadership

1   *Affirmation.* Affirmation is exhibited when a leader recognizes and celebrates school accomplishments, and, in addition, is able to acknowledge failures. In other words, when a leader is able to give an honest accounting of the school's achievements and failures, the leader is practicing the skill of affirmation. Creating this balance is not easy. Leaders may boast about their achievements but may have difficulty in acknowledging failures. The opposite scenario may also occur when leaders are too critical and fail to recognize the achievements of both their teachers and their schools.

2   *Change agent.* Effective leaders know when to challenge the status quo and when to leave things in place. They are not making changes just to make waves. They are principled and reasoned in challenging the status quo and in making this reasoning known to the stakeholders, such as teachers and parents. They know when to "disturb them [staff] in a manner that approximates the desired outcome" (Fullan, 2001, pp. 45–46).

3   *Contingent rewards.* This characteristic of effective leadership is associated with the extent to which a leader recognizes and rewards individual competencies. This behavior may seem like routine in most schools and programs, but it is not. In fact Marzano et al. (2006) report that individual recognition of both students and teachers is rare in K-12 education.

4   *Communication.* Effective leaders are pro-active in establishing strong lines of communication with teachers and with students. They also help facilitate communication between students and teachers. See Chapter 12 for a more in-depth treatment of communication skills for leaders. Leaders demonstrate skills in communication when they set up regular meetings with faculty and staff, provide various ways to give updates on program changes and news, such as via email or short memos, and initiate informal conversations and discussions with students, faculty, and staff.

5   *Culture*. Each school environment has its own culture and this culture is shaped by a combination of the values, beliefs, and feelings of the teachers, staff, and students. Effective leaders understand this phenomenon and build a culture that has a positive impact on learning. Creating a positive impact means that school leaders influence the culture of the school through their thoughts and actions. They establish policies to enable others to be effective.

6   *Protection*. Marzano et al. (2006) call this quality of leadership Discipline, but we prefer to use the traditional term *Protection* (Elmore, 2000; Youngs & King, 2002) that is also represented in Murphy's *Leadership IQ* (1996) and discussed in Chapter 1 in this volume. Specifically and in the U.S. public school context, it refers to the skills leaders develop to protect teachers from issues and influences that detract from their instructional time and focus. School leaders use this leadership skill when they create policies about when announcements can be made over the school intercom system or when they make decisions about the times that parents can talk to teachers.

7   *Flexibility*. Flexibility refers to personal behaviors of the leader. Derring et al. (2003) call it "mental agility." In their meta-analysis, Marzano et al. (2006) associate Flexibility with at least four distinct abilities: (1) the ability to adapt one's leadership style to fit different situations; (2) the ability to be either directive or nondirective as the situation warrants; (3) the ability to get people to express what is true for them even if the opinions may be diverse and contrary; and (4) the ability to be comfortable making major changes in how things have been done.

8   *Focus*. The leadership skill of Focus has to do with the "extent to which the leader establishes clear goals and keeps those goals in the forefront of the school's attention" (ibid., p. 50). Effective leaders must pursue goals with vast amounts of energy, and they must marshal all available resources towards achieving these goals. When leaders forefront goals in meetings, on posters, and in school literature, they are demonstrating the leadership skill of Focus.

9   *Ideals/Beliefs*. Bennis (2003) states that well-articulated beliefs are at the core of effective leadership. Effective leaders must share their ideals, beliefs, and opinions openly and explain decision-making processes in terms of these ideals and beliefs. In addition, they must practice what they preach (Cottrell, 2002) and demonstrate the behaviors they wish to see in others in their own daily lives. The behaviors they demonstrate must be consistent with these ideals.

10 *Input*. Input has to do with the extent to which leaders involve others in the design and implementation of important decisions and policies. Effective leaders seek input from others in the decision-making process and then keep others informed as the process evolves. They also demonstrate the attitudes of openness and interest in others' ideas and opinions so that faculty, staff, and students feel encouraged to share their ideas and opinions.

11 *Intellectual stimulation*. Intellectual stimulation refers to the extent to which a leader ensures that faculty are aware of the most current theories and research about teaching and learning. Leaders refer to this research in the decision-making process.

Intellectual stimulation also refers to the extent to which leaders are able to engage faculty in discussions about the relationship between research and practice. For example, faculty should know what a leader's position is on different approaches to reading or the different philosophies about creating best practices for English language learners.

12 *Involvement in curriculum, instruction, and assessment.* An effective leader must be involved in the design of curricular, instructional, and assessment activities. Stein and D'Amicio (2000) state that knowledge of subject matter and pedagogy should be as important to a leader as it is to the teachers. However, Schmoker (2007) states that school leaders do not have any formal mechanisms to accurately gauge the content teachers are actually teaching or how effectively they are teaching it (Marzano, 2003; Evans, 1996; Marshall, 2005). Some important questions that leaders should continually ask are the following: How can I get involved in helping the teachers design curricular activities? How can I help teachers address assessment issues? How can I help teachers address their instructional concerns?

13 *Knowledge of curriculum, instruction, and assessment.* A leader's knowledge of effective practices is important for teachers. Teachers should be able to rely on a leader's knowledge in order to facilitate the day-to-day tasks of teaching and learning. Leaders must not only have knowledge of effective practices, they must also feel comfortable in entering into discussions with their teachers and staff.

14 *Monitoring/Evaluating.* Effective leaders know how to monitor and evaluate both the systems they manage and the individuals within the system. Behaviors associated with this leadership skill are continually monitoring the effectiveness of the school's curriculum, assessment practices, and approaches to instruction. Effective leaders are aware of the impact the school's practices have on student achievement (Marzano et al., 2006).

15 *Optimizer.* Optimism is a critical characteristic of an effective school leader (Blase & Kirby, 2000). Leaders must inspire teachers to accomplish things that might otherwise be a bit beyond their grasp. They do this by becoming the driving force behind major initiatives and by demonstrating positive attitudes towards tasks and the people involved in the tasks needed to accomplish specific goals. The characteristics of optimizers are also considered in Chapter 5 on emotional intelligence.

16 *Order.* All schools and work environments need some sort of order. Order in the meta-analysis done by Marzano et al. (2006) refers to the extent to which a leader establishes a set of standard operating principles and routines. These operating principles and routines must be sufficiently rigid to provide the structure necessary for everyone to know what to do and when to do it, but they must also be flexible enough so that teachers, students, and staff do not feel constrained by the structure and are able to respond to new ideas and developments in creative and innovative ways. This idea is similar to the concept of chaos theory that Murray introduced in Chapter 1.

17 *Outreach.* Leaders must be able to communicate with individuals both inside and outside of the school environment and to establish partnerships with them. These

partnerships include all parents, local services, agencies, governments, churches, and businesses. The school leader represents the school to all of these different constituencies in the community. Effective leaders find ways of ensuring that the school and its accomplishments are highlighted in the community.

18 *Relationships.* Relationships refers to the extent to which a leader demonstrates an awareness of the personal lives of teachers, staff, and students. Effective leaders must rely heavily on face-to-face relationships and on forming emotional bonds with teachers, staff, and students. The ability to form these bonds successfully is also part of the concept of emotional intelligence that will be covered in Chapter 5.

19 *Resources.* The extent to which a leader provides teachers with materials and professional development opportunities necessary for the successful execution of their duties (Marzano et al., 2006, p. 60) is known as Resources. In order for leaders to know what teachers need, they must also establish processes for communicating with teachers about what they need. An effective leadership strategy for Resources would be for a leader to meet with each teacher on a regular basis (e.g., every other month) and visit classrooms often enough to be able to make a determination of needs.

20 *Situational awareness.* Situational awareness refers to a leader's awareness of the details related to how the school functions on a day-to-day basis. Leaders must be aware of both opportunities and also threats. Leaders who demonstrate the skill of situational awareness are able to make successful daily, weekly, and long-term plans. They can anticipate what could go wrong in a given day, develop a plan in advance, and avoid crisis management. Leaders who are adept at situational awareness are also willing to meet problems straight on, such as meeting with teachers who are unhappy regarding a decision that has been made.

21 *Visibility.* Leaders need to be visible. Visibility is the extent to which leaders are in contact with teachers, students, and parents. Fink and Resnick (2001) add that effective school leaders are in classrooms every day and in doing so, they have contact with teachers and students. In addition, they create ways in order to be visible to parents.

As we mentioned above, the individual characteristics of effective school leaders are not new to the literature on leadership. However, the meta-analysis done by Marzano et al. (2006), is the first time in the history of public school leadership in the United States that these 21 characteristics have been identified with a set of competencies needed for leadership to be successful in contributing to academic success of students. Although the list is a useful one for school leaders, the sheer number of items that needs a school leader's attention may be a bit daunting. In order to make the information useful and more manageable, we have created a self-inventory. This self-inventory appears in Appendix 3.1, p. 69. Leaders can use the self-inventory to help them target specific characteristics of effective leadership on which they want to work. They can also use the instrument to get feedback from teachers or other leaders in the school.

> **Task 3.1**
>
> Take the self-inventory that appears in Appendix 3.1, p. 69 on the characteristics of effective school leadership. Rate yourself from 0–2 on each one. Then, ask a colleague whom you trust to rate you on the same indicators. Find time to sit down with your colleague and review the indicators together. Discuss the indicators wherein your ratings were different. Based on the information that you receive in this process, select five indicators on which to work and make improvement.

While the research on the characteristics of effective school leadership was conducted in the United States, we believe that much of it is relevant to public school leadership in contexts outside of the United States because the leadership skills highlighted in this list are more about the nature of human interaction and the expectation of leadership behaviors within those interactions than they are about expectations that are culturally-based.

Sustainable Leadership

Even when leaders have the necessary skills defined in the meta-analysis by Marzano et al. (2006) and even when they routinely and purposefully implement the skills, there are still challenges with school leadership. For one thing, leadership is constantly changing. For example, Principal A may be very skilled in school leadership in terms of leadership characteristics, may have set high goals and standards for the school, and may have boosted the school's reputation by making the central district administration and school board aware of the school's success, only to see herself promoted to a new position in central administration. Principal B steps in, and within two years, the school can no longer boast of the qualities that once made it strong.

Unfortunately, scenarios such as this one are commonplace in public schools. Successful and innovative leaders are often transferred or prematurely promoted before their improvements and changes take hold or become part of the culture of the school. Leadership is not only about developing qualities and strengths within individual school leaders, it is also about creating sustainable leadership—creating long-lasting and widespread improvements. Sustainable leadership is predicated on principles. Hargreaves and Fink (2004), offer seven principles that they believe contribute to this sustainable leadership.

Principles for Sustainable Leadership

Principle 1. Sustainable leadership focuses on putting in place lasting, meaningful improvements in learning, rather than short-term fixes that may look good in the short term but not have lasting effects and consequences.

Principle 2. Sustainable leadership benefits all students—not just a few. Sustainable leadership is tied to issues of social justice. Leaders care not only about their own school, but also accept responsibility for how the actions of their school affect the wider educational and social environment.

Principle 3. Sustainable leadership embraces diversity and recognizes and cultivates many different kinds of learning, teaching, and leading. Sustainable leadership does not impose standardized templates on everyone. How to develop these skills will be dealt with in Chapter 5 on Emotional Intelligence.

Principle 4. Sustainable leadership is activist. Standardized reform initiatives have been potentially harmful to both traditional schools and to innovative schools, but activist leadership has the potential to bring about change that focuses on creating schools that can be the best they can be, whether that be traditional or innovative.

Principle 5. Sustainable leadership focuses on planning and preparing for one's successor, not as an afterthought, but from the first day of one's appointment. This concept may seem like an unusual idea to many leaders, but if the goal of leadership is to create successful schools and promote the academic success of students over the long term, then succession of leadership is an important principle. No innovations should rest solely with one leader. In the business world the concept of planning and preparing for your successor is known as "succession planning" and is now a major focus in many industries.

Principle 6. Sustainable leadership provides opportunities for leaders to network, learn from and support one another, and coach and mentor their successors. Rather than lavishing rewards on a few selected leaders, sustainable leadership works to develop the talents of all educators and encourages all educators to develop skills as leaders.

Principle 7. Leaders develop sustainability in leadership by committing to and protecting deep learning in their schools by fostering leadership in others and distributing leadership responsibility in teachers and staff.

Many of the principles of sustainable leadership can be identified in the work of Goleman and others on the importance of emotional intelligence in the workplace for both leaders and other workers. An interesting study was done in Ontario regarding the EQ requirements for school principals (See the website for Research on Emotional Intelligence in Organizations <www.eiconsortium.org> "Report on the Ontario Principals' Council Leadership Study" (by Stone et al., February, 2005.) The project sought to identify key emotional and social competencies required by school administrators (principals and vice-principals) to successfully meet the demands and responsibilities of the leadership positions they hold. Because there is a growing body of empirical evidence that the type of competencies most closely linked to emotional intelligence are strongly linked to an individual's ability to cope with environmental demands and uncertainties (Mayer et al., 1999), we believe these competencies also underpin sustainable leadership.

The results of the Hargreaves and Fink (2004) research indicate that sustainable leadership is based on principles and that it cannot be left to individual leaders, no matter how skilled they may be at demonstrating the characteristics of skilled leadership.

Leadership changes. In order to effect sustainable leadership, school and district leaders must consider this fact and be prepared for it. Leaders who can inspire others to join them in achieving goals leave the most powerful legacies. By creating teacher leaders and by distributing leadership responsibilities throughout a school, school leaders make it possible for effective goals and policies to continue and for sustainable leadership to be implemented. In Appendix 3.2, p. 72, we offer a checklist based on the principles of sustainable leadership that school leaders and teachers can use to monitor this concept in their own schools.

Task 3.2

Take the self-inventory on sustainable leadership in Appendix 3.2, p. 72. Rate yourself from 0–2 on each one. Then, ask a colleague whom you trust, to rate you on the same indicators. Find time to sit down with your colleague and review the indicators together. Discuss the indicators where your ratings were different. Based on the information that you receive in this process, select five indicators on which to work and make improvement.

Teachers as School Leaders

Sustainable leadership through the development of teachers as leaders has become not so much an innovation in education, but a necessity for effectively improving current school leadership. Once seen as being in a position of autonomy and authority, classroom teachers today may feel themselves dwarfed by the magnitude of curriculum mandates, standardized assessments, and measures of their own standing as professional educators. Much of the isolation, frustration at standardization, and feelings of helplessness with regard to accountability measures are magnified for teachers in public schools. Upon examination of today's teacher from the perspective of a hierarchical, top-down leadership style, teachers are in effect the recipients of a long line of bureaucratic assertions—from the federal level, as in the No Child Left Behind Act of 2001, to the state/province, institutional, and even departmental level within their schools. Without reform, this role of the teacher as an empty vessel can result in "learned powerlessness" (Lieberman & Miller, 2005), which threatens to negate school-wide initiatives, lower student outcomes, and result in high levels of attrition among professional educators. In Chapter 13 on building effective teams, Christison and Murray also refer to the dangers of this "learned powerlessness" and its effect on the overall performance of teams. They discuss Hargie's ideas that "Empowerment means managers identifying areas where they can relinquish power in favor of others—and then actually giving up those areas" (Hargie et al., 1999, p. 62). In school settings, empowerment means that principals and other district leaders must relinquish power in favor of teachers.

How, then, do we break the cycle of bureaucratic mandates and learned power-lessness among administrators and educators? First, we examine why education may be changing and how teacher leaders are a necessary element of this change. In addition, we review much of the literature surrounding teacher leaders that attributes specific characteristics to teachers who demonstrate efficacy as potential leaders. For a teacher-leader to possess certain characteristics is not enough for sustainable leadership; hence, we discuss how the school and district setting should reflect a certain environment responsive to the needs of teacher-leaders. Finally, we present various roles that teachers assume that enhance their own leadership skills and contribute to the professional learning community.

Outside Factors Influencing the Teacher-Leader Climate

In their 2005 article, Lieberman and Miller discuss four major societal changes that in turn affect education: changes in the world, changes in the economy, the role of the private sector in public schools, and the changing student/teacher demographic. Changes in the world, such as shifts in family structure dynamics, manifest themselves in the school setting, as do economic changes. Globalization has altered the balance between the need for manual labor versus the need for knowledgeable workers, in addition to increasing use of the Internet for course offerings and learning activities. Previously, a high school diploma may have been enough to obtain a fair job; post-secondary education is now more the rule than the exception. Global discourse centered around private sector values now infiltrate the public domain, as visible through lower public engagement and voter turnout, tax reductions, and less social responsibility (and more individual responsibility) overall (Lieberman & Miller, 2005).

A new power paradigm between the government and the private sector directly influences what we see in today's classrooms on a daily basis. Schools especially feel the pressure of the shift of the school as a public institution that is held to the norms of private business through standardized assessments for children and accountability measures for teachers. Alternative schools, such as private, charter, and magnet schools are examples of how education is shifting to take a larger part of the private (vs. public) agenda. An example of the private influence on public institutions can be seen in the State of Utah's recent move to implement a school voucher system, which would give families tax credits of up to $3000 for sending their children to private schools (Stricker, 2007). If passed, this would be the largest school voucher program in the United States that allows citizens to use public monies for private school tuition.

In the Australian public school system, such a change was made several decades ago. All private schools receive some public funding from the Federal Government, based on formulae that have changed over the years depending on the political climate at the time. Schools are state-regulated and the majority of funding for government schools is from the state. The original goal of this movement was to ensure equity in instruction for the many parochial schools. Now, schools as diverse as religious schools (including

Muslim, Jewish, and Christian) and elite schools with large foundations and high tuition still receive Federal funding.

The rationale behind the voucher program is that it would provide more school choices for parents, and could improve public schools by increasing competition among students and lessening class sizes in public schools. Objections to the program come from those who argue that public money should not be spent on private schools that are not subject to the same standardization and accountability measures, or can specifically select students based on religion, academics, or ability to pay private school tuition (ibid.). Regardless of opinions on the matter, this is a prime example of the influence of the private values of competition and individuality on the public, social institution of education. Along with the mission of schools as a public institution comes public opinion, which in recent years has diminished while, conversely, expectations for teachers and students have risen. Schools today must reconcile this public mission with the increasing influence of world-wide privatization (Lieberman & Miller, 2005).

The negotiation of public and private ideologies with respect to the school system, affects both student and teacher demographics. More teachers are leaving the profession than entering it, with attrition rates at high-poverty schools exceptionally high (Darling-Hammond, 2003). Teachers must now meet standards outside of their credentials as mandated by NCLB's "Highly Qualified" criteria, and possess a varied and profound skill set (such as foreign language proficiency and/or various licensure endorsements) to deal with more advanced content and widening student populations. Today's school-age children reflect a myriad of cultures, ethnicities, languages, and socioeconomic strata, conditions which should be addressed as part of the school system's public mission; yet, teachers are held accountable in a private manner for their capacity to integrate this new demographic into an older (albeit shifting) paradigm. A new currency of cultural capital is present between students in a classroom, and teachers must shift perspectives and roles and must continue to be engaged in ongoing professional development; nowhere is this new student demographic more visible than in the ESL/EFL classroom.

These outside factors may paint a bleak picture for the future of public education, but they also present advantageous conditions for schools to implement change. All of the variables mentioned above create weaker boundaries between institutions, fewer segregated roles, and render traditional borders irrelevant (Hargreaves & Fullan, 2000). This is not necessarily a negative aspect because increased fluidity characterizing the more dynamic relationship between schools and the outside community allows educators to work with more diverse groups, and see parents and community as sources of learning and support rather than interference. "Social geographies" of education also promote increased access for teachers to networks of professional learning and the many approaches to education possible via collaboration with outside groups (ibid.). Rather than looking at the role of teacher as a stagnant one within a stolid institution, these outside factors enable us to look at the development of the teacher as a leader and mentor capable of instigating the change that pushes the continual innovation of schools systems in our society.

Defining Characteristics of a Teacher-Leader

Upon review of much of the current research surrounding the characteristics of an effective teacher-leader, many commonalities exist. There seems to be almost a general consensus that the teacher as leader must demonstrate both the capacity and the commitment to contribute to education beyond the scope of his or her own classroom. In addition, a teacher leader must be willing to assume more responsibility, to assist in those school reforms that impact organizational and curricular processes, and to invest his or her time to improve the overall school climate (Beachum & Dentith, 2004). Anderson also makes these points in Chapter 7 in his discussion of understanding one's stewardship and the sphere of influence that individuals can have outside of the scope of a leadership position.

Table 3.1 illustrates qualities that teacher-leaders must possess if they are to be effective in bringing about change. The characteristic of teacher-leaders most frequently mentioned in the research is the willingness to take risks in regard to implementing changes within the school, including even personal inquiry on behalf of the teacher. Another frequently mentioned characteristic is the teacher's ability to include and draw from community and university resources. Indeed, willingness to take appropriate risks and to make use of existing resources are often skills that we as teachers seek to develop in our students, making the case for the teacher-leader as a learner, an important role as well.

Fostering an Environment for the Teacher-Leader

The teacher as leader is critical to achieving the goal of shared decision-making, community building, and professional empowerment (Wynne, 2001). In fact, much of the literature surrounding the creation of teachers as leaders cites common ideals that a school or institution must have in place in order to produce effective teacher leaders. In schools with successful teacher-leader programs in place, the administrators invest in teachers who seek to become leaders by treating their faculty as active and able contributors to the larger social environment of the school, rather than isolated individuals responsible for only a set number of students. Districts and administrators provide leadership training for teachers, as often teachers are given leadership roles without adequate preparation (ibid.). Fullan agrees, commenting that "the contemporary principal's role is largely inflated and overburdened due to the lack of leadership opportunities and training for teachers" (1993, p. 17).

A concrete way to promote these opportunities is for schools to offer incentives for teachers who invest time to improve their educational knowledge base. Administrators may opt for staff development programs that publicly recognize the skills and abilities of various staff members, and make curricular and policy decisions that are more enabling rather than prescriptive (Lieberman & Miller, 2005). Longitudinal staff development that makes use of teachers as leaders is a prime example of this ideal. Day-long or even week-long staff development conferences can promote teacher awareness

Table 3.1 Characteristics of the Teacher-Leader

Characteristic	Theoretical Support
High sense of ethics, moral purpose	Fullan, 1993; Wynne, 2001
Make/implement change	Fullan, 1993; Beachum & Dentith, 2004
Reflect/Maintain personal vision or personal philosophy of teaching	Fullan, 1993; Wynne, 2001; CSRI, 2005
Inquiry skills	Fullan, 1993; Wynne, 2001; Lieberman & Miller, 2005
Expertise/Mastery of Content and Methodology	Fullan, 1993; Wynne, 2001; CSRI, 2005
Collaboration	Fullan, 1993; Wynne, 2001; CSRI, 2005
Active Learning	Fullan, 1993
Work with all students	Fullan, 1993; Lieberman & Miller, 2005
Mentor	Wynne, 2001
Community involvement and use of higher education resources	Fullan, 2000; Wynne, 2001; Beachum & Dentith, 2004
Take risks in teaching and curriculum development/implementation	Fullan, 1993; Wynne, 2001; Beachum & Dentith, 2004; Lieberman & Miller, 2005; CSRI, 2005
Perform action research in schools and classrooms	Wynne, 2001
Discuss issues of power, race and class; social consciousness and political activity	Wynne, 2001; CSRI, 2005
Confidence in presenting self publicly	Lieberman & Miller, 2005
Connect leadership skills to classroom practice	Lieberman & Miller, 2005
Create safe environments for teachers and students to learn	Lieberman & Miller, 2005

of new trends in education, but allow little time for teachers to integrate the proposed strategy or method into their teaching practice. In order for change to truly impact the existing system, mastery of the concept is essential to being able to use it automatically as a personal practice, as well as to implement the concept when making changes to one's personal practice (Fullan, 1993). To draw upon Bloom's model for demands on cognition (1956), with only superficial exposure to a new concept, it is difficult to develop beyond knowledge and comprehension stage.

In a study of a nationwide top-down curriculum renewal exercise in Malaysia, Goh (1999) found that the cascade model (sometimes known as the training of trainers model) was ineffective because it was based on assumptions that were not warranted for most teachers in her setting.

The strategy assumed that the theory and the resultant practice of a complex curriculum innovation could be communicated both in a short space of time and using simple techniques of information-providing seminars . . . and that those teachers (now change agents themselves) whose task it was to communicate the changes to their peers in schools would have the skills, experience and status to do so successfully.

(Kennedy et al., 1999, p. 1)

The finding that complex curriculum innovation may not succeed if the only mechanism for dissemination is input through information seminars is consistent with other findings that have shown that transmission of knowledge and even skills does not necessarily lead to teacher growth and changes in classroom practice (for example, Bartels, 2005, and discussion above). In order that trained teacher trainers can themselves conduct training effectively, there is a need for longitudinal professional development that must include an on-going coaching and feedback sessions. However, by educating and coaching a cohort of teachers over time (one year or more) in a certain discipline or specialty, teachers have time to move beyond recognition and understanding of the method into applying it to their teaching practice in new ways (i.e., application and synthesis in Bloom's model).

Later, administrators may draw upon the first cohort to act as coaches in subsequent years for newer cohorts receiving the same training as the original cohort. District officials and administrators may perform needs-based assessments of their schools and faculties, and decide together which staff development programs will best meet professional learning and school goals. By distributing the weight of decision-making and professional education, the administrator is engaging leadership among teachers by eliciting opinion and delegating responsibility, which results in a unified staff working together toward common goals.

Values regarding the school environment an administrator wishes to create greatly influence the willingness of educators to assume leadership positions. If a teacher feels that administrators treat their opinions with respect, they may be more willing to initiate change without fear of failure or reprobation. Openness to ideas of change and innovation on behalf of administrators and school leaders may also promote teachers to independently seek change based on their own observations or action research, and in turn, take risks on programs that could possibly improve student achievement. Principals create this type of climate by conveying the expectation that teachers assume these roles as part of their professional identity. The underlying values of many schools with effective teacher-leader programs include a unity of purpose among faculty and staff, chances for teachers to build their individual strengths, reciprocal trust between teachers and administrators, and a strong sense of pride, community and social justice (Beachum & Dentith, 2004).

Implementing Practice as a Teacher-Leader

Due to the increasing complexity of the school system, the teacher as leader is not limited to traditional roles, such as a department chair or a grade-level team leader. Leadership roles vary from less intensive roles, such as observing colleagues or collaborating on projects, to serving as links between higher-level administration and the teaching faculty.

In more practical roles, teachers can occupy leadership positions by facilitating team meetings and/or taking notes at larger-scale school meetings where change and curriculum are discussed. Whether the head of a teacher team or part of a larger administrative organization, the teacher-leader can submit and publish the notes from their respective committee meetings, which helps with follow-up, accountability, and awareness of school-wide issues among colleagues. With respect to classroom practice, the teacher-leader might invite colleagues into the classroom to observe practices and provide feedback; administrators in turn support this by providing time outside of the preparation period for teachers to observe each other.

Administrators can further support this practice by providing observation training, and deciding with teacher-leader teams on a school-wide initiative on which to focus during observations. With the same school-wide initiative in mind, teacher-leaders can establish study groups or professional learning communities for continued and supported staff development by grade level, content area, or interest. Again, the publication and submission of minutes from these meetings to administrators and colleagues are essential to promoting the values of the professional learning committee throughout the school and/or district.

It is important that teacher-leader meetings or committees do not revert to always discussing strategies or venting about students and school problems. The teacher-leader can expand the focus of his or her colleagues by presenting text, books, video, etc. that are relevant to the committee goals and intellectually stimulating for adults, not only for students. Teacher-leader committees may also be ideal times outside of discussing school business to integrate issues of equity, culture, power, race, class into the discussion, particularly due to the shifting population demographic as mentioned earlier in this chapter.

Teacher-leaders also play a large part as they revitalize the profession itself. Through mentoring new teachers, becoming more involved at universities in the preparation of pre-service teachers, and conducting active research in classrooms and schools, teacher-leaders help shape the new culture of education and receive recognition for the wisdom they have garnered during their multiple years of professional participation. On the opposite end of the spectrum, novice teachers bring recent knowledge and practices straight from a university or teacher-preparation setting, and are eager to learn how their education translates into practical opportunities to engage students. Teacher-leaders can model this for them, as well as encourage them to join in the collegial conversation without the intimidation of being observed or evaluated by an administrator. Veteran teachers often approach new ideas in different ways due to the lens of their previous experience.

In an ethnographic study of 25 teacher-leaders from five different schools in the same Midwestern school district, certain structures and organizations promoting leadership development emerged. Prevalent among all five schools were teacher teams according to grade levels or content areas, teacher committees that addressed issues and events relative to everyday events in their schools, and teachers who held positions as "quasi-administrators." Individuals in this role spent some time during the day teaching, but also assumed responsibilities with regard to curriculum planning, instructional supervision and observation, mentoring, large field trips or school-wide projects, discipline and referral, special programs, and management of grant writing and funding (Beachum & Dentith, 2004). A variation on this position is what Lieberman & Miller (2005) call "leading in the 'middle space,'" where a teacher with specific expertise does not work in the classroom, but serves primarily as a liaison between classroom teachers and administrators with regard to supporting teacher leadership, learning, and student success. In this case, the teacher-leader does not necessarily view him/herself as an administrator, but instead as a teacher of adults.

Special thought should be put on the ESL teacher as a leader simply due to the nature and weight of their position within the larger school climate. We would be remiss not to count the trained ESL teacher as a potentially lone individual who also feels an impact of those changes and demands higher than that of his/her colleagues. Consider that the ESL teacher in U.S. public schools or the English teacher in public schools where English is not the medium of instruction, may be the *only* ESL or EFL teacher at his or her site or part of a cadre of only two or three teachers out of a faculty of 50 or 60 other educators. Having worked widely in the field with in-service teachers, and from our own personal experiences, we recognize that the English language teacher comes face to face with changes in global demographics, sometimes teaching students with anywhere from two to 20-plus different first languages at a time.

With regard to accountability, English Language Learners' scores are specifically disaggregated from No Child Left Behind (2001) data to determine whether or not a school has achieved Annual Yearly Progress (AYP), and are tested every year of their involvement in an ESL program to track their progress in English language learning. ESL teachers often possess the most expertise about ESL at their own sites, making it difficult for them to find models of teaching and curriculum development within their building or from administrators. They may act as consultants on curriculum and methodology for English Language Learners for this reason as well.

Due to their close interaction with ELL students and their families, ESL teachers are sometimes the only advocates for their student population in school and district decision-making processes. It is not difficult to see the necessity of fostering leadership skills among ESL teachers in public schools to help them effectively manage the additional duties they may encounter due to their specific and much-needed position.

In short, six domains exist where teacher-leaders can make the most impact: collegiality, context, continuous learning, management of change, sense of moral purpose, and teaching and learning (Fullan, 1993). With regard to helping manage school bureaucracy, many are hopeful that teacher-leader structures will aid in dissolving the tension between management and leadership in schools, and create a better combination that includes both perspectives among a larger group of professionals. Through their roles as leaders, teachers can inspire others, act as community facilitators, and help others organize themselves for the purpose of achieving short- and long-term goals. By acting as models, teacher-leaders at a site will hopefully lead through example, demonstrating classroom practice and professional community membership that exudes the values and beliefs of inquiry, advocacy, innovation, participation, and reflection.

Conclusion

In this chapter we have focused on key elements for understanding leadership in public schools, particularly the role that instructional leadership can play in the form of teacher-leaders. In order to accomplish this task, we have tried to tie the concept of teacher-leader into the already existing literature on public school leadership. We first reviewed the 21 characteristics of public school leaders that have an impact on student achievement. In addition, we presented the concept of sustainable leadership, the ability to create long lasting and wide spread improvements, and outlined seven principles for school leadership to follow. Finally, we turned to the concept of teacher as leader. By looking at the outside factors that influence the teacher-leader climate and the characteristics of effective teacher-leaders we were able to discuss how to foster an environment for teacher-leaders and implement an effective teacher-leader practice from both the standpoint of effectiveness within the school and the personal satisfaction one achieves from leadership experiences.

References

Bamburg, J. & Andrews, R. (1990). School goals, principals and achievement. *School Effectiveness and School Improvement. 2*, 175–191.

Bartels, N. (Ed.) (2005). *Applied linguistics and language teacher education*. New York: Springer.

Beachum, F. & Dentith, A.M. (2004). Teacher leaders creating cultures of school renewal and transformation. *The Educational Forum, 68*, 276–286.

Bennis, W. (2003) *On becoming a leader*. New York: Basic Books.

Blase, J. & Kirby, P.D. (2000). *Bringing out the best in teachers: What effective principals do* (2nd edn). Thousand Oaks, CA: Corwin Press.

Bloom, B. (1956). *Taxonomy of educational objectives, Handbook 1: Cognitive domain*. New York: McKay.

Cottrell, D. (2002). *Monday morning leadership*. Dallas, TX: Cornerstone Leadership Institute.

CSRI, The Center for Comprehensive School Reform and Improvement. Teacher leaders: The backbone of sustained improvement. *December 2005 Newsletter*. http:// www.centerforcsri. org/index.php?option=com.content&ask=view&id=259&itemid=5 Accessed May 27, 2007.

Darling-Hammond, L. (2003). Keeping good teachers: Why it matters, what leaders can do. *Educational Leadership, 60*, (8): 6–13.

Davidson, B. & Dell, G. (2003). A school restructuring model: A toolkit for building teacher leadership. Paper presented at annual meeting of the Educational Research Association. Chicago, IL.

Derring, A., Dilts, R., & Russell, J. (2003). Leadership cults and culture. *Leader to Leader. 28*, 31–38.

Eberts, R. & Stone, J. (1988). Student achievement in public schools: Do principals make a difference? *Economics of Education Review, 7*, 291–299.

Elmore, R.F. (2000). *Building a new structure for school leadership.* New York: Albert Shanker Institute.

Evans. R. (1996). *The human side of change.* San Francisco: Jossey-Bass.

Fink, E. & Resnick, L.B. (2001). Developing principals as instructional leaders. *Phi Delta Kappan, 82* (8): 598–626.

Fullan, M. (1993). Why teachers must become change agents. *Educational Leadership.* 50(6), 12–17.

Fullan, M. (2000). The three stories of education reform. *Phi Delta Kappan, 8*: 581–584.

Fullan, M. (2001). *Leading in a culture of change.* San Francisco: Jossey-Bass.

Gilpin, A. (1997). Cascade training. In I. McGrath (Ed.) *Learning to train,* (pp. 185–194), Englewoods Cliffs, NJ: Prentice-Hall.

Goh, C. (1999). Nationwide curriculum innovation: How do we manage? In C. Kennedy, P. Doyle & C. Goh (Eds.), *Exploring change in English language teaching* (pp. 5–18). Oxford: Macmillan Heinemann.

Hargie, O.D.W., Dickson, D. and Tourish, D. (1999). *Communication in management.* Aldershot, England: Gower.

Hargreaves, A. & Fink, D. (2004). The seven principles of sustainable leadership. *Educational Leadership, 61*(7), 8–13.

Hargreaves, A. & Fullan, M. (2000). Mentoring in the new millennium. *Theory into Practice, 39*(1): 50–56.

Hargreaves, A. & Goodson, I. (2004). *Change over time? A report of educational change over 30 years of eight U.S. and Canadian schools.* Chicago: Spencer Foundation, as referenced in A. Hargreaves, & D. Fink, (2004). The seven principles of sustainable leadership, *Educational Leadership, 81*(7): 8–13.

Kennedy, C., Doyle, P., & Goh, C. (eds) (1999). *Exploring change in English language teaching.* Oxford: Macmillan Heinemann.

Lieberman, A. & Miller, L. (2005). Teachers as leaders. *The Educational Forum, 69*, 151–162.

Marshall, K. (2005). It's time to rethink teacher supervision and evaluation. *Phi Delta Kappan, 86*(10), 727–744.

Marzano, R.J. (2003). *What works in schools: Translating research into action.* Alexandria, VA: Association for Supervision and Curriculum Development.

Marzano, R.J. (2005). A tool for selecting the "right work" in your school. [Online] http:// www.marzanoandassociates.com/pdf/schooleffect_09.pdf

Marzano, R.J., Waters, T., & McNulty, B.A. (2006). *School leadership that works.* Alexandria, VA: ASCD and Aurora, CO: McREL.

Mayer, J.D., Caruso, D.R., & Salovey, P. (1999). Emotional Intelligence meets traditional standards for an intelligene. *Intelligence, 27*, 267–298.

Murphy, E.C. (1996). *Leadership IQ.* New York: John Wiley & Sons, Ltd.

National Center for Education Statistics (2002). *Table 1: Projected number of participants in educational institutions by level and control of institution.* Fall 2002. [Online]. Retrieved March 1, 2007 from http://nces.ed.gov/ccd

Oakes, J. (1989). Detracking schools: Early lessons from the field. *Phi Delta Kappan*, 74, 448–454.

Scherer, M.M. (2004). Perspectives: What do leaders do? *Educational Leadership* 61(7): 7.

Schmoker, M. (2007). *Results now*. Alexandria, VA: Association of Supervision and Curriculum Development.

Stein, M. K. & D'Amicio, L. (2000). How subjects matter in school leadership. Paper presented at the annual meeting of the American Educational Research Association, New Orleans.

Stone, H., Parker, D.A., and Wood, L.A. February, 2005. Report on the Ontario Principals' Council Leadership Study. <www.eiconsortium.org> Accessed January 14, 2008.

Stricker, N. (2007). Do school vouchers belong in Utah? *The Salt Lake Tribune*. April 9, 2007. <http://www.sltrib.com//ci-5060104> Accessed January 7, 2008.

Wynne, J. (2001). Teachers as leaders in education reform. *ERIC Digest*, ED 462376.

Youngs, P. & King, M.B. (2002). Principal leadership for professional development to build school capacity, *Educational Administration Quarterly* 38(3): 643–670.

Appendix 3.1

Characteristics of Effective School Leadership

0 = ineffective 1 = moderately effective 2 = highly effective

Leadership Characteristics	Ratings		
	0	**1**	**2**
1. I recognize and celebrate the school's accomplishments.			
2. I recognize, celebrate, and reward individual teacher accomplishments.			
3. I can give an honest accounting of the school's achievements and failures.			
4. I know when to challenge the status quo and when to leave it in place.			
5. My reasons for challenging the status quo are principled.			
6. I am pro-active in communicating with the teachers.			
7. I set up regular meetings with the teachers.			
8. I am pro-active in setting up communication between students and teachers.			
9. I give frequent updates on program and administrative changes via email messages and short memos.			
10. I seek feedback from teachers on program and administrative changes.			
11. The policies that I establish in the school are designed first and foremost to enable teachers to be effective in creating optimal learning environments for students.			
12. I protect teachers from issues and influences that detract from their instructional time and focus.			
13. I try to adapt my leadership style to fit different situations.			
14. I try to get both teachers and students to say what is true for them.			
15. I am comfortable in making major curricular and administrative changes.			

continued

Leadership Characteristics	Ratings		
	0	1	2
16. I establish clear goals for the school.			
17. I keep the goals at the forefront of the school's attention.			
18. I share my ideals, beliefs, and opinions openly.			
19. I involve others in the design and implementation of important decisions and policies.			
20. I am aware of the most current theories and research about teaching and learning.			
21. I refer to the most current theories and research about teaching and learning in my conversations with teachers, students, and parents.			
22. I am involved in the design of curriculum, instruction, and assessment in my school.			
23. Knowledge of subject matter and pedagogy is important to me.			
24. I am knowledgeable of effective instructional practices.			
25. I know how to monitor and evaluate management systems within my school.			
26. I know how to monitor and evaluate individual teachers within my school.			
27. I can inspire teachers to accomplish the tasks on focus.			
28. I am effective at establishing a set of standard operating principles and routines.			
29. I can effectively communicate with individuals both inside and outside of the school environment.			
30. I am knowledgeable about the personal lives of the teachers, staff, and students.			
31. I provide teachers with materials and professional development opportunities.			
32. I meet with each teacher in my school on a regular basis.			

Leadership Characteristics	Ratings		
	0	I	2
33. I am aware of the opportunities and threats my school faces.			
34. I am able to make successful daily, weekly, and long term plans.			

Appendix 3.2

Principles for Sustainable Leadership

0 = ineffective 1 = moderately effective 2 = highly effective

Principles of Sustainable Leadership	Ratings		
	0	1	2
1. I try to put in place lasting improvements and put systems in place to sustain these changes.			
2. I accept responsibility for how the actions of my school affect the wider community.			
3. I embrace diversity.			
4. I cultivate different types of learning and teaching within the school.			
5. I continually focus on creating a school that is the best it can be.			
6. I focus on planning for my successor even though I may have no intention of leaving at this moment.			
7. The changes in my school do not rely solely on me to implement.			
8. I provide opportunities for teachers to network.			
9. I provide opportunities for teachers to develop and use their leadership skills.			
10. I am committed to distributing leadership responsibility throughout teachers and staff.			

Chapter 4

Innovation as the Hallmark of Effective Leadership

Fredricka L. Stoller

Introduction

Try imagining a language program that has experienced little, if any, change in the past 50 years. It is likely that we would not see instances of communicative language teaching, computer-assisted language learning, or project-based instruction. We might not see team teaching, student-centered lessons, or self-access centers. We probably would not witness students out in their communities engaged in service learning. Nor would we observe systematic attempts by teachers to integrate strategy instruction into classroom teaching. Students might be left to their own devices to build their vocabulary, without the help of word walls, semantic maps, and teachers' attempts at systematic recycling. Students might be simply asked to read, without the assistance of pre-, during-, and post-reading tasks, fluency practice, text-structure awareness activities, and sustained silent reading. Despite the absence of this representative sampling of classroom practices that could be considered commonplace in many instructional settings today, students would indeed be learning language, just as they have for millennia. But would the language program be as responsive to learner and teacher needs as it could be? Would learners be truly engaged? Would the program graduate students who could successfully continue learning on their own? Would the program have a good reputation and the competitive edge that accompanies that reputation? Would the program attract the best and brightest teachers? Unlikely.

Why, in fact, is such stagnancy uncommon? Why do so many language programs change over time? The answer is straightforward: Because change is a stable feature of organizational life. But changes do not necessarily ensure improvements. The implementation of team teaching, for example, does not always lead to positive results. Similarly, the adoption of communicative language teaching approaches is oftentimes superficial, with classes actually being very teacher centered and form focused. And computer-assisted language learning can still result in rote learning, with little carryover to students' meaningful language use. But some changes, of course, do result in true improvements in student learning, student motivation, teacher satisfaction, and language program management. Such changes are often referred to as innovations.

Although the terms *change* and *innovation* are often used interchangeably, it is useful to distinguish one term from the other. In all settings, including language programs, change is predictable and inevitable, resulting in an alteration in the status quo but not necessarily in improvements. Language programs experience change when, for example, faculty retire (or relocate), student enrollments decline (or increase), educational costs escalate, a favorite textbook goes out of print, and governmental legislation or institutional policies mandate new practices. Many of these changes occur without any planning or control on the part of the language program. Innovations, on the other hand, typically result from deliberate efforts to bring about improvements. Innovations are, therefore, key to improving language program learning, teaching, and management; in fact, innovations are essential to thriving and progressive language programs.

It is often said that behind every innovation is a supportive administrator or at least someone with decision-making powers. It is therefore important to explore innovation from a leadership perspective, with the resulting implications for language teaching professionals who hold official titles such as director, chair, head master, curriculum head, or level supervisor. The same implications hold true for teachers who have a vision of improved language program practices and who essentially assume leadership roles when they propose, plan, implement, and evaluate improved practices (often with the help of others). To explore the intricacies of innovation in the context of leadership, I briefly describe the complex nature of innovations, the symbiotic relationship between top-down and bottom-up innovations, impetuses for innovation, characteristics of more easily adopted innovations, and the cycles of innovation diffusion process. I conclude with 12 guiding principles for those wanting to inspire innovation in their language programs.

Task 4.1

Keeping in mind the distinction between the terms *change* and *innovation*, identify some changes and innovations that have taken place in the recent past in a language program with which you are familiar. Can you identify their causes and/or impetuses?

On the Nature of Innovations

Innovations are odd entities because what might be perceived as innovative in one setting might be seen as standard practice in another. Such perceptions reveal the importance of the local context. As an example, some programs have integrated language skills instruction for decades (combining, for example, listening and speaking, reading and writing, or listening and reading), whereas other programs are only now contemplating moving from discrete-skill to integrated-skills instruction. In one setting, integrated skills are accepted as the norm, while in the other they are viewed as innovative (and may, in fact, be causing discomfort among those who are perfectly content with discrete-skill instruction). As another example, in some programs language teachers have modified the mandated curriculum to include project-based learning, thereby engaging students in interesting, extended projects that lead to improved language abilities and content learning. In such settings, project-based learning is perceived as not only compatible with program goals, but also relevant to student needs. In another setting, we might have two brave teachers who have approached their supervisor to ask permission to pilot a modest project with their students; reception to the novel request might be mixed. In one setting, project work is a well-accepted practice; in the other, it is perceived as an innovation, at least by some. These examples reveal the context-specific nature of innovation.

Accompanying innovations of all types are new ways of thinking, adjustments in attitudes and behaviors (e.g., Kennedy & Kennedy, 1996), a willingness to abandon the relative comfort of the status quo, and the adoption (and possibly later adaptation) of new practices. As a result, innovations usually require increased workloads, some form of retraining, and costs in terms of time, energy, resources, and intellectual attention (Fang & Warschauer, 2004). Innovations oftentimes provoke discomfort (revealing itself as anxiety, insecurity, defensiveness, and sometimes disruptive turf battles) among those who are content with current practices. So while innovations bring about improvements, they almost always result in resistance as well. Being cognizant of these realistic outcomes is important for language program personnel who take the lead in ushering in innovative practices.

Task 4.2

Think of an innovation that might be appropriate in a language program that you are familiar with. If that innovation were to be adopted, how might teacher and/or administrative workloads increase? What types of retraining might be needed? What costs would have to be anticipated (e.g., monies, time, energy, resources)? Who might be inconvenienced by the innovation?

Top-Down and Bottom-Up Innovations: A Symbiotic Relationship

Innovations require leadership in some form (Hamilton, 1996); they can be proposed (or imposed) in a top-down fashion (e.g., by administrators, teacher supervisors, Ministries) or promoted in a bottom-up manner (e.g., by teachers in the trenches) (see Markee, 1997, for a discussion of teacher-initiated innovations). Because "monolithic central controls stifle innovation" (Hamilton, 1996, p. 3), top-down innovations are rarely successful without teacher enthusiasm and endorsement. Similarly, bottom-up innovations rarely sustain themselves without the support of the administration (see also Chapter 9 on planning strategically for further discussion of top-down, bottom-up processes). Support —in its many forms, including positive attitudes, resources, release time, retraining opportunities, and explicit recognition—is an essential prerequisite for successful and sustained innovations (see Carless, 1998; Kennedy & Kennedy, 1996; Rubdy, 2000). Davison articulates the need for administrative support by stating that "the active support and understanding of all key administrative staff and decision-making bodies can make or break an ESL program" (1992, p. 40). Without support, even teachers who are initially strong advocates of an innovation may become disillusioned.

Innovations that are successfully implemented, whether they are initially top-down or bottom-up propositions, essentially require some sense of ownership from those involved in and affected by the innovations. To develop a sense of ownership, all parties need to understand the underpinnings and actual applications of the innovation. Such understandings develop through training, open discussions, and dialogue, in open forums where questions can be asked, answers provided (or at least explored), apprehensions shared, and fears acknowledged.

Task 4.3

Most language professionals realize that bottom-up initiatives require top-down support and that top-down initiatives require the endorsement of teacher and staff. What forms of top-down support might be both realistic and effective? What steps can be taken to nurture teacher and staff buy-in?

Impetuses for Innovation

It is important for those in leadership positions to understand the types of environments that are most conducive to innovation. Some innovations "spring from a flash of genius" (Drucker, 1991, p. 9), others from a critical incident (de Lano et al., 1994), but "most stem from a conscious, purposeful search for innovation opportunities" (Drucker, 1991, p. 9). But what sort of environment provides the impetus for such searches (and the hard work that accompanies getting an innovation off the ground)? The impetus for innovation can emerge from a variety of circumstances, including dissatisfaction with the status quo, a stated (or unstated) desire for more professionalism, the recognition of new student needs, faculty interest and suggestions, and more top-down mandates from the higher administration, governmental legislation, and/or standards endorsed by professional organizations (see Stoller, 1997). Let's examine each of these impetuses in turn.

Some degree of dissatisfaction with the status quo—among teachers, students, staff, boards of directors, and/or higher administration officials—can provide a powerful impetus for innovation. Rubdy (2000) has observed that when dissatisfaction is dealt with in a thoughtful and self-reflective manner, "transformational possibilities" open up. Thus, for example, when teachers are dissatisfied with current textbooks, they are likely to be more willing to serve on a textbook selection committee and be more responsive to a mandate to recommend brand new materials for the program. When students exhibit frustrations with their oral skills, they may be more apt to entertain out-of-class conversation partner programs and service-learning opportunities. When faculty are unhappy with some aspect of the curriculum, placement procedures, exit criteria, working conditions, or outdated computer software, they may jump at the opportunity to become involved in discussions that lead to improvements, even if those discussions add to their busy schedules.

In other settings, a desire for more professionalism among faculty and staff can provide the needed impetus for innovation. When teachers state that they wish they knew more about reading strategy instruction, or the interface between self-access centers and their classes, or content-based instruction, as plausible examples, they are indirectly indicating a desire for access to new information. In settings such as these, teachers may be more responsive to new practices (e.g., the piloting of a new textbook series with a commitment to strategy instruction, a Friday bag-lunch speaker series, the institutionalization of action research) if linkages to stated interests are visible.

The recognition of "new" student needs (whether the needs are, in reality, new or not) often motivates innovation as well. There was a time when incorporating type-writing instruction into language curricula was considered innovative. Of course, such practices would be considered outdated (and hardly innovative) in most settings today. Yet, introducing students to word processing skills (in some settings) or perhaps corpus linguistics tools so that students can conduct their own computer-based language analyses (in other settings) might be considered an improvement in current practices and a response to students' needs. In other settings, it might be brought to the attention of language program personnel that students exiting the program have pronunciation that is incomprehensible to their employers. When such complaints are lodged, teachers may be more willing to attend workshops on pronunciation and restructure the curriculum so that more sustained attention to pronunciation runs throughout.

It is not uncommon for teachers to return to their home institutions after attending professional conferences or workshops with lots of new ideas. Those ideas are often revealed in casual conversations, in the form of questions such as these: Why don't we carpet classroom walls so that we can create easy-to-use word walls? Why don't we have a particular concordancing software in the computer lab? Why don't we collaborate with nearby schools and give our students the opportunity to introduce their cultures and countries to the local kids? How can we change the reading curriculum to accommodate students' reading fluency needs? Why don't our students create multi-skill portfolios for end-of-term assessment? It is often in the midst of such enthusiasm and questioning that innovations spring forth. Leaders should be poised to take advantage of the energy and openness that accompany such inquiries; it is in such environments that innovations receive a positive reception.

And, finally, the momentum needed to introduce and implement an innovative proposal may stem from external mandates (from the higher administration, a governing board, a ministry of education, or standards approved by a prestigious professional organization). In such cases, the mandate may inspire the energy required to rethink current practices and propose new and improved ones. Such mandates have led to credit-bearing courses for language students, the reconfiguration of curricula to align with standards, and/or more aggressive recruitment practices, to name just a few innovations that have stemmed from mandates "from above."

Whatever the impetus may be, those who take a lead in innovation diffusion processes need to be vigilant and responsive to conditions that will help them usher in new ideas and innovative practices. Building upon dissatisfaction, faculty readiness for professional development and/or the adaptation of ideas culled from outside sources, newly perceived student needs, and external mandates might foster the right conditions for introducing and then implementing new practices, even though those new practices are likely to upset the comfort of the status quo for some.

Task 4.4

Consider the language programs with which you have been associated (as either a student, teacher, and/or administrator). In which situations have proposals for innovations (small or large) been most warmly received?

Characteristics of More Easily Adopted Innovations

Although we must accept the fact that there may always be a few stalwart resisters to programmatic innovation, those numbers can be minimized if innovations are introduced in ways that maximize receptiveness by those impacted by the innovations. Much research on innovation diffusion, over the years, has determined that the adoption rates of innovations are partially dependent on perceptions (rather than realities) of the innovations themselves (e.g., Henrichsen, 1989; Markee, 1993, 1997; Rogers, 2003; Rogers & Shoemaker, 1972; Stoller, 1994, 1997; White, 1993). Thus, if an innovation is perceived to be difficult to implement (even if, in fact, it would not be that hard), the innovation is likely to fail. If the innovation is perceived to be incompatible with current practices (even if, in fact, it is compatible in many ways), the innovation is likely to receive a cool reception. It behooves those trying to introduce innovations to consider how to present them so that they are perceived in the most positive light early in the process. Demonstrating a match between the innovation and institutional philosophy, resources, and/or faculty and student needs is helpful (see Kelly, 1980). Explaining how the innovation is a response to current dissatisfaction is effective as well.

What this signifies for those in leadership positions is that they must take great care in how they introduce and present innovations to those who will be affected by them. In innovation research conducted in U.S. intensive English programs (see Stoller, 1997), it was determined that innovation adoption rates depend, in part, on middle-range perceptions, rather than perceptions that fall on extreme ends of different continua (e.g., a difficult-to-easy continuum, an incompatible-to-compatible continuum). That is, when certain attributes are perceived to be "sufficiently" present and fall within what has been labeled a *zone of innovation* (see Figure 4.1), adoption rates are likely to increase. Let's consider a few examples. When an innovation is perceived to be sufficiently compatible with current practices, favorable attitudes toward the innovation are likely to develop and thus motivate potential supporters. If, on the other hand, the innovation is perceived to be incompatible with current norms, the innovation will not be warmly received (see Fang & Warschauer, 2004). At the same time, if the same innovation is viewed as too compatible with current practices, those impacted might question why they should trouble themselves with something so similar to current practices. In other words, if an innovation is perceived to be a minor adjustment in or a simple tinkering with current practices, those affected may not want to invest the time and energy in the proposal.

Similarly, if an innovation is perceived as too complex, those affected are likely to be frightened away. Yet, if an innovation is seen as being too simplistic, the innovation may be regarded as not different enough from current practice. Consequently, those innovative efforts will not be seen as worthwhile. Similar reactions occur with innovations that are perceived as too explicit, flexible, and original. When an innovation is seen as being too flexible, for instance, it may be rejected on the grounds of not being explicit enough. And when an innovation is perceived to be too novel, therefore lying outside the realm of acceptable norms, conventions, and expectations, it is likely to be rejected. What leaders need to remember is that to earn support for their innovative ideas, innovations must be described so that they fall within the zone of innovation; in other words, they must be perceived as being neither excessively divergent from, nor too similar to current practices.

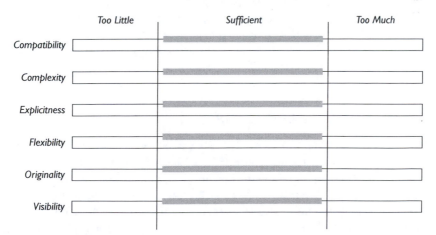

Figure 4.1 The Zone of Innovation

Issues related to perceptions, however, are not as straightforward as they might seem. Innovations are likely to influence stakeholders (e.g., teachers, students, parents, the community, the directorate) in different ways. Some innovations directly affect just a few individuals, while others radiate out to have broader consequences (de Lano et al., 1994). Thus, how one presents a given innovation might have to differ, depending on the audience. Without misrepresenting the innovation, those needing to gather support may have to plan various ways to introduce the innovation. Explaining how an innovation is likely to increase the revenue stream will only be persuasive to some; other attributes, of the same innovation, will need to be highlighted to gain the support of other stakeholders. For example, students' parents may be persuaded when they are told that the innovation will increase their children's competitive edge; teachers may be persuaded when they realize that the innovation actually gives them more freedom in terms of materials selection; program administrators might be swayed when they understand how the same innovation might help students perform better on mandated exams.

Task 4.5

Identify an innovative practice that you would like to see adopted in a language program that you are familiar with. How would you describe it to different stakeholders so that it falls inside the zone of innovation?

Task 4.6

Consider the following attributes of a particular innovation: The innovation is likely to enhance the visibility of the language program, improve perceptions of the program's academic legitimacy, assist students in developing autonomy, and help teachers plan instruction that extends beyond the confines of the traditional classroom. What innovation could it be? Which of these attributes would you share with which stakeholders to gain support?

The Cycles of Innovation Diffusion

The innovation diffusion process involves successive cycles that require long-term involvement, commitment, and support. (See de Lano et al., 1994, and Markee, 1997, for summaries of seminal works on this topic.) Although introduced here in a linear fashion, it should be noted that the process itself is rarely linear. Nonetheless, it is worthwhile considering the essential components of the process; after all, it is indeed a process. The first phase, sometimes referred to as the initiation phase, planning stage, or diagnostic phase, will involve the presentation and consideration of an innovative idea. At this stage, a "rational argument alone is generally not sufficient to bring about change" (Brindley & Hood, 1990, cited in de Lano et al., 1994, p. 492). More importantly, this phase requires needs analyses, the determination of a need for improvement, an evaluation of the proposed innovation in light of the needs analyses, the decision to proceed, the gathering of support, an assessment of available and required resources, and, finally, plans for implementation, including the building of a sense of ownership among those involved in the implementation process. It is at this stage when administrators, proposing top-down innovations, need to build acceptance among faculty, and when teachers, proposing bottom-up innovations, need to secure the support of administrators and their colleagues.

The implementation phase, the second part of the process, involves attempts to translate innovative ideas into practice. Carless (1998) has identified three factors as being particularly relevant to the implementation phase: teacher attitudes, teacher training, and teacher understanding of the innovation. Parallels surely exist with staff, students, parents, and other stakeholders. It should come as no surprise that when teachers have favorable attitudes toward an innovation, they are likely to be supportive of implementation efforts. Conversely, if teachers are reticent about the innovation, they are likely to exhibit resistance to implementation. But positive attitudes are not enough to ensure successful implementation. Teachers need both ongoing training and support (see Brindley & Hood, 1990); without them, teachers may become frustrated and disillusioned and then reject the project, thereby undermining implementation efforts. Carless (1998) emphasizes the importance of teachers having a thorough understanding of the principles and applications of the innovation. Without this understanding, the implementation phase may end in failure, with misconceptions being translated into mismatched applications.

During the continuation (or diffusion) phase, the innovation either becomes an integral part of the program, accepted by most, or it is discarded. It is during this stage when teachers are likely to reinterpret the innovation in light of their own knowledge and experience (Carless, 2004). Thus, over time, the original innovation may change into a "weakened" (or strengthened) version of the original. Such changes should not be viewed immediately as a failure; in fact, some of the changes may have strong justifications (e.g., context-specific pressures). Because innovations are likely to change during the continuation phase, leaders must establish and implement a system that will guide change rather than leaving the process to chance (Watson Todd, 2006).

Essential to the continuation phase are formative and summative evaluation. Different forms of evaluation, including classroom observations, will determine if there is support to continue and sustain the innovation or if abandonment is inevitable. Classroom observations are particularly revealing because it is only through observations that one can gain a real sense of "actual rather than reported behavior" (Kennedy & Kennedy, 1996, p. 360).

Key to the successful management of top-down and bottom-up innovations is the active engagement of stakeholders in all three stages of the process. Teachers, for example, should be involved in decision-making during the planning stage; they should be central to the implementation stage; and they should be granted some control during the continuation stage (Watson Todd, 2006). Equally important are relationships, as stated by Fullan:

> No amount of political advocacy or even technical support will generate success unless *relationships improve*. If I had to identify one and only one indicator of successful implementation, it would be whether or not relationships among participants improved.
>
> (1998, p. 257)

Relationships, like the process itself, become more complicated when stakeholders are members of different cultural groups or networks, a common phenomenon in language programs (see Carkin, 1997; Guariento, 1997; Kennedy & Kennedy, 1998; Rubdy, 2000). Thus, leaders need to be attentive to the potential complications that might arise in multicultural environments (see also Chapter 1 on intercultural issues in the workplace).

Task 4.7

Relationships have been identified as critical to a successful implementation phase. How might relationships at the planning and continuation phases influence the innovation diffusion process? What can leaders do to cultivate good working relationships?

Guiding Principles for Those Wanting to Inspire Innovation

The management of innovations, as challenging (and exhilarating) as the task may be, requires leadership. We conclude the discussion of innovation in the context of leadership with 12 principles:

1   View every innovation as an opportunity for professional development. Fullan and Stiegelbauer wisely remind us that "we cannot develop institutions without developing the people in them" (1991, p. 349).
2   Be willing to experience failure in the quest for innovative practices. According to Rogers (2003), 75 percent of all innovations fail. We need to be willing to fail on some attempts in order to succeed on others. What is critical is the learning that can occur from failed attempts.
3   Devote time to nurturing a sense of ownership among those who will be impacted by the innovation; innovations cannot sustain themselves without a team of steadfast supporters. Share responsibility by letting those impacted help shape the innovation and remain engaged in the implementation and continuation phases (see de Lano et al., 1994; Markee, 1994).

4 Identify faculty leaders and support risk-takers.

5 Remember that subjective perceptions of innovations are oftentimes more powerful than objective viewpoints. Therefore, take care in the ways that innovations are depicted to those who will be impacted.

6 Learn to live with resisters. Most language programs, like other work environments, have faculty and staff who are content with the status quo.

7 Be willing to let innovations follow their natural course. Initial conceptions (even if successfully implemented) are likely to change as people experiment with them, as the field changes, and as new faculty and students come into the program.

8 Grant freedom and flexibility to faculty. Allow for curricular fluidity and experimentation. Such an atmosphere requires trust and open lines of communication.

9 Communicate with stalwart resisters, rather than ignore them or be frustrated by them. If we force them to change their ways, they may become further disillusioned and energized to build an active resistance (see also Chapter 12 for a communicative toolkit).

10 Do not leave innovations to chance. Plan, strategize, and pilot, whenever possible (see also Chapter 9 on planning strategically).

11 Provide adequate administrative support. When leaders are supportive of an innovation, a positive message is transmitted.

12 Remember that innovations alter the status quo, undermining the security of some stakeholders. Leaders must help those impacted by the innovation see how they can overcome difficulties and reap the benefits of the innovation (or at least learn to live with them) (see also Chapter 2 and Murphy's concept of the "healer" role of leaders).

References

Brindley, G., & Hood, S. (1990). Curriculum innovation in adult ESL. In G. Brindley (Ed.), *The second language curriculum in action* (pp. 232–248). Sydney: National Centre for English Language Teaching Research, Macquarie University.

Carkin, S. (1997). Language program leadership as intercultural management. In M.A. Christison & F.L. Stoller (Eds.), *A handbook for language program administrators* (pp. 49–60). Burlingame, CA: Alta Book Center.

Carless, D. (1998). A case study of curriculum implementation in Hong Kong. *System, 26*, 353–368.

Carless, D. (2004). Issues in teachers' reinterpretation of a task-based innovation in primary schools. *TESOL Quarterly, 38*, 639–662.

Davison, C. (1992). Look out! Eight fatal flaws in team and support teaching. *TESOL in Context: Teaching English to Speakers of Other Languages, 2*(1), 39–41.

de Lano, L., Riley, L., & Crookes, G. (1994). The meaning of innovation for ESL teachers. *System, 22*, 487–496.

Drucker, P.F. (1991). The discipline of innovation. In J. Henry and D. Walker (Eds.), *Managing innovation* (pp. 9–17). Newbury Park, CA: Sage.

Fang, X., & Warschauer, M. (2004). Technology and curricular reform in China: A case study. *TESOL Quarterly, 38*, 301–323.

Fullan, M. (1998). Linking change and assessment. In P. Rea-Dickins & K.P. Germaine (Eds.), *Managing evaluation and innovation in language teaching: Building bridges* (pp. 253–262). London: Longman.

Fullan, M. & Stiegelbauer, S. (1991). *The new meaning of educational change* (2nd edn.). New York: OISE Press and Teachers College Press.

Guariento, W.A. (1997). Innovation management issues raised by a distance-learning project in Eritrea: Can such projects be successfully transplanted from one developing country to another? *System, 25*(3), 399–407.

Hamilton, J.A. (1996). *Inspiring innovations in language teaching*. Clevedon: Multilingual Matters.

Henrichsen, L.E. (1989). *Diffusion of innovations in English language teaching: The ELEC effort in Japan, 1956–1968*. New York: Greenwood Press.

Kelly, P. (1980). From innovation to adaptability: The changing perspective of curriculum development. In M. Galton (Ed.), *Curriculum change* (pp. 65–80). Leicester: Leicester University Press.

Kennedy, C., & Kennedy, J. (1996). Teacher attitudes and change implementation. *System, 24*, 351–360.

Kennedy, J., & Kennedy, C. (1998). Levels, linkages, and networks in cross-cultural innovation. *System, 26*, 455–469.

Markee, N. (1993). The diffusion of innovation in language teaching. In W. Grabe (Ed.), *Annual review of applied linguistics, 13: Issues in second language teaching and learning* (pp. 229–243). New York: Cambridge University Press.

Markee, N. (1994). Using electronic mail to manage the implementation of educational innovations. *System, 22*, 379–389.

Markee, N. (1997). *Managing curricular innovation*. New York: Cambridge University Press.

Rogers, E.M. (2003). *Diffusion of innovations* (5th edn.). New York: Free Press.

Rogers, E.M., & Shoemaker, F.F. (1972). *Communication of innovations: A cross-cultural approach* (2nd edn.). New York: Free Press.

Rubdy, R. (2000). Dilemmas in ELT: Seeds of discontent or sources of transformation? *System, 28*, 403–418.

Stoller, F.L. (1994). The diffusion of innovations in intensive ESL programs. *Applied Linguistics, 15*(3), 300–327.

Stoller, F.L. (1997). The catalyst for change and innovation. In M.A. Christison & F.L. Stoller (Eds.), *A handbook for language program administrators* (pp. 33–48). Burlingame, CA: Alta Book Center.

Watson Todd, R. (2006). Continuing change after the innovation. *System, 34*, 1–14.

White, R.V. (1993). Innovation in curriculum planning and program development. In W. Grabe (Ed.), *Annual review of applied linguistics, 13: Issues in second language teaching and learning* (pp. 244–259). New York: Cambridge University Press.

Chapter 5

The Role of Emotional Intelligence in ELT Leadership

Denise E. Murray and MaryAnn Christison

Introduction

In the Introduction, we noted that researchers and practitioners in a variety of fields have recognized the importance of the human element in the workplace, sometimes referred to as "soft skills," in contrast to more technical or "hard skills." While the ELT field has a long history of humanism in teaching, there has been less attention paid to the role of such skills in educational managers and leaders.

While other chapters in this volume provide technical skills (see, for example, Chapters 9, 10 and 11 on strategic planning, quality assurance, and performance management respectively), in this chapter, we focus on one aspect of soft skills, as discussed in Pink's recent work, in which he claims we need more high touch rather than high tech in the workplace: "High touch involves the ability to empathize, to understand the subtleties of human interaction, to find joy in one's self and to elicit it in others, and to stretch beyond the quotidian in pursuit of purpose and meaning" (2005, p. 52).

Why Emotional Intelligence?

To elucidate this perspective, we draw primarily on the work of Goleman (1998)[1] who has found this high touch ability critical to effective leadership and management. These abilities are critical for leading in the volatile, unpredictable world of language education (see Chapter 1 for a discussion of chaos theory and its effects). As Vince (1996, p. 73) puts it: "Increasingly, the challenge of managing and organising change will not be faced by finding solutions but by finding different ways of engaging with uncertainty and paradox, with the emotional and the irrational in organizations." He calls for a "shift in focus away from the rational into the relational" (ibid., p. 81). This chapter provides just such a shift. Goleman (1998) has found that for star performance in all jobs, in every field, emotional competence is twice as important as purely cognitive abilities. For success at the highest levels, in leadership positions, emotional competence accounts for virtually the entire advantage" (ibid., p. 34). In fact, he and colleagues found that "the higher level of the job, the less important technical skills and cognitive abilities were, and the more important competence in emotional intelligence became" (ibid., p. 33). Cooper and Sawaf (1997) have developed an EQ Map. This map comes from individuals completing a questionnaire, available in their book, a questionnaire that has been researched and tested on many executives. While their framework differs somewhat from that of Goleman, the questionnaire is a useful tool for any (aspiring) leader. In a study of highly effective urban principals and typical principals, Williams (2004) found that the characteristics that distinguished the highly effective were: self-confidence, self-control, conscientiousness, achievement orientation, initiative, organizational awareness, developing others, leadership, influence, change catalyst, conflict management, teamwork/collaboration, and analytical thinking, only one of which (analytical thinking) is a cognitive competence. Other researchers also found that the best principals exhibit competencies such as more conceptual thinking, team leadership, and organizational commitment than do average performers (Spencer & Spencer, 1993). The work on EQ is succinctly summarized by Senge: "People with high levels of personal mastery . . . cannot afford to choose between reason and intuition, or the head and heart, any more than they would choose to walk on one leg or see with one eye" (1994, p. 168).

From our experience, emotional intelligence (EI)[2] is a key competence for successful leadership and so this chapter provides an overview of EI; in addition, since EI is also key for star performance for all workers, leaders need to both understand the concept, develop their own EI and develop plans for professional development of their staff.

What is Emotional Intelligence?

Goleman's work builds on almost a century's work in applied psychology on the concept of social intelligence (Thorndike, 1920) and the notion that competence may be more important than intelligence (McClelland, 1973). Currently, there are three sometimes competing models (Bar-on, 2006; Emmerling & Goleman, 2003; Mayer et al., 2000) that approach the construct from different perspectives. We have found Goleman's approach to be transparent for educators and builds on the work of multiple intelligences (Gardner, 1985) already familiar in language education. Many of the competencies that constitute emotional intelligence (EI) are essential for the leader to fulfill the role of healer and protector that Murphy (1996) describes (see Chapter 2 for a discussion of this role). Importantly, both Goleman's work and that of others in the EI field are research-based.

Goleman's first set of studies involved general discussions around defining the characteristics of EI. Since then, he has conducted empirical research on the role of EI in the workplace. His research included a survey of what U.S. employers are looking for in their employees, and competencies essential to do 181 jobs in 121 companies and organizations worldwide. The research included 15 global companies, both public and private sector and countries in Latin America and Europe as well as North America. In addition, he commissioned other research into the components of EI and its role in the workplace.

He defines emotional intelligence as "the capacity to recognize our own feelings and those of others, to motivate ourselves, and to manage emotions well in ourselves and in our relationships." Edge and Clarke (Chapter 12 this volume) also take the position that leadership requires communication with others as well as communicating and understanding oneself. However, just because a leader has emotional intelligence does not mean it is used in practice. Like Gardner, Goleman also asserts that emotional competence can be learned. For him, emotional competence is "a learned capability based on emotional intelligence that results in outstanding performance at work." He therefore recently has preferred to use the term EI competence to indicate that emotional competence and EI are related, but not the same, with emotional competence being based on EI. Further, he and colleagues have found that EI competencies have both a developmental and neurological base. Dreyfus (2001), for example, found that people often build EI competence over the course of their lives, because of specific life experiences. Neuroscience has identified areas of the brain responsible for emotion; further, they have shown that emotional competence is dependent on the functioning of the wiring between the prefrontal and emotional centers.

In our own work as leaders and managers in ELT, we have found the conceptual framework Goleman[3] developed to be a powerful tool to learn emotional competence and to evaluate our own performance as leader managers. This framework has two dimensions, each of which we discuss in detail below: Personal competence and social competence.

Personal Competence

Goleman's studies have shown that personal competence includes those competencies that determine managing oneself, that is, self-awareness, self-regulation, and motivation, each of which we describe below.

Self-awareness

Self-awareness, which means knowing one's own internal states, preferences, resources, and intuitions, has three competencies:

1   emotional awareness, that is, recognizing one's emotions and their effects;
2   accurate self-assessment, that is, knowing ones' strengths and limits;
3   self-confidence, that is, having a strong sense of one's self-worth and capabilities.

To be emotionally aware includes what is often termed intuition, the feeling that a particular action, idea, or response is appropriate or not. Intuition has been widely studied and is built on years of experiences, something akin to what Dreyfus and Dreyfus (1986) refer to as expertise, the expert knowledge built up over years of experience. All this research notes that such expertise or intuition usually cannot be explained by the person who has it; it is not part of rational, conscious thinking. Knowing one's strengths and limits is essential. No leader is perfect; the key is to recognize areas of weakness and work to improve them. Within the field of language teaching, self-reflection has been promoted as a means to changing teaching practice (for example, Richards & Lockhart, 1994).

As well as self-reflection, leaders can learn much about their own practice through 360 degree evaluations, that is, evaluations from managers, peers and subordinates. Of course, such evaluations need to be conducted in an atmosphere of trust and openness, with no resulting effect on the evaluators. Questionnaires that are completed anonymously by peers and subordinates are therefore useful. However, assessment by managers should be part of regular performance management (see Chapter 11 for details on performance management). Self-confidence is not arrogance; rather, it is based on honest self-assessment. Leaders lacking self-confidence find decision-making difficult, if not impossible. Effective leaders have confidence in their decision-making and its implementation, despite opposition and difficulties.

Self-regulation

Self-regulation, which means managing one's internal states, impulses, and resources has four competencies:

1   self-control, that is, keeping disruptive emotions and impulses in check;
2   trustworthiness, that is, maintaining standards of honesty and integrity;
3   adaptability, that is, flexibility in handling change;
4   innovation, that is, being comfortable with novel ideals, approaches, and new information.

Being self-aware is not sufficient. Leaders also need to be able to regulate their emotions. This does not mean denying emotional states and feelings, but using them positively. Thus, the leader needs to control those emotions that would disrupt the workplace or affect others negatively. When emotions take over, the rational brain shuts down, resulting in the "flight or fight" response developed for life-threatening situations. So, for example, bullying or outbursts of temper are inappropriate for the leader. In such situations, the brain's resources needed for other work are not available and furthermore, the effects on co-workers can be catastrophic. Self-control extends to developing the resilience necessary for dealing with stress. But, as well as controlling disruptive emotions, self-regulation includes positive competencies that build trust and allow the leader to operate successfully even in changing circumstances. To build trust, the leader needs to be ethical, not only in words, but in deed. The leader needs to set the example in the workplace. One way of setting the example is to admit to mistakes immediately, to follow through on a promise, be careful and conscientious, and to be discreet with the confidences of others. The effective leader capitalizes on change and innovation and takes risks (see Chapter 4 for further information on innovation and change). Flexibility is a key characteristic of leaders who exhibit this competence. The effective leader doesn't just react appropriately to change, but provides opportunities for innovation and creativity among staff.

Motivation

Motivation, which means having the emotional tendencies that guide or facilitate reaching goals, has four competencies:

1   achievement drive, that is, striving to improve or meet a standard of excellence;
2   commitment, that is, aligning with the goals of the group or organization;
3   initiative, that is, readiness to act on opportunities;
4   optimism, that is, persistence in pursing goals despite obstacles and setbacks.

All effective leaders are internally driven to achieve but the balance with the other personal competencies ensures that this driving does not negatively affect others in the workplace. Part of the drive is the continual desire to learn. While English language teaching is about learning, not everyone in an organization has the desire to learn, nor is everyone committed to the goals of the organization, especially in an era of casualization and lack of commitment from employers (see Chapter 9 for tools for developing shared goals and values). While intrinsic motivation is essential for star performers, the leader also needs to exercise tools such as performance management to ensure standards of excellence in teaching and all other aspects of the organization's work (see Chapter 11 on managing performance). Leaders with initiative find new ways of doing things, do not take the bureaucratic or "rule" approach. Optimism has been found to be an essential characteristic of all successful leaders. They act from a sense of "this is achievable", rather than "this won't work." They consider obstacles as a normal part of operation and seek to find ways to solve the problem.

Task 5.1

Use the personal competencies checklist in Table 5.1 to rate your own competence. For each competency, state whether your level of competency is *low, average* or *high* and *how important* that competency is for your work—whether it is *slightly important, important,* or *very important.* Which competencies do you need to develop to match those needed for your work?

All of these competencies that constitute personal competence interact. For example, accurate self-assessment prevents the leader from hubris that self-confidence and optimism could generate. Trustworthiness prevents the leader from being so driven that the ends justify the means.

Social Competence

Goleman's research has shown that social competence includes those competencies that determine how one handles relationships, and consists of empathy and social skills, each of which we describe below:

Empathy

Empathy, which means being aware of other people's feelings, needs, and concerns, consists of five competencies:

1   developing others, that is, sensing other people's development needs and bolstering their abilities;
2   service orientation, that is, anticipating, recognizing, and meeting customers' needs;
3   leveraging diversity, that is, cultivating opportunities through different kinds of people;
4   political awareness, that is, reading a group's emotional currents and power relationships.
5   understanding others, that is, sensing other people's feelings and perspectives, and actively being interested in their concerns.

As can be seen from the list of competencies above, empathy includes putting oneself in the situation of clients/customers, colleagues, and the organization as a whole. Effective leaders do not take all the credit themselves, nor do they micromanage; rather, they develop an understanding of the strengths and weaknesses of staff, and build on people's strengths, while working to develop areas of weakness. Mentoring is a key skill in this area, a skill that has also been shown to be effective in language teaching situations (Wallace, 1994). Additionally, this understanding of staff is vital for the role of selector that we have described in Chapter 2, and described more fully by Murphy (1996). As well as empathy for colleagues, a leader also needs to know what customers want, even when they themselves are not sure of their needs. Leveraging diversity is more than acknowledging and hiring people with different cultural, linguistic, and religious backgrounds, but recognizing that they can bring new ways of looking at the world and new ways of behaving that can be a positive influence. As we saw in Chapter 1, different national cultures have different constellations of values, which need to be recognized and incorporated into an organization's ways of behaving. The leader has a responsibility to prevent and sanction intolerance and stereotyping. Within our own experience as leaders, we have witnessed the powerful effect of having non-native speaker teachers teaching English. Not only do they provide a role model for learners, but also such teachers help colleagues see their students through different lenses (Murray & Garvey, 2004). The last competence in empathy refers to the ability to detect the subtle (and sometimes not so subtle) informal systems and alliances. Effective leaders recognize

Table 5.1 Personal Competence Checklist

		Rating of Your Level of Competence				Rating of Level of Importance of the Competency for Your Work		
		Low	Average	High		Slightly Important	Important	Very Important
Self-awareness	Emotional awareness							
	Accurate self-assessment							
	Self-confidence							
Self-regulation	Self-control							
	Trustworthiness							
	Adaptability							
	Innovation							
Motivation	Achievement drive							
	Commitment							
	Initiative							
	Optimism							

their existence as inevitable, but do not react to it emotionally. They are objective, trying to capitalize on it, not for self-interest, but to improve teaching and learning.

Social Skills

Social skills, which means adeptness at inducing desirable responses in others, have eight competencies:

1   influence, that is, wielding effective tactics for persuasion;
2   communication, that is, listening openly and sending convincing messages;
3   conflict management, that is, negotiating and resolving disagreements;
4   leadership, that is, inspiring and guiding individuals and groups;
5   change analyst, that is, initiating and managing change;
6   building bonds, that is, nurturing instrumental relationships;
7   collaboration and cooperation, that is, working with others toward shared goals;
8   team capabilities, that is, creating group synergy in pursuing collective goals.

Social skills are those through which the leader can influence the direction of the organization and ensure commitment from staff. Many of the competencies that constitute social skills are detailed in other chapters of this volume (see Chapter 12 on communication and Chapter 13 on building teams). Here, we would like to stress the importance of building bonds and nurturing instrumental relationships (see also Chapter 2 and the role of the connector). We have found that effective leaders consider all stakeholders—from the university president to a student's parent to a funding agency to a janitor—need to be nurtured. There is an adage in China that the most powerful person in any organization is the person who has the keys. Although this may be a lowly position in the hierarchy, if you can't find the person to open the classroom or meeting room, then the school or university can't serve its clients. Additionally, we want to stress that influence and managing change and nurturing relationships should be done from a commitment to the goals of the organization, not as manipulation to exert power.

Task 5.2

Use the social competencies checklist in Table 5.2 to rate your own competence. For each competency, state whether your level of competency is *low*, *average* or *high* and *how important* that competency is for your work—whether it is *slightly important*, *important*, or *very important*. Which competencies do you need to develop to match those needed for your work?

Table 5.2 Social Competence Checklist

		Rating of Your Level of Competence				Rating of Level of Importance of the Competency for Your Work		
		Low	Average	High		Slightly Important	Important	Very Important
Empathy	Understanding others							
	Developing others							
	Service orientation							
	Leveraging diversity							
	Political awareness							
Social skills	Influence							
	Communication							
	Conflict management							
	Leadership							
	Change catalyst							
	Building bonds							
	Collaboration and cooperation							
	Team capabilities							

Task 5.3

In Chapter 2, we provided a survey to help leaders examine their own practices. Question 8 provides the following scenario and possible actions.

8. You have just been hired as the director of an intensive English program. One of the instructors, Carlos, has been teaching in the program for over 15 years. In reading the personnel files, you notice that he had always received excellent student evaluations until the last two quarters. In your first meeting with all the faculty you notice that he seems withdrawn and unenthusiastic. You arrange to have lunch with each instructor to get to know them better. After some general conversation with Carlos, you say:

a. "You've clearly been an excellent instructor here for many years, so your last two semester student evaluations really seem odd. But, I don't want to talk about them first—let's talk about you. How do you feel about the program? About the students and your job?"
b. "You've clearly been an excellent instructor here for many years, so your last two semester student evaluations really seem odd. Let's go over all the students' comments and find out what's going wrong with your teaching."
c. "You've clearly been an excellent instructor here for many years, so your last two semester student evaluations really seem odd. When I see a sudden change like this, I get very worried. Perhaps it's time for you to think about a change. As you know, I do have to ensure the whole program provides excellent instruction for all our students."

Murphy notes that this involves the role of selector, and that the most effective workleaders choose a.

What emotional competencies are these workleaders exhibiting when they choose a?

Developing Emotional Competence

Although emotional competence has both a developmental and neurological base, it is not fixed genetically, nor is its development limited to childhood. Those who do not have the life experiences that develop EI competence can develop any of the competencies listed above through appropriate teaching and learning. Additionally, excellence in performance does not require people to excel in all the competencies. Different jobs require high levels in different competencies. For example, outstanding school principals need the ability to seek out feedback from teachers and parents. In addition, leaders require sufficient competence in most to be effective.

Professional Development

However, traditional professional development, which is based on cognitive, explicit learning, is ineffective in developing EI competence, because the emotional brain learns differently from the rational brain. Within English language teaching, many (for example, Freeman, 1998; Richards, 1998) have noted that training approaches that focus on transmission of knowledge and skills are inadequate and that to grow professionally teachers need to become reflective practitioners by studying their own practice and using the data from such study to evaluate and change their practice as appropriate. "One insight that emerges consistently from these studies of language teachers at work is that teachers learn by doing, by reflecting and solving problems, and by working together in a supportive environment" (Yates & Brindley, 2000).

Since emotional intelligence relies on the emotional centers of the brain that learn differently from the rational centers, developing EI competencies in oneself or one's staff also requires a different approach to teaching and learning. Based on an examination of training and other literature, Goleman, Cherniss and Cowan (n.d.) developed guidelines for best practice in training in EI competencies, specifically for the EIConsortium. These guidelines correspond to the four phases of the EI competency development process: preparation, training, transfer and maintenance, and evaluation.

1   *Preparation.* The preparation phase includes a needs analysis, of both the organization and those to be trained, the latter assessment requiring sensitivity to people's feelings. In other words, the manager/leader who is requiring the professional development needs to exhibit all the EI competencies themselves. The needs analysis has to take into account the potential trainees' readiness for training and provide the opportunity for people to choose whether to undertake the training or not. Organizations need to encourage professional development and link it to individual's personal goals.

2   *Training.* Trainers need also to exhibit EI competence, demonstrating empathy and engagement with the trainees. They also suggest giving staff as much control over their own training as possible, setting clear goals and breaking them into manageable chunks, providing experiential learning opportunities and feedback on practice, providing models and support. For those of us in English language education, many of these characteristics of best practice are ones we ourselves use in our own teaching and training. As research in our field has shown, the most effective professional development is one that involves self-reflection and provides ongoing support. "Teachers learn[ing] from their practice of teaching, by trying to make sense of it and developing their own principled understandings of their own practice" (Wigglesworth & Murray, 2007).

3   *Transfer and maintenance.* Goleman and his colleagues stress the importance of encouraging the use of the new skills in the workplace and developing a culture of learning. Within English language teaching, carry over from training into practice has been found to be dependent on ongoing support, enquiry and reflection, and

what Edge (2002) calls cooperative development (see Chapters 12 and 16 in this volume).

4   *Evaluation.* As with all successful professional development programs, evaluation is vital to ensure the program met its goals and also to assess changes for future offerings.

Task 5.4

In Tasks 5.2 and 5.3, you evaluated your own personal and social competence. Now try to think about ways you can develop those competencies, given the guidelines presented above. Write an action plan for developing those competencies you consider essential for your work, but in which you have not yet become proficient.

Conclusion

In this chapter, we have explained the importance of EI competence for superior performance of all staff and its vital importance for leaders. While we have summarized Goleman's approach and applied it to the English language teaching context, we highly recommend that readers read Goleman's work for themselves —both his book and the guidelines for best practice in professional development available on the web, even though the examples he provides are from the business world.

Notes

1   A number of "how to" books have been developed on EQ competence, such as Bradberry & Greaves (2005) and Cooper & Sawaf (1997). See also the Emotional Intelligence Consortium website: http://www.eiconsortium.org for research articles and discussions on the concept.
2   We will use the abbreviation EI, rather than EQ, in line with the terminology used by the major consortium for research in emotional intelligence.
3   As discussed above, the concept of EI was developed by Mayer and Salovey; but it is the *framework* developed by Goleman that we have found useful in our work.

References

Bar-on, R. (2006). The Bar-on model of emotional-social intelligence. Retrieved February 8, 2007, from http://www.ieconsortium

Bradberry, T., & Greaves, J. (2005). *The emotional intelligence quickbook.* New York: Simon & Schuster.

Cooper, R.K., & Sawaf, A. (1997). *Executive EQ: Emotional intelligence in leadership and organizations.* New York: Grosset/Putnam.

Dreyfus, C. (2001). Scientists and engineers as effective managers: A study of the development of interpersonal abilities. Unpublished PhD, Case Western Reserve University.

Dreyfus, H.L., & Dreyfus, S.E. (1986). *Mind over machine*. New York: The Free Press.

Edge, J. (2002). *Continuing cooperative development: A discourse framework for individuals as colleagues*. Ann Arbor, MI: University of Michigan Press.

Emmerling, R.J., & Goleman, D. (2003). *Emotional intelligence: Issues and common misunderstandings*. Retrieved February 8, 2007, from http://www.ieconsortium.org

Freeman, D. (1998). *Doing teacher research: From inquiry to understanding*. Pacific Grove, CA: Heinle and Heinle Publishers.

Gardner, H. (1985). *The theory of multiple intelligences*. New York: Basic Books.

Goleman, D. (1998). *Working with emotional intelligence*. London: Bloomsbury.

Goleman, D., Cherniss, C., & Cowan, K. (n.d.). *Guidelines for best practice*. Retrieved February 18, 2007, from http://www.eiconsortium.org/research/guidelines_for_best_practice.pdf

Mayer, J.D., Salovey, P., & Caruso, D. (2000). Models of emotional intelligence. In R.J. Sternberg (Ed.), *Handbook of intelligence*. Cambridge: Cambridge University Press.

McClelland, D.C. (1973). Testing for competence rather than intelligence. *American Psychologist, 28*, 1–14.

Murphy, E.C. (1996). *Leadership IQ*. New York: John Wiley and Sons, Ltd.

Murray, D.E., & Garvey, E. (2004). The multilingual teacher: Issues for teacher education. *Prospect, 19*(2), 3–24.

Pink, D. (2005). *A whole new mind*. New York: Riverhead Books.

Richards, J. (1998). *Beyond training*. Cambridge: Cambridge University Press.

Richards, J., & Lockhart, C. (1994). *Reflective teaching in second language classrooms*. Cambridge: Cambridge University Press.

Senge, P.M. (1994). *The fifth discipline: The art and practice of the learning organization*. New York: Currency Doubleday.

Spencer, L., & Spencer, S. (1993). *Competence at work: Models for superior performance*. Hoboken, NJ: Wiley.

Thorndike, E.L. (1920). Intelligence and its uses. *Harper's Magazine, 140*, 227–235.

Vince, R. (1996). *Managing change: Reflections on equality and management learning*. Bristol: The Policy Press.

Wallace, M. (1994). *Training foreign language teachers: A reflective approach*. Cambridge: Cambridge University Press.

Wigglesworth, G., & Murray, D.E. (2007). Opening doors: Teachers learning through collaborative research. *Prospect 22*(1), 19–36.

Williams, H.W. (2004). A study of the characteristics that distinguish outstanding urban principals: Emotional intelligence, problem-solving competencies, role perception and environmental adaptation. Unpublished PhD, Case Western Reserve University.

Yates, L., & Brindley, G. (2000). Editorial. *Prospect, 15*(3), 1–4.

Chapter 6

On the Edge
Leading From the Periphery

Andy Curtis

Introduction

Where am I?

When we first enter the TESOL field, we may be somewhat overwhelmed by the tremendous range of language teaching and learning methodologies, approaches, techniques, etc. Similarly, when we move from teaching to senior level administration in a language teaching organization (LTO) or add such roles to our existing teaching responsibilities, the number of possibilities can be equally overwhelming. As Denise E. Murray and MaryAnn Christison state in the opening chapter of this volume, leadership theories include: "transactional, transformational, instructional, personal, servant, situational, change, and instructional leadership" as well as other aspects such as "leadership IQ, and total quality management."

According to Andrew DuBrin, "about 30,000 research articles, magazine articles and books have been written about leadership in the 20th century" (1998, p. 2). This is the equivalent of four articles on leadership published every five days, week after week, month after month, year after year—for nearly one hundred years. This is a humbling thought, and there appears to be no sign of this output slowing down. For example, ScienceDirect, the online database of Elsevier publishers (www.sciencedirect.com), provides electronic access to 2,000 peer-reviewed journals. A search of these journals revealed that approximately 500 articles on leadership were published in 2006 alone, i.e., more than one article on leadership every day for the entire year. In January 2007, the online bookseller Amazon (www.amazon.ca) listed more than 22,000 books on leadership available at that time. By now, that number has almost certainly increased.

There are at least two ways of viewing such figures. Either, these tens of thousands of books and articles can be seen as already providing everything we need to know on leadership, in which case leadership may simply be a matter of finding the right material. Or, these figures can be seen as an indication of how tremendously challenging it is to lead. It may be that both ways of viewing are accurate, so that, as with teaching, although finding the most appropriate material is essential, so too is understanding the great complexity of what we are attempting to achieve and to enable.

This raises the question of how to deal with so much input and information. One way to cope with such complexity is to seek the simplicity which follows complexity rather than vice versa. As Alan Perlis, the prominent American computer scientist and Yale professor, put it: "Simplicity does not precede complexity, but follows it." One way of rediscovering this simplicity is to ask fundamental questions such as: Where Am I?

Many real estate agents still subscribe to the idea that the three most important factors in selling a property are: location, location, location (see, for example, Rebane, 2005). This may or may not still be true in the property market, but it is certainly true in educational leadership. As an experienced teacher, in a classroom, you usually know where you are. However, in an LTO leadership role, you could be anywhere.

The goal of this chapter is to revisit the well-established leadership positional metaphor of "leading from the front," and to suggest that this may not necessarily be the most effective position for an LTO leader. Instead language educators in leadership positions are encouraged to consider alternative positions, such as "leading from the edges" and to encourage LTO leaders to be aware of which position they are taking and why.

Metaphor as Method in Leadership

In Chapter 1 of this volume, Denise E. Murray describes an "ecology of leadership in language education", using "the metaphor of ecology to help us examine the context of our leadership in English language education." She also makes use of spatial metaphors: "Murray (2001), borrowing Liddicoat and Crozet's (2000) notion of 'intercultural space' to describe the environment for English language teaching, proposes several strategies for creating such a space for language learners."

Perhaps the best-known proponents of the power of metaphor are George Lakoff and Mark Johnson, whose book *Metaphors we live by* (1980) is still required reading for those working in the field nearly 30 years after it was first published. In one of the most often-quoted lines from the book, they state that: "metaphor is pervasive in everyday life, not just in language, but in thought and action. Our ordinary conceptual system, in terms of which we both think and act, is fundamentally metaphorical in nature" (ibid., p. 3). According to Lakoff and Johnson, "the essence of metaphor is understanding and experiencing one kind of thing in terms of another" (ibid., p. 5). Chapter 4 in their book focuses on what they refer to as 'Orientational Metaphors' also known as positional metaphors.

Positional metaphors are based on spatial orientations and physical structures, such as the human body. For example: up or down; in or out; front or back, as in "I'm feeling *up*. That *boosted* my spirits. I'm feeling *down*" (ibid., p. 15). Another reason for employing metaphors in conceptualizing leadership in language education is the importance of metaphors in language teaching, as Steve Darn and Ian White recently put it:

There is one single reason why metaphor is important to the English language and language teaching. It is impossible to communicate naturally and effectively without

employing this device. Metaphors are an essential part of our everyday language, used to give physical qualities to the non-physical . . . To the language teacher and learner, it is this elementary level of significance which is important.

(2006, p. 1)

Darn and White go on to state that: "Metaphor, then, can be taught and learned in the same way as grammar and lexis, but also has a role as a tool in teaching other facets of the language" (ibid., p. 1).

In the same way that metaphor can be a tool in language teaching, it can also be a useful method of conceptualizing leadership in LTOs. In the next chapter in this volume, Chapter 7, Neil Anderson makes use of the front-back positional metaphor when he wrote about 'leading from behind'. In this chapter, I will make use of the reverse positional metaphor, i.e., 'leading from the edges' or 'leading from the periphery', but before journeying to the edge, it is necessary to first re-visit the best-known and commonly employed positional metaphor in leadership: 'leading from the front'.

Leading from the Front

In meritocracies and other achievement-oriented cultures, being at the front is generally considered the most desirable position. This belief appears to have influenced the majority of models and metaphors of leadership that also promote the idea that the front is the best place to be. For example, in 1998, Gareth Lewis and the Institute of Management (based in the UK and founded in 1992 following the merger of the British Institute of Managers and Institute of Industrial Managers) produced a 96-page handbook, *Leading from the front*. The book, designed for self-study certificate and diploma courses in management, is a clear and concise introduction to leadership, but it does not examine the idea that being at the front may not necessarily be the most effective position all of the time.

Interestingly and rather unusually, later that same year, Mike Gatting and Angela Patmore published a book with the same title *Leading from the front* (1998). However, this book is an autobiography of the England cricketer, Michael William Gatting, who was the captain of the national team between 1986 and 1988. This may provide a clue to why being at the front is considered the ideal position, as winning the game or the race is usually based on being the first past the finishing line. In this view of the world, coming second is failing and may be seen as being not that much different to coming last.

The interest in leading from the front has continued as shown by books such as David Garic's *Leading from the front: Answers for the challenges leaders face* (2002). At just 64 pages, this is an even briefer introduction than Lewis' handbook, but the brevity of such books is also an acknowledgment of the fact that busy leaders generally do not have the time to plough through heavy tomes on theories of leadership. Rather, they want practically-oriented answers to complex questions, hence the subtitle and focus of Garic's book. In the opening chapter, "The Selfless Servant," Garic lists some of the many complex and demanding roles, responsibilities, and challenges facing leaders: "Leaders are expected to be psychologists, problem-solvers, communicators, politicians, resource managers, delegators, evaluators, referees, facilitators, and more. Plain and simple, this is hard work" (ibid., p. 1).

Garic also refers to the point made below, regarding the definition of edge as being 'between a rock and a hard place':

> A duality lies at the core of the organizational leadership challenge. It requires leaders to continuously balance the needs and desires of individuals and groups under their charge against the demands placed on them by the organization. In other words, leaders serve two masters: the people they lead and the purpose of the organization to which they belong.
>
> (ibid., p. 1)

This on-going interest in leading from the front can be seen in more recent books for educators, for example, Jim Donnelly's *Managing urban schools: Leading from the front* (2003). In his explanation of the book's title, Donnelly explains that: "The thesis of this book is that managing is not enough and that school leaders must raise their heads above the parapet if they are to be fully effective" (ibid., p. 3)). In terms of personality and character, he goes on to explain that educational leadership is "no job for 'shrinking violets' and neither is it a job for those who do not have strong convictions" (ibid.). In terms of positioning and placement, Donnelly argues that "leadership needs to exist everywhere in the school, and that it is not something that is vested only in the senior management team" (ibid.). This statement is interesting as this is potentially in conflict with the notion of leading from the front, or it could be a reference to the idea of leadership as "everywhere and nowhere" (see below).

Given the popularity and predominance of the metaphor of leading from the front, it is necessary to consider why an alternative positioning, such as leading from the periphery, may be more relevant to LTO leaders.

Task 6.1

List some of the advantages and limitations of leading from the front. Where do you (or where would you) like to position yourself as an LTO leader and why?

An Alternative Positioning

In his review of George Braine's edited collection *Non-native educators in English language teaching* (1999), Jim Bame wrote that: "ELT is not the property of native speakers who reside in the Center (defined as the United States, Canada, England, Australia and New Zealand, as opposed to *the Periphery—amazingly, everywhere else*) (2001, p. 1;

emphasis added). Bame goes on to explain that: "He [Braine] explains that the periphery status is not only in geographic location of teaching."Where, then, does this leaveTESOL professionals taking on the roles and responsibilities of leadership?

As Braj Kachru (1985, 1992, 1996) and others have pointed out, the number of non-native speakers of English (NNSE) in the world has for some time been greater than the number of native speakers, and given the growing number of NNSE teachers of English globally, it is likely that more and more NNSE will be in LTO leadership positions. However, it is not necessary to be an NNSE to be on the periphery in the field of TESOL. As Curtis (2006) notes, though he is a native speaker of English, as the director of an intensive EAP (English for Academic Purposes) program at a small, white university in a small white town in eastern Canada, he was on the periphery as a result of being "one of the only persons of color, one of the only non-Canadians and one of the only males at the school" (ibid., p. 20). There are many ways to be marginalized.

As the notion of peripheral positioning in relation to language and culture may be unfamiliar to those in the cultural, racial, and linguistic majority, one way of developing an in-depth understanding of this concept is through case studies and narrative inquiry, such as those found in Curtis and Romney (2006), for example, the account of Carmen Chacón, a TESOL professional of color in Venezuela (2006, pp. 49–63).

In terms of English language education, popular culture, and the periphery, Chacón finds a relationship between the popularity of the Barbie doll in Venezuela, "the English hegemony perpetuated by the spread of English as an International Language" (ibid., p. 52) and Phillipson's position that "English is the language of the USA, a major economic, political, and military force in the contemporary world" (1992, p. 24). As a result of these forces, Chacón believes that "people on the periphery (e.g., Venezuela) take for granted the legitimacy of the dominant ideas and images [e.g. Barbie as the feminine ideal] that come from the center" (2006, p. 52). In relation to location, Chacón refers to Phillipson's geopolitical mapping, in which linguistically peripheral countries "are peripheral in the sense that norms for the language are regarded as flowing from the core-English speaking fountainheads" (1992, p. 25).

For Chacón, it was during her doctoral studies that she started to think about the social, cultural, and linguistic impact on how she was perceived and how she perceived herself. In relation to Braj Kachru's work on World Englishes and the Other Tongue (1992), Chacón describes how she:

> started to "see" and understand why my status as a Latina in the center is perceived as inferior not solely because of my race but also because I come from the periphery. I started to "see" that generalizations and stereotypes are rooted in the education we receive in the expanding circle (Kachru, 1992).
>
> (2006, pp. 52–53)

The relationship between being a non-native speaker of English and being on the geopolitical and linguistic periphery is a constantly recurring theme in Curtis and Romney's recent *Shades of meaning* collection (2006) of narratives from TESOL professionals of color, interpreted in relation to Critical Race Theory. For example, Chacón describes how, as part of her self-re-evaluation, she "read the work of scholars (e.g. Amin, 1997; Braine, 1999; Kachru, 1982; Pennycook, 1994; Phillipson, 1992; Tang, 1997) and engaged in a dialogic critical reflection with other NNESTs [Non-Native English-Speaking Teachers] from the periphery" (2006, p. 55). More specifically, in relation to native and non-native accents of English and where these place TESOL professionals, in terms of the center or the periphery, Chacón came to the realization that "coming from the periphery, I think my accent is not perceived with the same privileges of someone coming from Australia or Great Britain" (ibid., p. 56).

This account by Chacón highlights the importance of the periphery in relation to language and culture, specifically the different cultures of English language teaching and learning. However, the periphery is usually characterized, almost by definition, as an undesirable position, but there may be some advantages of being here, as the examination of meaning below shows.

Task 6.2

Do you agree or disagree with Chacón's statement that: "coming from the periphery, I think my accent is not perceived with the same privileges of someone coming from Australia or Great Britain"? Give reasons for your response.

Defining the Periphery

As language educators, we know that the meaning we assign to words is a critical component of how we think and conceptualize. Therefore, in the context of LTO leadership metaphors, it is necessary to consider the different meanings of the two metaphorical terms, *edge* and *periphery*.

The online *Cambridge Advanced Learner's Dictionary* (CALD) lists no fewer than 15 meanings of edge, including phrases such as: bleeding-edge, leading edge, cutting edge and knife-edge. A more manageable list is provided in the online *Compact Oxford English Dictionary* (COED) definitions of the noun *edge*, including "the line along which two surfaces of a solid meet." This is a more relevant definition than it might at first seem to be, as teaching professionals in leadership roles often find themselves at the interface between teachers and senior levels of administration, such as deans, heads of department, and owners of private, for-profit language schools. Being at this interface can sometimes be described by the expression 'between a rock and a hard place' (see Garic's note above, on duality) meaning to be in between two positions, both of which are difficult and neither of which is particularly desirable. At such times, the leader's role is often to mediate between the two parties and help them reach mutually acceptable positions, even if the solution is far from what either party would consider ideal.

The fifth online COED noun definition of *edge*—"a quality of factor which gives superiority over close rivals"—may also be relevant, as many LTO leaders are working in organizations actively competing for students. This is no longer only true of private, for-profit chains of English language schools, but increasingly government-funded universities and colleges are also competing for students, with each other and with the private sector. Therefore, according to this definition, being at the edge may be an advantage. The second verbal meaning of edge given by the OED relates to "moving carefully or furtively," and while moving furtively may not be necessary, moving carefully will always be necessary.

Although the two terms are sometimes used interchangeably and their meanings do overlap, there are some important differences between *edge* and *periphery*. In terms of overlap, the COED defines *periphery* as "the outer limits or edge of an area or object" and the CALD similarly defines it as "the outer edge of an area." However, it is the meanings of periphery that relate to relevant importance that show some significant differences. According to the COED, the second use of the noun *periphery* means "a marginal or secondary position," but the CALD gives perhaps the most interesting definition: "the less important part of a group or activity," adding that the adjective *peripheral* "describes something that is not as important as something else."

The reason that the CALD definitions may be especially important in this context is that they raise the essential but highly provocative question: How important is a leader? This question has been seriously considered in recent years, giving rise to books such as Jeffrey Nielsen's *The myth of leadership: Creating leaderless organizations* (2004), which question the whole notion of traditional, hierarchical models of leadership, though Nielsen does not claim that leaders are not important. In fact, he reiterates the importance of leaders, but puts forward a peer-based model of peer councils and rotational leadership. Combining the dictionary definitions with Nielsen's book shows that leaders do not have to be at the front or at the top of an organizational structure. Also, being on the periphery does not necessarily mean being less important.

The View from the Edge

Being at the edge and leading from the periphery does imply, for some authors at least, a sense of uncertainty or even impending chaos, which may come from the notion of stepping over the edge into the unknown. For example, about his book, *Leading at the edge of chaos: How to create the nimble organization* (1998), Daryl Connor writes: "Chaos is a frightening word, but you will have to get used to it if you desire or hold leadership positions in today's organization" (2003, p. 1). From a language education perspective, Connor's work is relevant as he takes a somewhat linguistic approach to the topic: "Snuggle deeper into the lexicographical security blanket. If you prefer 'turbulence' or 'unrest', 'conflict' or 'confusion'—fine. Whatever term you've chosen, my point is that stability is no longer the prevalent condition of our age" (ibid., p. 1).

Although it seems unlikely that stability has been the prevalent condition of any age, Connor does make some important points, for example, he defines a nimble organization as one which is capable of "adroitly responding to the chaotic conditions produced by constant change" (ibid., p. 1) and in terms of the challenges that such change creates, he write that: "Decades of deeply ingrained procedures, traditions, attitudes, and cultural biases about managing change must be jettisoned. In their place, new perspectives and frameworks must be embraced" (ibid., p. 1). The reference to cultural biases is especially relevant, as many leaders in language education are leading multilingual and multicultural groups and therefore must be sensitive to cultural biases—their own as well as everyone else's.

This relationship between being on the edge, managing change and coping with chaos is also the focus of Shona Brown's and Kathleen Eisenhardt's *Competing on the edge: Strategy as structured chaos* (1998) based on "in-depth field research on 12 businesses in Asia, Europe and North America" (ibid., p. 128). According to the authors, "the edge of chaos is a key concept in complexity theory that describes where systems can most effectively change" (ibid., 28). Brown and Eisenhard give five characteristics of the edge:

1   Complicated behaviours occur here.
2   A few rules (like priorities) exist that are "not arbitrary and that are not compromises between extreme values."
3   Work needs to maintain a balance on the edge of chaos because it is a "dissipative equilibrium."
4   Surprise occurs here because "control is not tight" and because systems are "adapting in real-time to unpredictable changes."
5   Mistakes occur here because "systems at the edge of chaos often slip off the edge" (ibid., p. 28).

In terms of metaphors and models, Brown and Eisenhard make much use of the musical metaphor of improvisation, such as "the jazz musician who plays the wrong note" but sees the opportunity to "turn mistake into advantages" (ibid., p. 28). In relation to the third point above, the notion of *dissipative structures* was first put forward by the Belgian scientist Ilya Prigogine, who won the Nobel Prize for Chemistry in 1977. Such structures are open systems in which energy and matter are exchanged and in which complex and chaotic structures are formed. Perhaps one of the most useful aspects of this characterization of the edge of chaos is the idea of improvising in order to turn mistakes into opportunities, as this is how language teachers often approach their students' mistakes, i.e., as indicators of what the student knows as well as what they have yet to learn.

Gordon McKibben's book, *Cutting edge* (1998), describes what he refers to in the book's subtitle as *Gillette's Journey to Global Leadership*. The book is an engaging narrative account of the rise of the Gillette shaving company. McKibben describes the early life of John Symons, who was key player in Gillette's business in the 1980s: "Symons was born in 1930 in London's East End . . . just at the time of the Great Depression, which made life marginal for many in the crowded neighborhood" (ibid., p. 105). In this description, we can see some important relationships between leading from the edges, being at the leading edge and being on the periphery.

It is possible that being at the edge or on the periphery has some advantages, for example, from the point of view of perspective. One problem with leading from the front is that the leader has to be always looking over their shoulder to see where their followers are. However, from the edges, it is possible to see without constantly turning back. This raises the question of what it means to lead from the edge.

Task 6.3

List some of the advantages and limitations of leading from the edges in your language teaching and learning organization.

Leading from the Edge

The metaphor of life as a journey is perhaps one of the best-known metaphors, for example, as used in Robert Frost's very popular poem, *The Road Not Taken*, published in 1915. Indeed, the metaphor is so popular that some may claim that it is overused. However, its longevity and popularity suggest that life as a journey may be a powerful and pervasive means of understanding (Ortony, 1993; Kovecses, 2002). Of all the recent accounts of leading at the edge, one of the most widely read in recent years has been an account based on a journey. Although Dennis Perkins' *Leading at the edge: Leadership lessons from the extraordinary saga of Shackleton's Antarctic expedition* (2000) does not have the short, catchy title of many books on leadership and management, it does contain a great deal of potentially useful guidance for anyone who is interested in leading from the edges and who ascribes to the notion of life—and leadership—as a journey.

The book is based on the difficult and dangerous but ultimately successful expedition to the South Pole led by Ernest Shackleton in 1914 (at the same time Frost was writing his *Road Not Taken*) during which the entire crew survived on the ice with very few supplies and little hope of rescue after their ship drifted off course and was destroyed by the ice and snow. To show how dangerous such a journey was, Perkins contrasts Shackleton's success with a disastrous Canadian expedition launched the previous year, in 1913. Although Perkins accepts that this is a very dramatic analogy—most leaders will not face life-threatening conditions of the kind faced by Shackleton and his team— as a former Marine lieutenant, Perkins argues that leaders can learn from both successful and unsuccessful expeditions. To that end, and in the manner of most books on leadership and management, Perkins presents a list of ten learning points, each of which forms the basis for a chapter in his book:

1   *Vision and Quick Victories*: Never lose sight of the ultimate goal, and focus energy on short-term objectives.

2   *Symbolism and Personal Example*: Set a personal example with visible, memorable symbols and behaviors.

3   *Optimism and Reality*: Instil optimism and self-confidence, but stay grounded in reality.

4   *Stamina*: Take care of yourself: Maintain your stamina and let go of guilt.

5   *The Team Message*: Reinforce the team message constantly: "We are one—we live or die together."

6   *Core Team Values*: Minimize status differences and insist on courtesy and mutual respect.

7   *Conflict*: Master conflict—deal with anger in small doses, engage dissidents, and avoid needless power struggles.

8   *Lighten Up*! Find something to celebrate and something to laugh about.

9   *Risk*: Be willing to take the Big Risk.

10 *Tenacious Creativity*: Never give up—there's always another move.

Task 6.4

Select one or two items of the ten listed by Perkins that are most relevant to your LTO context. Explain why these are especially relevant to your situation.

In an interview (undated, online) about his book, Perkins explains that a major part of his life "has been spent trying to understand what it really means to be a leader—particularly under conditions of adversity, uncertainty, and change." It is likely that at least one or two of these three conditions can be found at most LTOs today, so leaders in LTOs need to be able to develop a high tolerance for ambiguity within themselves and within their staff. In relation to leading from the edge, Perkins goes on to say:

> I decided to look for leadership lessons in stories of groups that have been to the outer limits of human endurance—the place I call *The Edge* . . . By studying *The Edge*, we can learn the things needed to lead organizations to their full potential, and we can remember these principles when we ourselves are stretched, stressed, and challenged.

Perkins concluded the interview by stressing his belief that: "*the key critical message to take from the Shackleton saga is that leaders do make a difference—a critical difference.*"

The desire to make a positive difference is what encouraged many of us to become language teacher educators. Similarly, the desire to make such a difference is why many language teachers become LTO leaders. Where we position ourselves is an important part of making that difference, so LTO leaders need to be aware of where they are and why they are there. It is, then, appropriate to conclude by returning to the last lines of the Robert Frost poem:

> Two roads diverged in a wood, and I
> I took the one less traveled by,
> And that has made all the difference.

Task 6.5

Describe some of the differences you would like to make as a leader in your language teaching and learning organization.

References

Anderson, N. (2007). Chapter 8: Leading from behind. In M. Christison & D. Murray (Eds.), *Leadership in English language education: Theoretical foundations and practical skills for changing times* (pp. 110–122). New York: Routledge.

Bame, J. (2001). Review of *Non-native educators in English language teaching* by George Braine. *TESL EJ* 5(1), 1–3. http://www-writing.berkeley.edu/TESL-EJ/ej17/r9.html

Braine, G. (1999). *Non-native educators in English language teaching*. Mahwah, NJ: Lawrence Erlbaum Associates.

Brown, S., & Eisenhardt, K. (1998). *Competing on the edge: Strategy as structured chaos*. Boston, MA: Harvard Business School Press.

Cambridge Advanced Learner's Dictionary. (2006). http://dictionary.cambridge.org/

Chacón, C.T. (2006). My journey into racial awareness. In A. Curtis, & M. Romney (Eds.), *Colour, race and English language teaching: Shades of meaning* (pp. 49–63). Mahwah, NJ: Lawrence Erlbaum.

Christison, M. & Murray, D.E. (2007). Introduction. In M. Christison, & D. Murray, (Eds.), *Leadership in English language education: Theoretical foundations and practical skills for changing times* (pp. 1–10). New York: Routledge.

Compact Oxford English Dictionary. (2006). http://www.askoxford.com/dictionaries/compact_oed/

Connor, D.R. (1988). *Leading at the edge of chaos: How to create the nimble organization*. Hoboken, NJ: John Wiley & Sons, Ltd.

Connor, D.R. (2003). Interview with Daryl Connor. *Integral Leadership Review*, (3)2, 1. http://www.integralleadershipreview.com/archives/2003_02.html

Curtis A. (2006). Dark matter: Teaching and learning between black and white. In A. Curtis, & M. Romney (Eds.), *Colour, race and English language teaching: Shades of meaning* (pp. 11–23). Mahwah, NJ: Lawrence Erlbaum.

Curtis, A., & Romney, R. (Eds.) (2006). *Colour, race and English language teaching: Shades of meaning*. Mahwah, NJ: Lawrence Erlbaum.

Darn, S., & White, I. (2006). Metaphorically speaking. *Humanising Language Teaching, 8*(5), 1–6. http://www.hltmag.co.uk/sep06/sart01.htm

Donnelly. J. (2003) *Managing urban schools: Leading from the front*. London: Kogan Page.

DuBrin, A. (1998). *Leadership: Research findings, practice, and skills*. Boston, MA: Houghton Mifflin.

Garic, D. (2002). *Leading from the front: Answers for the challenges leaders face*. London: Trafford.

Gatting, M. & Patmore, A. (1998). *Leading from the front*. London: Macdonald.

Kachru, B.B. (1985). Standards, codification and sociolinguistic realism: The English language in the outer circle. In R. Quirk, & H. Widdowson (Eds.), *English in the world: Teaching and learning the language and literatures* (pp. 11–36). Cambridge: Cambridge University Press.

Kachru, B.B. (1992). World Englishes: Approaches, issues and resources. *Language Teaching,* *25*(1), 1–14.

Kachru, B.B. (1996). Norms, models and identities. *The Language Teacher Online, 20* (10). http://langue.hyper.chubu.ac.jp/jalt/pub/tlt/96/oct/englishes.html

Kovecses, Z. (2002). *Metaphor: A practical introduction*. New York: Oxford University Press.

Lakoff, G., & Johnson, M. (1980). *Metaphors we live by*. Chicago: University of Chicago Press.

Lewis, G., & Institute of Management (1998). *Leading from the front*. Oxford: Elsevier Pergamon.

McKibben, G. (1998). *Cutting edge: Gillette's journey to global leadership*. Boston, MA: Harvard Business School Press.

Murray, D.E. (2007). Chapter 1: The ecology of leadership in ELT. In M. Christison, & D. Murray (Eds.), *Leadership in English language education: Theoretical foundations and practical skills for changing times* (pp. 13–26). New York: Routledge.

Nielsen, J.S. (2004). *The myth of leadership: Creating leaderless organizations*. Mountain View, CA: Davies-Black.

Ortony, A. (1993). *Metaphor and thought*. New York: Cambridge University Press.

Perkins, D.N., with Holtman, M.P., Kessler, P.R., & McCarthy, C. (2000). *Leading at the edge: Leadership lessons from the extraordinary saga of Shackleton's Antarctic Expedition* (2000). New York: American Management Association.

Perkins, D.N. (Undated). Interview with Dennis Perkins. The Goodman Speakers Bureau. http://www.goodmanspeakersbureau.com/articles/perkins_interview. htm

Phillipson, R. (1992). *Linguistic imperialism*. New York: Oxford University Press.

Rebane, B. (2005). The key to a successful franchise? Location, location, location. Globe and Mail Business Section Online. June 30, 2005. http://www.theglobeandmail.com/servlet/story/RTGAM.20050630.wrebanecol0701/BNStory/special SmallBusiness

Chapter 7

Leading From Behind

Neil J. Anderson

Introduction[1]

Learning about Leadership

During my graduate MATESL program, I took a seminar class from Harold S. Madsen, a professor at my university who had already established himself as a leader in the field of second language testing. One of the objectives he had for the course was for us to become familiar with the names and areas of expertise of the Presidents of the TESOL (Teachers of English to Speakers of Other Languages) Association. Many of these TESOL presidents had written the textbooks that we were using in our MATESL program. I also came to realize that, in addition to their scholarly contributions, they were role models of strong leadership. I felt inspired by their work and their lives and remember this exercise as the catalyst that spurred my interest in leadership. At the time that I participated in this course activity, I didn't hold a leadership position; however, as a result of my participation, I became interested in leadership and wanted to continue studying about it. Of course, I hoped to have a position of leadership one day, but, more importantly, I wanted to foster the behaviors in myself that I thought were representative of effective leaders even if I didn't have a leadership position.

Traditionally, leadership responsibilities have come with one's title or position within an organization. The title of this chapter is meant to focus your attention away from leadership as defined by one's title or position and towards leadership as defined by one's behaviors. Kouzes and Posner state: "Leadership is not a place, it's not a gene, and it's not a secret code. The truth is that leadership is an observable set of skills and abilities" (2003, p. 97). If leaders can be defined by the behaviors and characteristics they exhibit, rather than by position, then it is possible that each person can be a leader, regardless of the title or position that person holds. Kouzes and Posner further define leadership as relationships, reflecting the role of emotional intelligence in leadership (see Chapter 5, this volume). They say, "Leadership is about caring—about relationships, and about what you do" (ibid., p. 1). Neither view of leadership—the skills and abilities view nor the relationship view—is wedded to a title or a position.

Kouzes and Posner also provide further support for the idea of defining leadership through behaviors by dispelling two common myths about leadership. The first myth is that leadership is reserved for only a few people. If we define leaders by their behaviors, then clearly there could be an unlimited number of people in any organization who could be leaders. The second is the myth that leadership is always associated with title or position. The idea many people have about leadership is that when one gets elected or appointed to a position, then one becomes a leader. However, if leadership is defined by behaviors of leaders, then there could be some people with title and position who are not leaders because their behaviors are inconsistent with the characteristics of effective leaders. In addition, it is quite possible that it is the leaders in the "background," the ones without title or position, the ones who are leading from behind, who can be the most influential in moving others towards accomplishing their goals.

In this chapter, I will focus on how you, the reader, might go about developing your own leadership skills even though you may not hold a position of leadership and may never intend to do so. First, I will ask you to consider your own behaviors relative to the behaviors of effective leaders. Then, I will ask you to focus on developing the specific skills needed so that you can develop your skills independent of formal training in leadership.

Leadership Journal

One tool that I believe is extremely effective in developing skills as a leader is keeping a leadership journal. I will refer to this strategy throughout the chapter. Writing and answering reflective questions in a journal is one way in which you can gain insights into your own experiences as a leader and the experiences you have with leaders. As you consider the ideas in this chapter, I would encourage you to record your impressions in a journal. I would also like to suggest that you keep the journal solely for this purpose and use it to record your development and growth as a leader.

Task 7.1

Before you read the next section in this chapter, write answers to the following questions in a small notebook:

1   What characteristics do effective leaders possess?
2   How are leadership skills developed?
3   Do you consider yourself a leader? Why or why not?

Write your responses in your leadership journal. If you can, share your responses with a friend or colleague.

Identifying Characteristics of Effective Leaders

If you believe in the premise that leading from behind has merit and if you are interested in how you might develop behaviors that mirror effective leaders, then you will want to have a set of leadership characteristics to guide you. In Chapter 2 and Chapter 3 in this volume, two different models are introduced and reviewed. In these models, characteristics of effective leadership are identified and dealt with in different contexts. Leadership IQ has it roots in business with the work of Murphy (1996) and has since been translated into educational contexts (see Chapters 2 and 14 in this volume and also Murray & Christison, 2004). The model introduced in Chapter 3 comes from U.S. public school leadership and stems from the meta-analyses done by Marzano et al. (2006) in which behaviors of effective school leaders are correlated with student academic achievement in schools. In addition to these two models, Hoppe (2004) reports on research at the Center for Creative Leadership that identifies 22 universal characteristics of outstanding leaders. This list includes leader behaviors such as trustworthiness, honesty, foresightedness, team building, and problem solving. If you study the three lists side-by-side, you will see many crossover behaviors on the three lists. It is not the aim of this chapter to propose yet another list from which you might work, but rather to suggest that you select a list and work with it. Any one of the lists mentioned above would be useful and provide you with a good place to begin examining your own behaviors in the workplace in relationship to behaviors of effective leaders (see also Chapter 5 on emotional intelligence for a list of behaviors that promote effective leadership).

Working with Leadership Characteristics

Task 7.2

1. Work with the list you have selected on qualities of effective leadership. Write down three behaviors or characteristics on which you want to work and think about each one carefully.
2. Identify a leader you have known who exhibited these behaviors. Write down specifically what these leaders did when you noticed them exhibiting these three behaviors.
3. Think about yourself and whether you are skilled in these three behaviors. Using a Likert scale from 0-3 (0 = not effective and 3 = highly effective) evaluate yourself on each of the characteristics you have selected.
4. Think about your workplace and the influence that you can have within the sphere of your responsibility. What are three specific ways in which you can see yourself demonstrating these characteristics in your workplace?

As you work with leadership characteristics, it is important to remember that leadership is not about position. It is your attitude and desire that can help you move your organization or program forward in accomplishing its goals. McCauley and Van Velsor emphasize that:

> Rather than classifying people as "leaders" or "non-leaders" and focusing our work on developing "leaders," we believe that all people can learn and grow in ways that make them more effective in the various leadership roles and processes they take on. This process of personal development that improves leader effectiveness is what we understand leader development to be all about.
>
> (2004, p. 3)

I encourage you to place this list of characteristics on which you want to work in a visible place in your office. If you regularly review a list of the behaviors that you are seeking to develop within the workplace and you understand clearly your sphere of influence, you will be more effective in demonstrating these leadership characteristics in environments where you can make a difference in outcomes.

Developing Skills for Leading from Behind

Once you have identified the characteristics of effective leaders on which you want to focus, the next step is to develop the necessary skills for manifesting these behaviors. Identifying specific behaviors and characteristics that you believe are important is an important first step, but it is not sufficient. You will need to develop the specific skill subsets that underpin the behaviors and characteristics with which you want to work. McCauley and Van Velsor define leader development as "the expansion of a person's capacity to be effective in leadership roles and processes. Leadership roles and processes are those that facilitate setting direction, creating alignment, and maintaining commitment in groups of people who share common work" (2004, p. 2). Notice that with this definition, McCauley and Van Velsor focus on the growth that individuals experience in their leadership roles (see Chapter 15, this volume for a study on what TESOL presidents learned as a result of their leadership role), so it is probably not surprising to realize that the skills you need for leading from the background are not so different from the skills you must develop in order to be effective in a position of leadership.

I have identified five different activities that can be useful in developing your skills to be effective in leading from behind. They are the following:

1   Participate in leadership development activities.
2   Learn about the program or organization in which you work.
3   Learn about the limits of your stewardship.
4   Support colleagues performing well in their individual stewardships.
5   Evaluate the effectiveness of the work toward the established direction.

The time you take to develop leadership skills for the workplace will enable you to be more effective in all aspects of your life (Cashman, 1999; Palmer and Christison, 2007).

Participate in Leadership Development Activities

The first step in developing skills for leading from behind is to participate in leadership development activities. The more time you spend focused on leadership and on developing leadership skills, the greater the possibility is that you will develop your skills. I offer three suggestions for how you can take responsibility for your own development:

1   Attend workshops and seminars on leadership development.
2   Read books and articles on leadership development.
3   Access leadership websites on the Internet.

Attend Workshops and Seminars on Leadership Development

Workshops and seminars on leadership development are an ideal opportunity to focus your attention on how you can develop as a leader. Many organizations (e.g., TESOL[2]) offer short, reasonably-priced sessions that specifically teach skills like building effective teams (see Chapter 13 in this volume for more detailed information on building effective teams), time management, and communicating effectively with co-workers (see Chapters 5 and 12 in this volume for more detailed information on communication). Leadership skills do not develop overnight, but on-going exposure to principles of leadership and practice in developing specific skills are essential to the process.

Read Books and Articles on Leadership Development

There are numerous books on leadership and leadership development. In order to verify the truth of this statement, one only has to "google" the term "leadership development" to get over a million hits on the first try. Much of the information is focused on published books and articles that contain an array of topics related to leadership development. In order to help you navigate this abundance of information on leadership more effectively, I would like to highlight four books that have particular reference to the concept of leading from behind.

1   *The servant-leader within: A transformative path* (2003) by H. Beazley, J. Beggs, and L.C. Spears. Beazley, Beggs, and Spears are colleagues of R.K. Greenleaf (the author of *Servant-leadership: A journey into the nature of legitimate power and greatness*). *The servant-leader within* contains three sections: (1) Greenleaf's original edition of his article, "The servant as leader." The concept of a leader serving others is outlined in this section. (2) The second section is also a paper written by Greenleaf, "The teacher as servant." Greenleaf highlights the important roles that teachers can play as leaders and as role models for their students. (3) The third section contains

a 1984 commencement speech that Greenleaf delivered at Alverno College, a Catholic women's college in Milwaukee, Wisconsin, U.S.A. The book provides exceptional insights on how one can develop leadership skills through leading from behind.

2   Cashman, K. (1999). *Leadership from the inside out: Becoming a leader for life.* The central message of this book is to "remind us that our ability to grow as a leader is based on our ability to grow as a person" (p. 15). The book encourages a reflective approach to transforming ourselves into the type of leader we wish to be. One aspect of the book that I particularly like is the space provided to record your impressions while reading, much like the leadership journal. Cashman identifies seven pathways for mastery of "leadership from the inside out:"

(a) *Personal mastery*: The on-going commitment to unfolding and authentically expressing who we are (p. 31).

(b) *Purpose mastery*: The on-going discovery of how we express our gifts to add life-enriching value to the world (p. 63).

(c) *Change mastery*: Embracing the purposeful learning contained in the unending, creative flow of life (p. 83).

(d) *Interpersonal mastery*: The dynamic blending of personal power with synergy power to create value and contribution (p. 107).

(e) *Being mastery*: Connecting with the silence and peace of the innermost depth of one's character to support more dynamism, effectiveness, and contribution (p. 131).

(f) *Balance mastery*: The dynamic centering of our life to build resilience and to enhance effectiveness and fulfillment (p. 153).

(g) *Action mastery*: The ongoing commitment to creating value through enhanced authenticity and self-expression (p. 175).

Reading the book enabled me to identify areas in my life that I need to master to be effective in my individual leadership role or in leading from behind.

3   Nair, K. (1994). *A higher standard of leadership: Lessons from the life of Gandhi.* Gandhi is perhaps one of the greatest examples of leading from behind. He was not an elected political leader nor was he an appointed religious leader. He chose to live principles of leadership and help others see how individuals can have a powerful influence within society. This book outlines how to successfully apply leadership lessons from Gandhi's life. The book is divided into three sections: A Single Standard of Conduct, the Spirit of Service, and Decisions and Actions Bounded by Moral Principles. Nair emphasizes that we are all leaders. Each one of us is setting an example for someone else, and each one of us has a responsibility to shape the future as we wish it to be. But we must have ideals to guide our conduct if we are to make a positive difference (p. 139).

4   Covey, S. R. (2004). *The 8th habit: From effectiveness to greatness.* Building on the international success of *The seven habits of highly effective people,* Covey has recently

added an eighth habit. This additional habit highlights finding your own voice and inspiring others to find theirs. Covey encourages each of us to provide models for others, to empower others to lead, and to use our voices wisely to serve others. This book is helping me see the importance of sharing my voice with developing leaders in our profession and how I might serve as a mentor to help other leaders share their voice.

Access Leadership Websites on the Internet

Another tool you can use to help you develop your skills for leading from behind is the Internet. I have identified five sites that contain information on being a leader in the background:

1   *The Center for Creative Leadership*: http://www.ccl.org/
    This website has a particularly useful link to new publications on leadership development. This, as well as many other websites, can alert us to new publications that may help us in our quest to develop as leaders. I recently purchased the *Handbook of leadership development*, edited by McCauley and Van Velsor, from the Center for Creative Leadership.
2   *Journal of Academic Leadership*: http://www.academicleadership.org/
    This online journal is particularly valuable because it addresses leadership in academia. The vast majority of material on leadership development focuses on the field of business. Because TESOL professionals are engaged in academic pursuits, I have found this site valuable in helping me to translate business principles into an academic context.
3   *Leadership for a Changing World*: http://leadershipforchange.org/
    This site offers a valuable online forum for discussing leadership development. The discussions are archived so that you can see the comments even if you were not able to engage in the discussion yourself.
4   *The Greenleaf Center for Servant-Leadership*: http://www.greenleaf.org/
    This site offers a free downloadable article on servant and teacher leadership, and it lists the Greenleaf Center's international offices in Japan, Korea, the Philippines, and Singapore. The fact that the Greenleaf Center has offices outside the United States indicates that it is trying to reach beyond a leadership model based in a single country.
5   *The 8th Habit: From Effectiveness to Greatness*: http://www.stephencovey.com/8thHabit/8thhabit.html
    This site provides valuable resources for those reading the book, but they are just as useful for those who are not. It has tools to gain insights into developing your leadership voice and helping you to recognize leadership potential in others.

Learn about the Program or Organization in which you Work

Perhaps one of the most effective ways in which individuals outside of leadership positions can influence the programs or organizations in which they work is to have both a broadly defined and an in-depth knowledge of the make-up of the program or organization. Perhaps one of the best ways to do this is to participate in strategic planning exercises. The process of strategic planning is dealt with in detail in Chapter 9 in this volume, so rather than outline the entire process here, I will offer an interesting twist on some strategic planning activities that can be done individually.

Personal Mission Statements

A mission statement is a statement about what a program or organization is and what it believes are the unique contributions it can make. We should be able to articulate the mission statement for the organization or association for which we work and should know it well enough that we can not only recite it verbatim to another person or colleague but also talk about what it means and means to us personally. When you understand a program or organization's mission statement, you understand what is at the core of that program or organization. The same is true for individual mission statements. If you want to get to know yourself and how you best contribute to the program or organization, you should formulate a personal mission.

Covey (2004) refers to these unique contributions we can make to a program or organization as passions and encourages us to identify and create passions in our lives. He says, "The key to creating passion in your life is to find your unique talents and your specific role and purpose in the world" (ibid., p. 76). Writing a personal mission statement gives us an opportunity to do this. In writing a personal mission statement we must reflect on our personal passions. The task gives us an opportunity to take an in-depth view of what we believe we can contribute to the world and how we can be effective in the different roles that we might assume, roles that might include son, brother, father, husband, grandfather, teacher, researcher, professor, and program administrator. A personal mission statement is a living, dynamic document to be reviewed and updated regularly. By creating a personal mission statement, we can develop a more complete understanding of our roles in the programs or organizations for which we work.

Participate in an Historical Sign-in

Find out when your program or organization was founded or began. Then make a time-line and place five or ten-year markers on the time-line. Then, ask yourself the following questions and mark your answers on the time-line.

- When were you first aware of the program or organization in which you now work?
- When and how did you first become involved?

- When did you first accept a job with your program or organization?
- Who were the key individuals in the program or organization when you first became involved? When you first accepted a job? What roles did these individuals play?
- What major events have occurred in your program or organization during your tenure with the program or organization?

Once you answer these questions and mark them on the time-line, you begin to get a more complete understanding of the historical information for your program or organization and how the different events fit together. The time-line may also give you more information about decisions and policies. This can be particularly true if you choose to participate in this historical sign-in activity with other people with whom you work.

Participate in a Personal SWOT Analysis

SWOT stands for *strengths*, *weaknesses*, *opportunities*, and *threats*. A personal SWOT analysis is an activity that encourages you to examine your own strengths, weaknesses, opportunities and threats (see Chapter 9 on planning strategically for using this tool in the organization). Strengths and weaknesses are internal, while opportunities and threats are external. In conducting a personal SWOT analysis, focus on the following:

- **S**:   List three of your strengths.
- **W**:   List three of your weaknesses.
- **O**:   List three opportunities that you can take advantage of in the next 3–5 years.
- **T**:   List three major threats you will face in the next 3–5 years.

You can learn a great deal about yourself and your potential contributions in the workplace by performing an honest appraisal of yourself in these four areas. Once you have completed your own SWOT analysis, focus on collecting the same information for your own program or organization.

Learn about the Limits of your Stewardship

Merriam-Webster Online (2005) defines *stewardship* as "the office, duties, and obligations of a steward; the conducting, supervising, or managing of something; especially the careful and responsible management of something entrusted to one's care." In order to be effective as a leader, one must recognize both the obligations and limitations of one's stewardship. It is impossible to manage and supervise everyone and everything that arises. Effective leaders make choices and decisions. As mentioned earlier, Patterson et al. stress that "leadership is an act of balancing competing *wills*" (1996, p. 5). Leaders work with groups of individuals, each of whom may have demands that compete with the demands of others in the group. The leader works to bring some degree of harmony to the competing demands. Teachers face competing wills in every class they teach. I am reminded of this fact in my own classroom, an upper-intermediate reading class that I am currently teaching. I have a small class of 11 students; each has different needs and desires. Each places a certain demand on me to help him or her accomplish his or her individual will to develop reading skills. I'm not just a teacher. I am a leader, balancing the competing wills of the students in my classroom. The degree of success that I have in balancing those wills is related to my understanding the limits of my stewardship and what influence I can expect to have.

Help Colleagues Perform Well in Their Individual Stewardships

One of the most powerful ways that we can serve as leaders is to identify others who have strongly developed leadership skills and help them to perform well in their stewardship. In implementing this aspect in my own life, I have found the following questions helpful.

- Whose responsibility is it to nurture new leaders in my educational context?
- What can I do to nurture leadership skills and knowledge in others?
- Have any members of my group benefited from my leadership input as a mentor?
- Have any members of my group benefited by serving as a mentor to someone else?

Task 7.3

Record answers to these four questions in your leadership journal. How do your answers help you develop as a leader?

We can help colleagues perform well in their individual stewardships through personal encouragement and reinforcement and by setting examples for effective leadership behavior. I have benefited from being mentored and have been greatly influenced by five TESOL presidents—Donald Freeman, Denise E. Murray, MaryAnn Christison, Kathleen Bailey, and David Nunan. These five individuals have served as examples to me of effective leadership. Each of these leaders extended personal invitations to me to participate in activities to develop my skills as a leader. I have also been a mentor. I have seen leadership qualities in different TESOL members with whom I have worked on various projects and encouraged them to consider leadership roles in TESOL, such as Suchada Nimmannit, who became a member of the Board of Directors 2004–07, and Jun Liu, who became TESOL President 2006–2007.

   We can benefit greatly both from being mentored and being a mentor, not just in terms of mentoring that results in an individual pursuing a leadership position, but also in mentoring that results in our developing skills to effectively lead from behind.

Mentoring is about helping others find a leadership voice (Covey, 2004). The second half of Covey's book focuses on mentoring and the role that each of us can play in helping others find their leadership voice. For me, finding a leadership voice means developing the skills to effectively lead from behind. Sometimes we are on the giving end of the mentoring and at other times we are on the receiving end.

Evaluate the Effectiveness of the Work Toward the Established Direction

The final aspect of leadership development that I will address involves the importance of on-going, formative assessment of your success in developing leadership skills. As mentioned earlier, a journal may be an effective tool to help you to reflect on your progress. As you consistently keep a journal over time, it will provide you with a historical record of your development.

A journal enables you to perform a critical review of your leadership direction. My own review involves a careful analysis of my personal mission statement. In addition, I review my strengths, weaknesses, opportunities, and threats so that I can once again assure myself that I am going in the established direction.

A critical, self-reflection and evaluation of your work can often help you prepare for major changes in your life. For example, when I changed jobs, I used my mission statement and the self-assessments of my progress as tools to help me make decisions about new job opportunities. I am confident that this process helped me in accomplishing my goals and making progress in my professional life. None of us wants to be stagnant; we need tools to help us grow and develop.

Conclusion

When I interact with English teachers around the world, and we discuss their ideas about leadership development, I find that the vast majority of teachers do not consider themselves leaders. They say, "I'm just a teacher." This is a phrase that I wish we could eliminate from our discourse. All teachers have ideas about how classes should be taught, about how learners should learn, about how tests should be written. Lieberman and Miller state that because of this knowledge base "teachers should become leaders in curriculum, instruction, school redesign, and professional development and that the real power to improve achievement [lies] with teachers" (2004, p. 8). We all have opportunities each day to influence someone within our profession. When we look at leadership in this way, we need to wonder if we are having a positive or a negative influence on others.

I encourage language educators to make a list of characteristics of leaders and place the list in a visible place in their offices. If we regularly review a list of the characteristics that we are seeking to develop within our roles as leaders, we will be more effective in developing those characteristics. The time that we take to develop as leaders will enable us to be more effective in all aspects of our lives.

In this chapter, I have highlighted five aspects that English language teachers and program administrators can use to lead from behind; (1) know the direction of the program and recognize when to make course corrections; (2) develop your own skills as a leader; (3) know the limits of your stewardship; (4) help colleagues perform well in their individual stewardships; and (5) evaluate the effectiveness of the work toward the established direction. Leadership is not about position. It is about the attitudes that we have toward our stewardships and ourselves. All English language teachers should view themselves as leaders who will have a significant impact on both the learners in their classrooms and on the colleagues with whom they work. I challenge you to find ways to enhance your development as a leader and to use this information to lead from behind.

Notes

1 The tone of this chapter is different from Chapters 1–6 in this part of the book. This chapter is meant to read like a guidebook for individuals who are interested in the concept of leading from behind and wish to develop these skills and implement them in their individual workplace environments.
2 TESOL also offers a Leadership Development Certificate Program in conjunction with their annual conventions. In addition, a number of TESOL's affiliates (e.g., TESOL Arabia) are also offering their own certificate program to promote the development of leaders in the profession.

References

AcademicLeadership.org (2005). *Journal of Academic Leadership*. Retrieved February 17, 2005, from http://academicleadership.org.
Beazley, H., Beggs, J., & Spears, L.C. (2003). *The servant-leader within: A transformative path*. New York: Paulist Press.
Cashman, K. (1999). *Leadership from the inside out: Becoming a leader for life*. Provo, UT: Executive Excellence.
Center for Creative Leadership (2004). Retrieved February 17, 2005, from http://www.ccl.org/
Covey, S.R. (2004). *The 8th habit: From effectiveness to greatness*. New York: Free Press.
Greenleaf Center for Servant-Leadership (2002). Retrieved February 17, 2005, from http://www.greenleaf.org/
Hoppe, M.H. (2004). Cross-cultural issues in the development of leaders. In C.D. McCauley, & E. Van Velsor (Eds.), *Handbook of leadership development* (2nd edn.) (pp. 331–360). San Francisco: Jossey-Bass.
Kouzes, J.M., & Posner, B.Z. (2003). *Academic administrator's guide to exemplary leadership*. San Francisco: Jossey-Bass.
Leadership for a changing world (2005). Retrieved February 17, 2005, from http://leadershipforchange.org/
Lieberman, A., & Miller, L. (2004). *Teacher leadership*. San Francisco: Jossey-Bass.
Marzano, R.J., Waters, T., & McNulty, B.A. (2006). *School leadership that works*. Alexandria, VA: ASCD.

McCauley, C.D., & Van Velsor, E. (2004). *Handbook of leadership development* (2nd edn.). San Francisco: Jossey-Bass.

Merriam-Webster. (2005). *Merriam-Webster Online*. [Web site]. Retrieved February 17, 2005, from http://www.m-w.com/

Murphy, E.C. (1996). *Leadership IQ*. New York: John Wiley & Sons, Ltd.

Murray, D.E., & Christison, M.A. (2004). Developing Leadership IQ. Paper presented at the Annual TESOL Convention, Long Beach, California, March 31–April 3.

Nair, K. (1994). *A higher standard of leadership: Lessons from the life of Gandhi*. San Francisco: Berrett-Koehler.

Palmer, A., & Christison, M.A. (2007). *Seeking the heart of teaching*. Ann Arbor, MI: University of Michigan Press.

Patterson, K., Grenny, J., McMillan, R., & Switzler, A. (1996). *The balancing act: Mastering the competing demands of leadership*. Cincinnati, OH: International Thomson.

Part II

Skills for Leading

Introduction

Part II focuses on developing the requisite skills for leading. In the process of determining what should go into this section of the book, we thought about the skills that we ourselves wanted to develop and believed were essential to the work that we were doing as part of our leadership responsibilities, such as the skills needed to plan for the future of the programs. We also wanted to develop skills to ensure program quality, build teams, improve our communication skills, and manage performance within the entity. We have included all of these skills as chapters in Part II.

Leaders need to develop skills related to organizational structure in order to determine how best to organize their programs to achieve their objectives. In Chapter 8, Denise E. Murray and MaryAnn Christison introduce readers to organizational structures and the idea that organizational structures should reflect the vision and goals of the entity and should facilitate information flow, the decision-making process, curriculum development, services to students, and communication with all stakeholders.

In Chapter 9, Denise E. Murray and MaryAnn Christison explore the soft and technical skills that support a leader's capacity to plan strategically for an organization. They help leaders understand why it is important to plan strategically and how a strategic plan provides a baseline against which to make decisions. In addition, they also cover the process of planning strategically.

In Chapter 10, Colin McNaught introduces readers to the concept of ensuring quality programs and on what motivates programs to focus on standards of quality. He also discusses how programs go about establishing systems to ensure the quality of their teaching programs and services associated with these programs. Three different approaches to quality assurance as also covered in this chapter.

In Chapter 11, McNaught focuses on the practices and skills needed to manage performance in English language education. He does this by situating the skills leaders need within a broad framework for performance management and identifying the processes required to establish this framework. The theory is related to practice by focusing on one key process—the performance review.

There is nothing more basic to effective leadership than the development of one's communication skills. In Chapter 12, Julian Edge and Mark A. Clarke offer readers a toolkit for improving communication. They examine communication as a function of leadership—acts of leadership based on understanding and driven by communication. However, Edge and Clarke take communication one step further, by asserting that learning about oneself improves one's ability to communicate effectively with others. They also offer specific tools for improving communication in the form of specific guiding principles that are practical and grounded in ecological principles of teaching and teacher education.

The final chapter in Part II focuses on the skills needed to build effective teams. In Chapter 13, MaryAnn Christison and Denise E. Murray explore the concept of team building within the educational context. They offer guidelines for building effective teams and guidance for leaders who are in charge of teams. In addition, they cover skills associated with motivating teams, determining roles and responsibilities of team members, understanding the critical factors in developing effective teams, as well as the skills needed to run effective team meetings.

Chapter 8

Organizational Structure

Denise E. Murray and MaryAnn Christison

Introduction

As leaders, we need to understand, predict, and work with behavior at individual, group and institutional levels. In other chapters we have discussed individual behavior (see, for example, Chapter 5 on emotional intelligence and Chapter 12 on communication) and group behavior (see Chapter 13 on building teams). In this chapter, we examine behavior at the institutional level. To lead an organization requires an understanding of its organizational structure and culture and, oftentimes, the capacity to change the structure. Many of us in language education have worked in organizations where we have felt the structure inhibits our ability to achieve our goals and those of the organization. As leaders we need to evaluate the structure of our organization to determine whether the structure facilitates our work. We have seen new leaders appointed, who immediately change the structure, appointing different people in different roles and creating different reporting structures. While every leader seeks to inspire their organization with their own vision of its future, we would caution against hasty change. In our own experience, we have found it is essential to first conduct an environmental scan of the organization, internally and externally, as in a strategic plan (see Chapter 9). If the organization doesn't have a strategic plan, then this is the time to embark on such a process of consensus building. If it already has one, it is time to evaluate it. If there are compelling reasons to change the structure (for example, the resignation of key managers), then take the time to first analyze the situation before introducing changes. This is sound advice, not only because staff may automatically resist change from a new leader, but also because it takes time to know the hidden, informal cultures and structures as well as the formal structures and systems.

The Role of Organizational Structure

The organizational structure should reflect the vision and goals of the entity and should facilitate information flow and decision-making across the organization. Additionally, the structure of any organization reflects its culture. In the literature, organizational structure and organization culture are often used interchangeably. Mead (1994), for example, demonstrates how the multiplicity of meanings attributed to the term "organizational culture" leads to confusion among scholars and practitioners. In this chapter, we will discuss both aspects.

Within an English language education context, the structure needs to facilitate curriculum development, teaching and non-teaching staff discussion, services to students, and communication with all stakeholders, whether parents, recruiting agents, deans, or textbook suppliers. The strategic plan (see Chapter 9) sets out the direction for the organization's future, but the goals cannot be achieved unless the organization's structure clearly establishes individual competencies, roles and responsibilities, which constitute the organization's overall capacity. In Chapter 9 we see how one step in the process of planning strategically was to determine the organization's current capability. This capability includes the organizational structure and culture. McNaught, in Chapter 11's discussion on performance management (PM), shows how leaders conduct the PM process. The organizational structure, which delineates roles, provides input to the role descriptions used for PM, as well as delineating the lines of reporting. The roles that include leadership and management need to include the competencies described in Chapters 1 through 7, where several authors describe the qualities of effective leaders. There is, therefore, a symbiotic relationship among leader/manager and other staff competencies and the organizational structure and culture.

The structure of an organization, however, also reflects its context. As we saw in Chapter 1, different national cultures favor different approaches to the workplace. So, for example, one would expect that cultures that value power distance and uncertainty avoidance would tend to have hierarchical structures, while those that value low power distance and uncertainty avoidance would tend to have flatter structures. Researchers and others have posited two approaches to the relationship between national culture and organizational culture. The position taken by Hofstede (2001), Mead (1994), and others is that all management practices are culturally dependent and therefore the structure and culture of an organization reflect the national culture. On the other hand, others (Gray & Mallory, 1998; Van Dijk, 1995) have argued that there is in fact a convergence of organizational behavior, largely as a result of globalization. From this perspective, organizations share common values, which are of more importance than national cultural differences. As we saw in Chapters 2 and 5, research into aspects of leadership intelligence have found commonalities across different national cultures. Differences, they have shown, are more in relative weightings of the various competencies of EQ or roles requisite for effective leadership. This position is supported by studies specifically examining the role of national culture on organizational culture. A study of PR China, Hong Kong SAR, and Canada by Vertinsky et al. (1995), for example, found differences in internal competition, participation, and formal structure, but none in strategic adaptiveness, centralization, democratic organization, or management skills. Their finding of differences in structure have been supported by others such as Hofstede, who have found that Confucian values of harmony, order, control, and building relationships support formal and clearly articulated organizational structures, along with centralized authority, with leadership ascribed by role rather than achieved through merit. Further, with globalization both in product development and in management science, many countries have adopted an Anglo-American approach to organizational structure, but, as Mead (1994) warns, the structure may be in name only, with no attendant change in cultural values. Thus, the structures may not reflect actual practice and cannot be relied on. The research then, supports both points of view—that national culture controls organizational culture and that organizations have commonalities across cultures. In the discussions that follow, we suggest that readers consider both the impact of national culture as well as the universality of the human experience.

Other external influences on an organization's structure might be a result of government or other legal requirements. If the organization is accredited, it may have to abide by certain structures imposed by the accrediting agency. Even if the agency doesn't require a particular structure, it might require particular roles, such as a Board of Directors, a Chief Financial Officer, and so on, all of which become part of the structure. The unit may be part of a larger organization such as a university or a large chain of English language schools. In such cases, some of the structures are determined by the larger entity. However, leaders of a unit still have some flexibility in designing structures within their own unit. In an era of change such as the twenty-first century and in open systems such as education, whatever organizational structure is chosen, it needs to be flexible, able to cope with innovation and change in internal and external circumstances, and the resistance of staff.

Models of Organizational Structure

There is a plethora of different descriptions of the structures of organizations. They all seek to illuminate the way organizations operate. Since organizations have task needs, group needs and individual needs, the various models seek to explain how these (sometimes conflicting) needs are met through organizational structure. The models vary somewhat in the number of dimensions incorporated, from Baldridge's (1971) three dimensions (bureaucratic, collegial, and political) to Bolman and Deal's (1997) four-cornered frame (structural, human resource, political, and symbolic) to Birnbaum's (1988) five dimensions (bureaucratic, collegial, political, anarchical, and cybernetic). Organizational structures can be based on product, function, geographical location or a mixture of each. Here we will focus on those models that have the greatest relevance to language education. One theme is the dichotomy between flat and hierarchical structures. White and his colleagues (1991) are some of the few writers on leadership and management in language education and so we will draw on their work here. Another strand of the literature attempts to describe the culture of organizations. To illustrate this aspect of organizational structure, we will describe the work of (Handy, 1985). A model that we have found useful in describing language education institutions is that of Cope (1989), which draws on the models listed above, but is closest to that of Birnbaum. In work we have done internationally, we have found that this model resonates with most teachers and leaders in our field. These perspectives are not mutually exclusive, but rather overlap and interact.

Flat or Hierarchical Structures?

Many of us are familiar with the pyramidal structure typical of the organizational chart of many businesses. Many researchers have noted that a rigid hierarchical structure leads to what is called a "silo" mentality, where staff only think about and value those in their direct reporting line. Kanter (1983) especially has identified that those companies that are nimble and innovative have horizontal structures. While vertical structures facilitate control, horizontal structures, whether formal or informal, facilitate coordination and cooperation and are more responsive to change. While Kanter's research was within business, in the 1990s, the Pew Charitable Trusts sponsored The Pew Higher Education Roundtable, which examined the structures of institutions of higher education and how to make them responsive to the new demands of limited resources and accountability. Their findings indicate that the academic departments are the essential "building blocks" and need "to become effective service-providers that collectively design, monitor, and control the delivery of effective, cost-efficient courses and programs" (The Pew Higher Education Roundtable, 1994, p. 11A). However, they rejected the silo mentality that this might imply, requiring that faculty, president and trustees develop close, working relationships, that they develop partnerships, rather than the more usual adversarial relationship. White et al. (1991) note that schools have traditionally used a pyramid structure, although some school reform in the United States has followed a flatter, less hierarchical structure, giving teachers a large role in decision-making at site level, not just within their own classrooms.

Others have noted that a flat structure reflects the cultural values of low power distance, tolerance for ambiguity and high individualism, while a hierarchical structure reflects the cultural values of high power distance, need for certainty, and collectivism (Hofstede, 2001). In research in Thailand, Mead found that Thai workers expected a hierarchical structure, "in Thai culture people are used to looking up and waiting to be told what to do" (1994, p. 320). Further, in such high power distance cultures, people consider managers who delegate to be a "dereliction of duty" (ibid., p. 320). This doesn't necessarily imply an "either–or". If the structure is vertical, the leader needs to establish mechanisms, both formal and informal, that allow for cross-fertilization. For example, one of us, working in a large institution with several layers of management responsibility across very different work groups—book publishing, online courses, intensive English programs, graduate courses, research, and a large library—established horizontal committees with membership across sections, but reporting to a committee within the hierarchical structure that represented all sections of the organization. These horizontal committees provided for information flow and creativity, while still ensuring the innovations and ideas were responsive to the organization as a whole. Additionally, if an idea came from one area, but there were staff in another area who could contribute, she put together a task force. Leaders can also provide informal opportunities for staff from different areas to interact, such as social events, shared lunch/coffee break areas, and a culture of communication. Leaders need to model this behavior by themselves occasionally "walking the corridors" and talking with staff from different areas and choosing people from different areas to work on projects.

When such a structure is formalized, it can be called a matrix structure (Narayanan & Nath, 1993), which combines a functional structure with a divisional one. A functional structure is hierarchical, while the divisional structure is flatter, being built around product line. The matrix, by combining the two other types, seeks to combine efficiency (a hallmark of a hierarchical structure), with market responsiveness (a hallmark of a flatter, divisional structure).

Task 8.1

Draw an organizational chart for the organization you are working in (or know well). Is it hierarchical or flat? What mechanisms exist to prevent a "silo" mentality? If none exist, what would you institute to create interaction and innovation?

Organizational Culture

Organizational structures reflect the culture of the organization, while, at the same time imposing a way of behaving and meaning.

> The culture of an educational organisation is expressed in the attitudes and behaviour of people towards customers and each other. Organisational culture is influenced by the patterns of communication and codes of behaviour defined by the organisation's management, or the organisational structure.
>
> (White et al., 1991, p. 7)

Thus, one of the most common descriptive models is that of Handy (1985), who posits four types of organizational culture: power culture, role culture, task culture, and person culture.

- *Power or Club Culture.* While some national cultures value high power distance, as identified by Hofstede (2001), as we noted in Chapter 1, these national tendencies do not exclude the existence of institutions with values that differ from those of the national norm. Power cultures are characterized by strong leaders who choose effective teams that meet the needs of the leader. Members of the "club" exhibit loyalty to the leader and defer to him or her. Thus, these organizations have a very personal, almost cult-like culture. Since the leader is the ultimate power, communication is usually through the leader and informal, with little adherence to formal meetings with minutes or other records: "owner-managed schools, in particular, tend to embody a club culture, with the owner-principal occupying a central role" (White et al., 1991, p. 18). Change is embarked on only at the behest of the leader.
- *Role Culture.* In a role culture, the person in the position (or role) is not as important as the role's function itself. The role continues, regardless of who fills the position.

People define themselves and their work through their roles. Roles therefore need to be clearly defined and processes and procedures are also usually well defined. Consequently, role cultures are slow to change. In English language education, sometimes the role culture operates in parallel with a personal culture. The administration may be a role culture, relying on procedures for student enrollment, fee collection, supplies ordering, utilities payments, and so on, while the teachers operate in a power/club culture, clustering around the leader/head. When these different cultural orientations exist in the same organization, there is often conflict, as administrators seek to have teachers follow rules and procedures, but teachers feel exempt from such formal, organized behaviors.

- *Task Culture*. In a task culture, the focus is on the outcomes of projects. People form groups to participate in particular projects and meet certain goals. Consequently, the structure is often flat and responsive to changing customer needs. Such organizations tend to be challenging and stimulating, but, being built around projects, may be less stable for individuals than other cultures. English language schools that have a wide range of different course offerings tend to operate a task culture, with teams for each of the different courses. Unless there is some permeability across these teams, teachers and curriculum developers may not have opportunities to work on different areas. As mentioned above under flat or hierarchical structures, a task culture can exist in parallel with other cultures, with specific teams established for particular projects, but within a more role or power culture.

- *Person Culture*. In a person culture, the individual is valued for his or her skills. Person cultures are characterized by stars and the structure of the organization tends to be quite loose and management subservient to the stars. This type of culture is typical of research and development labs in industry or researchers in academia. While such a culture may pervade some areas of an English language educational institution, schools require team work, which is incompatible with a person culture.

Cultural types arise as a result of the size of an organization, the national culture, and the history of the organization. Role cultures tend to emerge over time and especially in large, stable organizations. All of these cultural types are, of course, prototypical and a "pure" case rarely exists in real educational institutions. They do, however, help us as leaders to examine the culture of our own organizations and decide whether the predominant culture is responsive to educational change and innovation.

Task 8.2

Identify an organization you are familiar with for each of Handy's organizational cultures. Describe the characteristics that helped you make this identification.

Five Types of Organizational and Information Structure

As indicated above, organizational structure is designed to facilitate information flow, whether that is for production of goods or for management of the organization, such as performance management. Within English language education, that information flow includes decision-making about central concerns such as curriculum development, student assessment, professional development, research directions, and accountability reporting to various stakeholders, such as deans, school owners, boards of directors, or government. Cope's (1989) model describes five structural types. In identifying each type, he describes features of the organization: its personnel, values, decision-making, and the type of information typical of each type:

1   *Bureaucratic.* The bureaucratic organization is formally structured, with people's roles clearly defined, regulations predetermined, and procedures clearly established. In such organizations, information is the province of specialist offices. This information is highly detailed and internally oriented. Each office justifies its position because of the specialist information it holds and doesn't share. Mead (1994), for example, illustrates the bureaucratic model by describing a Greek university where an instructor in the school of business needs information concerning names and ranks of academics. She needed this because an official from the overseas university from which she had graduated was going to visit Greece and hoped to catch up with former students, some of whom were now working at her Greek university. Because the institution is bureaucratically organized, she needs to ask the department secretary, who then makes the request in writing, explaining what is required and why, to the Assistant Director, who passes the written request on to the Director, who in turn passes it on to the Director of Personnel, who passes it to the Assistant Director, who then passes it to a Personnel Assistant. The Personnel Assistant finds the information and passes it back through the same chain of comment, first, through her management line and then down through the School of Business. At each stage, the request and/or information was checked. Mead points out that in other types of organizational structures, the instructor would have been able to contact the Personnel Assistant directly. But, in a bureaucratic organization, all decisions and requests for information must follow prescribed channels. This type of bureaucratic machinery requires a large support staff, including a legal office, to ensure compliance with rules and regulations.
2   *Collegial.* The collegial organization consists of experts who participate in decision-making, share values and are committed to the organization and work together collaboratively to achieve consensus. The structure is quite flat with minimal status differentiation. Information is technical, narrow, and value-laden. Hence, information flow tends to be project-based. Shared values and open communication sustain such structures. The traditional Western academic department is often cited as the typical collegial structure, a community of scholars. However, some researchers (Massey et al., 1994) have called it a "hollowed" collegiality. They found

that course assignments, decisions about promotion and tenure, and the sharing of research findings were all conducted on a collegial, democratic and participative manner. However, while important, this collegiality is superficial since it doesn't extend to core issues such as improving undergraduate education of making departments more effective. "[C]ollegiality remains thwarted with regard to faculty engagement with issues of curricular structure, pedagogical alternatives, and student assessment" (ibid., p. 19). Discussion of these substantive issues would require open and frank disagreements. These are avoided through this "hollowed" collegiality. They contend that the collegial model is insufficient for academic departments to be effective in the current climate of limited resources, and student and other stakeholder demands for accountability and calls for a focus on continuous quality improvement or total quality management in academic departments (see Chapter 10 for in-depth discussion of quality management). Yet others have found that different organizational structures co-exist in universities. The central administration may, for example, be a bureaucratic and hierarchical decision-making process, while the academic senate may involve a collegial process.

3   *Political*. The political organization assumes that conflict over goals, values, and preferences is natural. Decisions, therefore, are negotiated compromises. They are usually arrived at informally, through behind-the-scenes negotiations and deals, but are formally ratified. Information revolves around issues and is disseminated through factions. Holding of information constitutes one measure of power. In such organizations, forming coalitions is the only way to achieve one's own group's goals, even if the coalition partners have few common interests and values. These coalitions are constantly changing as interests and needs of groups change. Power is therefore diffused and emergent. People agree, at least publicly, on the major missions of the organization, such as the importance of teaching, research, and service, but specific programs are highly contested. For example, discussions over what course to include as core in an MA TESOL or PhD program may have more to do with individual desires to keep one's job than in what employers of graduates require. For individuals to achieve their own goal (ensuring their preferred courses are required) they might align with faculty espousing a completely different educational philosophy, but in a quid pro quo "deal" support each other's positions.

4   *Anarchical*. An anarchical organization is dominated by professionals, who have ambiguous goals, a loose system of rewards, and lack connectivity between the professionals. Their coming together is more for convenience than for a perceived belief that the whole is greater than the sum of the parts. Consequently, management in such an organization is not based on rational, goal-oriented decisions and plans. Information is not shared as there is little value assigned to the information held by others of the organization, since each is a professional, master of his or her own area. There are no leaders or those who do have positional leadership roles do not seek to influence the organization. In such an organization, groups are semi-autonomous and so able to be innovative, not having to answer to other parts of the organization. Individuals also have autonomy and so are often highly

motivated and fulfilled by their work. Law firms and research institutes often operate in this loose manner, their coalition being more for marketing (to get more clients or more grants) and some reduction in overheads, than for sharing of information. Some have claimed that many university departments have traditionally operated in this manner, especially where the head is a rotating position, regardless of individuals' expertise or interest in leadership. With more accountability expected and limited resources in many countries, such a model has become ineffective.

5   *Rational.* The rational organization is driven by seeking opportunities for strategic choices. These choices are logically determined through careful analysis of the environment, internal, but especially external. Information is organized through management information systems, whether careful paper filing or, more recently, complex, logically-derived computer-based databases and other systems such as online forms. Information is disseminated according to need. While this model has been the one underlying much management literature in the United States, the United Kingdom, and Australia, its applicability to other cultural groups has been questioned. Chinese culture for example, values common sense, rather than logic because it is more realistic (Hofstede, 2001). Mead (1994), also claims the rational approach is an American-Anglo perspective, based on cultural values such as analysis, rational decision-making, deliberate processes, acceptance of competition, and a preference for the linear . He compares this with family companies in areas of the world such as South East Asia, quoting Porter who says such "companies don't have strategies. They do deals. They respond to opportunities" (1996, p. 314). In other words, their strategic directions are emergent. Interestingly, recent work in systems theory (see Chapter 1, this volume), has noted that organizations that are open to emergent, unpredictable behavior are more effective in this current era.

Task 8.3

Identify an organization you are familiar with for each of Cope's organization types. Describe the characteristics that helped you make this identification.

There is some evidence that other characteristics, in addition to national and organizational culture, affect organizational structure. For example, the collegial model is difficult to implement in a large, complex organization. Bureaucratic characteristics often are introduced as organizations grow, have more specialized programs and departments, and fewer opportunities for all staff to communicate to reach consensus. These bureaucratic characteristics are usually introduced to standardize activities and actions by structuring means of interaction (e.g., through committees) and controlling behavior (e.g., through performance management). This standardization also serves to ensure equality of treatment of all staff as far as possible. Bureaucratic structures therefore work quite well for routine situations, but, being less flexible, are ineffective in changing, innovative, and unpredictable contexts. As a result, those working in bureaucratic organizations seek to avoid change and unpredictable situations. When confronted with the need to change, they tend to seek small aspects to change. In language education, for example, if student enrolments are declining and students are asking for new courses, staff tend to tinker with current programs, making minor changes to existing courses, rather than engaging in the holistic strategic planning process discussed in Chapter 9. This type of organization is compatible with national cultures that value large power distance, hierarchical control, and low uncertainty avoidance.

Conclusion

In this chapter we have examined the interplay between national culture, organizational culture, and organizational structure. Few organizations can be characterized entirely by one cultural or structural type; most have different types co-existing within the organization. While the literature suggests various models and often shows preference for some, the structure and culture of an organization are organic, dependent on the organization's goals, size, past history, ownership, and the national, political, and economic environment of the time. Examining the culture and structure are essential in the strategic planning process to ensure fit between the culture/structure and variables that impact on it.

References

Baldridge, J.V. (1971). *Power and conflict in the university: Research in the sociology of complex organizations*. New York: John Wiley & Sons, Ltd.

Birnbaum, R. (1988). *How colleges work: The cybernetics of academic organization and leadership*. San Francisco: Jossey-Bass.

Bolman, L.G., & Deal, T.E. (1997). *Reframing organizations: Artistry, choice, and leadership* (2nd edn.). San Francisco: Jossey-Bass.

Cope, R.G. (1989). *High involvement strategic planning*. Oxford: Basil Blackwell.

Gray, D., & Mallory, G. (1998). *Making sense of culture*. London: Thompson Business Press.

Handy, C.B. (1985). *Understanding organisations* (3rd edn.). Harmondsworth: Penguin.

Hofstede, G. (2001). *Culture's consequences* (2nd edn.). Thousand Oaks, CA: Sage.

Kanter, R.M. (1983). *The change masters: Innovation and entrepreneurship in the American corporation*. New York: Simon and Schuster, Inc.

Massey, W.F., Wilger, A.K., & Colbeck, C. (1994). Departmental cultures and teaching quality: Overcoming "hollowed" collegiality. *Change, July/August*, 11–20.

Mead, R. (1994). *International management*. Oxford: Blackwell.

Narayanan, V.K., & Nath, R. (1993). *Organization theory: A strategic approach*. Homewood, IL: Irwin.

Porter, M.E. (1996). It's time to grow up. *Far Eastern Economic Review*, March 14.

The Pew Higher Education Roundtable (1994). To dance with change. *Policy Perspectives, 5*(3), 2–12.

Van Dijk, J. (1995). Transnational management in an evolving European context. In T. Jackson (Ed.), *Cross-cultural management*. Oxford: Butterworth-Heinemann.

Vertinsky, I., Tse, D., Wehrung, D., & Lee, K. (1995). Organisational design and management norms: A comparative study of managers' perceptions in the People's Republic of China, Hong Kong and Canada. In T. Jackson (Ed.), *Cross-cultural management*. Oxford: Butterworth-Heinemann.

White, R., Martin, M., Stimson, H., & Hodge, R. (1991). *Management in English language teaching*. Cambridge: Cambridge University Press.

Chapter 9

Planning Strategically

Denise E. Murray and MaryAnn Christison

Introduction

In this chapter, we describe the technical skills that support a leader's capacity to plan strategically for the organization. However, the application of these technical skills requires the soft skills of leadership, innovation, vision, and emotional intelligence. It requires flexibility and adaptability to plan in a complex system such as education, which can be characterized as the open system described in the Introduction. We have deliberately called this chapter "planning strategically," rather than "strategic planning." For us, the former conveys the notion of process and flexibility, while the latter, more common term, implies a linear, static process. Others sometimes use the term "action plan" to ensure that the strategic plan doesn't just sit on a shelf, but details activities, people responsible, and due dates. We include action plans in our approach to strategic planning. The literature on strategic planning in the business world falls into two approaches—those who view strategic planning as a means of controlling the future by predicting it and those who consider the future to be so volatile and chaotic (in systems theory terms), that there is no point in planning for such uncertainty.

Despite this uncertainty, "the firm learns from the environmental feedback; and subsequent strategy reflects this learning" (Wiltbank et al., 2006, p. 985). In our own work in various countries, we have found that organizations that engage in strategic thinking and use their strategic plans as roadmaps for the future are the most successful in achieving their goals. Those that do not plan strategically tend to be reactive, unable to respond to change or innovation without creating stress for the organization and its staff or, they try to maintain the status quo. The process of strategic planning we describe below serves not only to develop a roadmap, but also to engage the entire organization in collaborative thinking about the organization's role in the field of language education. The strategic plan then becomes both a map for directing the future of the organization, and for developing a shared vision of that future. It provides the benchmark for developing annual work plans and the yardstick for measuring the performance of the organization. While there are technical skills and instruments to help achieve this, planning strategically in open systems such as education requires competent, innovative leaders who are flexible and exhibit high levels of emotional competence.

Why Plan Strategically?

We want to distinguish between planning strategically and program planning, which is a regular part of many language program's calendar. We have ourselves been involved in such regular five-year program planning exercises. However, they do not have the comprehensive, goal-oriented focus of the strategic planning we discuss here. While they may involve program evaluation, it is often restricted to an internal evaluation of the current program, especially curriculum content, followed by a decision to change the curriculum content. Suggested changes are usually based on staff intuitions. Planning strategically is a more systematic, objective analysis of the entire current situation and a decision about the organization's future directions, based on several analyses, not just staff perceptions or desires. For example, the program planning process is often hijacked by staff who want to ensure that their particular course (phonetics, English for doctors or pronunciation) is maintained or introduced or their particular orientation to language or learning is imposed on all staff (e.g. task-based learning, systemic functional grammar, competency-based syllabus design). We are not suggesting that any of these approaches are inappropriate, just that the planning process needs to provide opportunities for open, frank discussion about the theoretical bases of the curriculum and its implementation, along with discussion about attitudes to customer service and interaction with suppliers. Strategic planning is not designed to either maintain the status quo or provide a platform for individual's pet projects.

Plans for the future need to be strategic so they position the organization and, as Peter Drucker (1993, p. 16) has succinctly stated, "the best way to predict the future is to create it," even if that future is uncertain. Therefore, for a language educational organization to plan strategically means it will understand itself, and its relation to other organizations in the field, and create its own future in ways that differentiate it from its competitors. Its plans then are comprehensive, goal driven, the result of conscious decision-making (Kanter, 1983), rather than drifting into new ideas or falling back on old ones. Kanter, along with most researchers and commentators on management and leadership, recognizes the danger an organization faces if it lurches from new idea to new idea without an articulated purpose, or embeds itself in past practice, without contemplating the possibilities of new ideas. The plans are not reactive to specific, singular threats or opportunities, although they provide mechanisms to evaluate such threats and opportunities. Since language education is an open emergent system, the approach we take is of "planned emergence" (Wiltbank et al., 2006), that is

> Rational planning can focus on predictive strategies that set the stage for fast adaptation. Organizations can rationally plan and develop systems that facilitate innovation and change, for example, through modular organizational structures that smooth significant organizational challenges to change, and/or establish formal but simple rules that guide the evaluation and pursuit of emergent opportunities.
>
> (ibid., p. 986)

Such an approach focuses more on what an organization can control than on what it can predict. To achieve this, strategic planning usually involves envisioning where the organization would like to be in five to seven years, understanding the organization's current strengths and weaknesses, investigating the local and global environment in which it operates, and then creating a plan that will help the organization move from its current position to its newly envisioned one. It therefore includes the allocation of both human and physical resources to achieving the goals. But, given the volatile nature of open systems, that plan has built-in flexibility, in the way the organization develops its annual plans based on the strategic plan, and in how it monitors its performance.

The strategic plan provides a baseline against which to make decisions. For example, if an Intensive English Program (IEP) is approached by an academic department within its university, to develop a discipline-specific course, the IEP needs to evaluate the proposal against the plan. Does it fit the plan? Would it require re-allocation of resources, both human and material? What effect would that have on achieving the already agreed-upon goals? If it doesn't fit the plan, should the plan be modified or should the organization reject the proposal? The values (see below) of the organization can be used in performance management and in hiring. When a new person is hired into the organization, they can be requested to agree to the values, which are then used as one measure of their performance. So, for example, if one of the organization's values is a focus on customer service, a new receptionist can be required to exhibit certain types of behaviors that are consistent with customer service such as polite interactions with all clients and suppliers, or ensuring if she/he doesn't know the answer, he/she will ensure that the referral is to someone who can truly help the client, rather than buck passing to move the client on.

Although planning strategically has been widely adopted within education, it has often been resisted because of its origins in the business world or has been adopted uncritically. The business world may seem alien to many educators, because of its major drivers of delivering products to customers, making a profit, and outperforming the competition. Yet, the world of ELT has become increasingly competitive and the survival of many programs is no longer assured, but is dependent on attracting students and research funding and meeting the expectations of stakeholders such as boards of directors, owners, or deans and presidents. Our view of strategic planning is that it helps an organization improve its services and in turn improve the learning outcomes for students.

The Process of Planning Strategically

As Covey says about how organizations need to prepare for their future:

> The solutions are basically the same for any situation, any field. We gather complete and balanced data to get a clear picture of where we are now. We analyze it to diagnose our strengths and weaknesses. We select objectives, we identify and evaluate our options and make some decisions. We identify critical action steps,

implement the plan, and then compare results against the objectives, which takes us back to the beginning of the process.

(1990, p. 197)

In this chapter, we will describe a process we have been involved in that is both top-down and bottom-up. While we have found that this approach has been most successful in the environments in which we have worked, because of national cultural differences or the cultural history of an educational institution, this approach may not always be most appropriate. A top-down approach is one in which the managers or others (e.g., owners) in position of structural power develop a strategic plan and present it to staff. There is usually no discussion; rather, staff are required to abide by the plan. In a bottom-up approach, all staff participate and drive the ideas that end up in the plan. We have found there are advantages and disadvantages to both approaches. A top-down approach is efficient, but may be rejected by staff who have had no input. This rejection may be subtle non-compliance. We have seen top-down approaches where managers have decreed a specific language teaching methodology, for example, communicative language teaching. However, what happens in the classroom, behind closed doors is the same grammar-translation that teachers are most comfortable with. The bottom-up approach is time-consuming and can lead to frustration if staff have ideas they value and advocate for, but are not included in the final plan. Staff may also have different perspectives from management and there is no process for these to be negotiated. However, it can lead to dialogue within the institution and a sense of ownership by all who participated. Therefore, we and others (for example, Cope, 1989) have found that a combined top-down, bottom-up process is usually the most effective. The process needs to be centrally managed and supported with vision and resources (top-down), but involve all staff in an iterative process of discovery and evaluation (bottom-up). We have found one way of ensuring this ongoing dialogue is to commission a team to take responsibility for the process (not the final plan—that is everyone's responsibility). Such a team needs to be appointed by management to ensure members do the following:

- Understand the organization;
- Understand the field of language education, i.e., can see the big picture;
- Are able to work together as a team;
- Are able to "think out of the box;"
- Are able to facilitate work teams.

These are essential skills for a team that will drive the process and work collaboratively with management, teachers and non-academic staff. See also Chapter 13 for a discussion on creating and leading teams.

> **Task 9.1**
>
> Think about your culture and the culture of your organization. How would bottom-up and top-down approaches fit your cultures? How is buy-in achieved in your organization? Do all staff commit to or just give lip service to strategic directions?

Having chosen the approach that best fits the organization, you can then embark on the steps of the planning process. While terminology in the research in strategic planning differs, most experts consider three main steps as essential in the overall process (for example, Ansoff, 1979; Bennis & Nanus, 1997; Cope, 1989; Covey, 1990; Klinghammer, 1997): assessing the internal and external situation, determining the organization's goals, and deciding on a path for getting from the present to the goal at some point in the future. In our experience, using a top-down/bottom-up process means involving all staff in the various analyses discussed below. Such discussions need to be focused, operate as teams, be led by members of the strategic planning team, have clear outcomes, and be managed as teams (see Chapter 13 for how to manage teams effectively). We will use the term staff below as a shorthand for all people employed in the organization, whether teachers, clerical staff, accountants, janitorial staff, or managers.

Assessing the Situation

Assessing the situation has two important strands—evaluating the organization and examining the external context. The latter is often referred to as an environmental scan. The most common tool for assessing the situation is the SWOT analysis, that is a determination of the *strengths* and *weaknesses* of the organization and the *opportunities* and *threats* from outside. Because most people are familiar with the SWOT analysis for assessing the situation and because it is a rather blunt instrument, we will introduce some other tools we have found useful and that provide a finer grained analysis.

Evaluating the Organization

The evaluation of the organization requires examining the capability of the organization. This will therefore include an examination of both its strengths and weaknesses. Strengths refer to the resource capacity the organization has, both human and material, while weaknesses are areas where it doesn't have capacity currently, but could capacity build, if that were a considered direction for the future. For example, if an organization has no staff with expertise in TOEFL (Test of English as a Foreign Language) preparation and yet many potential students want to sit for TOEFL, it is vital in the strategic planning process that this lack be identified. Then, when considering goals, the organization can determine whether it wants to capture this market. If so, the path may be to hire new, expert staff, or retrain current staff. A tool we have found useful for evaluating capability is adapted from that of Bruce (2000), who describes the organizational setting in which enterprises operate as involving three key elements: the organization's culture, its structure and systems, and its competencies and experiences. He calls the interaction among staff and these elements the Capability Platform. For an organization to plan strategically, it needs to assess its existing capability platform.

- *People*: The commitment and creativity of staff are the most valuable resources in any language education enterprise. Therefore, in defining the capability platform, all individuals and groups must be honest and open, while still valuing each other. If the group meetings gloss over weaknesses in current staff, they will not be able to make a realistic appraisal of the current capability. Also, if they use the meetings as an opportunity to push their own personal agendas and likes and dislikes of colleagues, the meetings will not be productive. Therefore they must be conducted in an atmosphere of trust and mutual respect and where leaders model appropriate behavior (see Chapter 5 on emotional intelligence for some strategies for creating such an atmosphere). To assess the capability of staff (both managers and non-managers) in the organization, the following questions need to be asked:

  - How risk-averse or risk-tolerant are staff?
  - How conservative (in the sense of conserving the status quo) are staff?
  - What skills do staff have?
  - What is staff commitment to the organization?
  - What is management commitment to staff?
  - How emotionally competent are staff?
  - What is the level of staff's soft skills?

- *Culture*: While Bruce focuses on the culture of the organization, in a global field such as English language education, national culture is also a consideration (see Chapter 1 for an analysis of the impact of culture on the workplace). To assess the culture of the organization, the following questions need to be asked:

  - How responsive is the organization to change?
  - How innovative/creative is the organization?
  - How entrepreneurial is the organization?
  - How focused is the organization on the following?

    a. soft skills
    b. meeting stakeholder needs
    c. excellence
    d. leveraging diversity

  - How bureaucratic is the organization?
  - How are decisions made?
  - Is the culture based on positional power, the charisma of the leader, achievement of common goals, or mutual trust?
  - Are all staff valued, no matter their role?

- *Competencies/experience*: The goal in this assessment is to determine what the current organization can do, not what you hope it might do in the future. As well as qualifications and skills of all staff, competencies include relationships with stakeholders and reputation. Questions that need to be answered include:
  - What is the organization most renowned for?
  - Why do students or other customers choose the organization?
  - Why do people want to join the staff?
  - What is the **range** of teaching/research/administrative skills among staff?
  - How knowledgeable are staff about the needs of students and other stakeholders?

- *Structure and systems*: Staff do not work in a vacuum. All organizations develop policies and systems to facilitate (or not) their work. Clearly, the culture of the organization affects structures and systems, but in this analysis, the meetings need to focus only on structures and systems, not on the culture that might have produced them. Therefore, questions to ask might include:
  - Do the systems promote quality (of instruction and any other work)?
  - Are procedures and policies communicated to all staff?
  - Are policies applied equally or in an ad hoc manner?
  - Are policies and procedures flexible?
  - Are information and communication systems transparent?
  - Is the structure hierarchical or flat? Is it horizontal or vertical?

Figure 9.1 illustrates the interaction among the elements of capability.

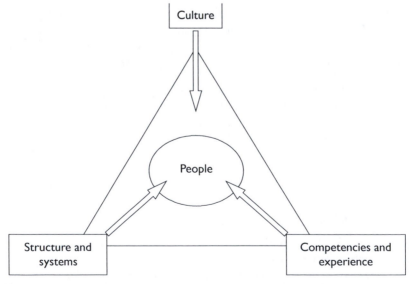

Figure 9.1 The Capability Platform
Source: After Bruce (2000).

Task 9.2

For each of the elements above, list 4–5 words or phrases that define the capability of the organization you work with. As far as possible, choose descriptive words such as hardworking, time poor, band-aid approach, compartmentalized, friendly/ fun, all terms used in a planning exercise we were involved in.

Environmental Scan

The environmental scan is designed to evaluate the external context in which the organization does its work. A number of tools can be used for this, such as the SWOT analysis. In the SWOT analysis, the "O" and "T" refer to the external context.

- *Opportunity*: For example, visa regulations may have recently changed, making it easier for students from certain countries to enter and specifically to study English in a non-matriculated program. Does the school, therefore, want to capture this market or does it want to continue on its traditional path of only accepting students who are accepted into their degree programs?
- *Threat*: There may be a new school or department that has recently emerged; there may be new government policies in another country that might lead to international students choosing that country over your own. For example, English-speaking countries such as the USA, Canada, Australia, Great Britain, and New Zealand, that have long been destinations of choice for students wanting to learn English or receive an English-medium degree, are now facing competition from Singapore, India, and the Philippines as they provide such education cheaper.

One tool we have found effective is Bruce's (2000) five industry forces. While his model was developed for use in determining industry profitability, it can be usefully adapted for education and provides a sharper lens than the threats and opportunities criteria of the SWOT analysis. We discuss the five forces below:

- *Threat of substitutes*: The threat of substitutes may seem to be minimal in our field. We don't have products such as artificial sweetners to replace sugar, ATMs to replace (or at least compete with) over-the-counter banking, or downloadable music to replace audiotapes and CDs. However, we have seen the move towards developing "intelligent" computer assisted language learning programs that do not require a teacher's intervention. We have also seen the growing accuracy of machine translation, which could obviate the need for many people to learn English. We have also seen the growing demand for teaching Mandarin.
- *Threat of new entrants*: Bruce explains that new players who enter the industry, like current participants, have to evaluate the context—whether they can scale up for

the new product, whether they can differentiate their product from existing ones, what resources they need, whether government regulation permits them to offer the new product, and whether they have access to the marketplace. Within many government-regulated language education contexts, new entrants can be very unlikely, but even established university programs, for example, can find a new player in their region. With online education being promoted, educational providers in other regions can often offer programs that compete with existing ones.

- *Bargaining power of buyers*: While we often do not think of our students as buyers, they (or their families or government through scholarships) are in fact buying a service when they pay tuition fees to attend our classes. Many in our field have observed organizations that offer language programs more cheaply, or at times that learners prefer. The students who come to our programs often have a variety of programs from which to choose. To remain viable each program needs to find its own niche. On p. 145 we provide a tool that helps staff decide what factors will help them find and maintain their niche.

- *Bargaining power of suppliers*: Bruce's fourth factor, suppliers, is one we don't often think about in language education. Probably the most significant supplier is the teaching force. In trying to meet the requirements of students for lower fees, we have to consider the effect this would have on staff salaries and other resources such as convenient and attractive premises, or providing computer labs.

- *Rivalry among existing firms*: We have noticed in recent years, much greater competition across all sectors of English language education—whether English language programs, teacher education programs – and in many regions of the world. In many places, there has been a paradigm shift from cooperation and friendly sharing of information, to market-driven win-lose competition. While we may consider this to be detrimental to our educational ethos, in many cases, it has lead to greater transparency for learners and other stakeholders. Whatever our ideological position regarding competition, in planning strategically, it is vital to consider the competition from other educational providers. Below, we will provide another tool that helps focus this competitiveness so each entity can find its own niche.

Task 9.3

Table 9.1 provides a grid of Bruce's five industry forces. We have provided one example for each force. Write down three or more examples from your own language education context.

Table 9.1 Five Industry Forces in English Language Education

Threat of Substitutes	Threat of New Entrants	Bargaining Power of Buyers	Bargaining Power of Suppliers	Rivalry Among Existing Firms
Dominance of the Chinese language, rather than of English	For-profit, non-educational companies offering English classes	Changes in government policy (e.g. charging higher fees for students in graduate programs)	Union agreements for higher faculty salaries	Cheaper, but lower quality courses at XYZ School

Stakeholder Views

An additional source of information about the environment is stakeholders. We have found it useful to develop a questionnaire and mail out to stakeholders. For this information source to be useful requires staff to think broadly about who the stakeholders are. For example, if your institution gets grants, then the granting agency would be a stakeholder; if you have students or teachers from outside your country, then the Immigration Department would be a stakeholder. A brainstorming session is useful here. As well as identifying the stakeholders, it is important to identify the needs and wants of those stakeholders. Klinghammer (1997), for example, identifies a number of stakeholders in an intensive English program at a university, such as faculty, sponsors (such as host families, community sponsors and embassies/agencies/companies). In an area of concern such as program delivery and quality, each stakeholder group may have different wants, needs and expectations. Faculty may want reasonable workloads and adequate resources such as videos and computers, while sponsors may be more interested in program flexibility, such as the ability for students to enter at any time. Often these different wants and needs are in conflict; however, it is vital to conduct a stakeholder analysis, and not just an armchair analysis. We suggest questionnaires and focus groups with major stakeholders.

Finding Your Niche

Once having learned as much as possible about the environment, "the organization can develop a sense of its purpose, direction and desired future state" (Bennis & Nanus, 1997, p. 198). We have suggested above that one of the goals of planning strategically is for an organization to find its particular niche, its particular future direction. To achieve this, the planning process includes examining the organization's vision, mission, and values. While some commentators on strategic planning begin with the vision and mission, in our experience, this examination will be based on realistic knowledge and assumptions if the environment is studied first.

Strategy Canvas

We have found one particular tool helpful in establishing the vision, mission and values, the strategy canvas of Kim and Mauborgne (2002). The purpose of the strategy canvas is to have staff draw a profile of their entity and compare it with what they consider to be the greatest competitor. In this exercise, we have found it useful for groups to meet according to areas of work because the exercise requires everyone to consider factors of competition. For example, the National Centre for English Language Teaching and Research (NCELTR) at Macquarie University has a range of products and services: research, professional development, English language teaching, book publishing, and a library/resource center. The factors of competition and the main competitor for the English language teaching program are different from that of the book publishing unit, and so on. Therefore, each section needs to undertake a strategy canvas, before all are brought together. Each work group then needs to brainstorm the main factors of competition, the goal being to eventually find its special niche. Factors might include cost, quality, facilities (this may, for example be subdivided into factors such as position, quality of premises and technology). The factors chosen will be those important for the particular context. Staff, through facilitate meetings, develop their list of factors and then rate their own organization against these factors. They then agree on their most important competitor and rate it on the factors.

Below we have created a context to demonstrate how the strategy canvas works. We have chosen an intensive English language program context, with My-IEP being the organization engaged in planning strategically. This is a university-based preparation program for students prior to entering an English-medium university degree program. Staff have chosen six factors as being important to their clients and rated them on a 20-point scale (Figure 9.2). The factors are cost, student support, staff qualifications, variety of programs, facilities, and quality of programs. They have chosen two different competitors: Uni-IEP, the major university-based competitor to My-IEP, and Private-IEP, a non-university-based IEP program in a commercial organization. If My-IEP has a variety of programs (for example, IELTS preparation, TOEFL preparation, discipline-specific courses), staff might choose to do a strategy canvas for each program since the rating of each factor for different programs could be different. In this case, to involve all staff, they might workshop staff in each program to help them develop their program's strategy canvas, rather than having the strategic planning committee developing each one. For our example, we have only rated the three IEPs overall on the six factors.

The next step for the My-IEP strategic planning committee would be to decide where the organization should be in each of these categories in five or so years. So, for example,

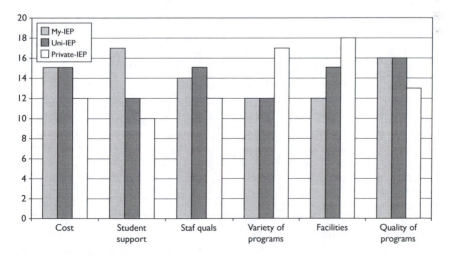

Figure 9.2 A Strategy Canvas for Three Different IEPs

the group might decide that, while their costs are higher than those at the commercial IEP, it is in keeping with other university IEPs and they cannot afford to decrease course fees and still maintain quality and high levels of student support, which is one of the principal values of the organization. On the other hand, they might decide that, to be competitive, they really need to upgrade staff qualifications and so might plan for that to rise to 17/18 on a scale of 20. The strategy canvas and the situation assessment provide the backdrop against which staff can define their vision, mission and goals. Within the literature and especially within education, there is considerable confusion about the definition of these terms. We follow Kouzes and Posner (1987), among others, who use vision to refer to the overarching direction, while mission is used as the "time-bound (2–5 years), action-based part of the vision" (Klinghammer, 1997 p. 64).

Vision Statements

Most strategic planners agree that the wording of a vision statement should be brief, clear, descriptive, and compelling. Vision statements say what, not how. "Because you want what you create to be unique, you differentiate your organization from all the others that produce the same product or perform the same service. Yours is a distinctive vision" (Kouzes & Posner, 1987, p. 87). Kouzes and Posner provide four guidelines for a vision: it needs to be future oriented, provide an image, provide a sense of the possible, and be unique. Vision statements are used to communicate the organization's vision to the outside world and so appear on websites, letterheads, and business cards. Here we provide examples of three vision statements in English language education:

AMES Victoria (AMES Victoria, 2006) provides a variety of English language programs, as well as job training and other services for immigrants and international students in Australia. Vision statement = *Full participation in a cohesive and diverse society*.

NCELTR (NCELTR, 2007) provides research, professional development, English-only courses, courses for university-bound students, book publishing, and a library. Vision statement = *International leadership in English language education*.

TESOL Inc.[1] (TESOL Inc., 2007) is the international professional association for teachers of English to speakers of other languages, headquartered in the United States. Vision statement = *A global education association*.

Mission

If the organization already has a mission and goals, then the first step is to review them. If the organization doesn't have a mission and goals, then the first step is to develop them. Mission statements are descriptions of (1) how the organization should operate, and (2) how students or clients benefit from the products and services of the organization. Most mission statements serve this dual purpose. Thus, it is based on the vision and is an expanded, action-oriented, achievable statement of goals. While the vision may have vague and lofty language, the mission needs to be achievable. If the organization is part of a larger one or affiliated with a larger one, the mission needs to be aligned to the larger one. So, CATESOL (CATESOL, 1998) (the California-Nevada affiliate of TESOL) defines its mission as shown in Figure 9.3.

CATESOL's mission is to promote excellence in education for English language learners and a high quality professional environment for their teachers. CATESOL represents teachers of English language learners throughout California and Nevada, at all levels and in all learning environments. CATESOL strives to:

- improve teacher preparation and provide opportunities which further professional expertise
- promote sound, research-based education policy and practices
- increase awareness of the strengths and needs of English language learners
- promote appreciation of diverse linguistic and cultural backgrounds.

Figure 9.3 CATESOL's Mission Statement

Values

Many organizations do not develop agreed upon values as part of their planning. We have found, however, that such values provide the guiding principles for the organization's behavior, both internal and external. For example, the values can be used in both hiring decisions and performance management (see Chapter 11 on managing performance). If the organization values diversity, then it may choose to hire staff from different backgrounds. Or, for example, if one of the organization's values is a focus on customer service, staff can be required to exhibit certain types of behaviors that are consistent with customer service such as polite interactions with all clients and suppliers. Values can include both moral principles and practical actions, as can be seen by the values of ACL, the largest private provider of English language education in Australia (Figure 9.4).

The Plan

Having surveyed the environment, tapped into the knowledge of stakeholders, and determined the niche the organization wants to develop, the next step is to develop specific, achievable, measurable objectives and goals. Again, the literature and especially education have used these terms quite differently. We have chosen the term strategic directions as the overall category of direction, which derives from the vision and mission, goals as the next level and projects as the action plan activities. The action plan includes performance indicators, timelines and responsibilities and each year serves as

---

ACL's values

- **We understand and act upon our clients' needs** – Our relationship with clients is an ongoing dialogue aimed at meeting their needs.
- **We foster innovation and creativity** – We are solutions-focused, using innovation, creativity and expertise to meet needs and solve problems.
- **We deliver on our promises** – We aim to meet our commitments and are accountable for what we do.
- **We deliver value** – We believe in delivering long-term value in our relationships, programs and services.
- **We celebrate cultural diversity** – We celebrate working across cultures and actively develop, use and promote the cross-cultural perspectives, experiences and skills of our staff and clients.
- **And we believe in achieving together** – We believe the best results come from working in partnership. We want people to feel they have gained from their association with us, be they students, staff or partners.

Figure 9.4 ACL's Values

the basis for the annual workplan. Performance indicators are essential to ensure measurement of progress and that everyone means the same thing by the project.

Thus, for example, NCELTR developed five strategic directions: client focus, leadership in English language education, organizational capability, building relationships and partnerships, and business management. Through working meetings with staff in different sections of the organization, led by the strategic planning committee, goals were developed for each strategy. The goals from each group then needed to be brought together to develop consistency across the entire organization and ensure high achievement, but realistic goals. The criteria shown in Figure 9.5 help guide decisions about whether goals are achievable, but stretch the organization towards its vision.

Criteria for Setting Goals

1. Are the goals clear and measurable? Will you know when you have achieved your goal? Can the goals be realistically achieved?
2. Is there a clear and sensible timeframe for achieving the goals?
3. Is there goal congruency (i.e., the goals combine with each other in order and support the vision statement)?
4. Is there a plan to revisit and revise the goals?
5. Will reaching these goals advance the strategic plan?
6. Will they generate rewards for people?
7. Do the organization goals translate into individual goals for staff?
8. Who will have overall responsibility for each goal?

> 9. Does the organization have the resources, both human and financial to carry
>   out the goals?

Figure 9.5 Criteria for Setting Goals

So, for example, NCELTR's strategic direction of "client focus" included the follow-ing goals:

- Ensure high levels of customer satisfaction.
- Maintain a high quality teaching and learning environment.
- Provide timely, accurate, and state-of-the-art information services.
- Provide a supportive environment to help students participate fully in university and wider community life.
- Monitor and be responsive to the changing needs of our clients.

Once there are agreed goals for each strategic direction, staff need to establish the actual projects that will help achieve the goals. Since this is not a one-year plan, there will be many projects, not all of which are achievable in the short term. Therefore, decisions need to be made about the timeline for projects in an action plan. Table 9.2 shows how NCELTR's plan moves from vision to action. We have provided some sample projects, performance indicators, who would be responsible for the activity, and timeline. The sample projects show that this objective crosses several sections of the organization—the IELTS test centre (projects 1, 5 and 8), the publications section (projects 5, 6 and 7), and the English language teaching unit (1, 2, 3, 4, and 5). Several would require team work across sections, such as projects 1 and 5. The timeline also shows that new initiatives (project 4) do not have to have immediate results. When new programs are started, there is often a time-lag before they become profitable and this should be built into the plan, along with evaluation steps along the way. At each evaluation point, decisions can be made whether to continue, add resources, abandon the program, or scale it back. These decision-points allow for the changing, volatile, unpredictable nature of open systems such as English language teaching.

The plan becomes the basis for annual workplans, which include projects, perfor-mance indicators, who is responsible and due dates. As can be seen from the samples given, not everything will be achieved in the first year, but each year, the plan needs to be revisited, performance indicators used to evaluate progress thus far and adjustments made based in changing circumstances. Thus, the plan drives the activities of the organization from committee structure to budget to staffing (Luther, 1995).

Table 9.2 Sample Strategic Plan

NCELTR's vision: International leadership in English language education

NCELTR's mission: To provide leadership to the English language teaching community and to promote excellence in English language education through innovative and high quality programs, services, products and research

Strategic Directions	Sample Objective	Sample Projects	Performance Indicators	Person(s) Responsible	Due Date
Client focus					
Leadership in English language education	Establish NCELTR as a leading comprehensive IELTS centre	1. Have additional teachers trained as IELTS examiners	12 teachers trained	ELTS Administrator & IEP Director	6 trained 2007 6 trained 2008
		2. Develop evening and weekend IELTS preparation courses			
		3. Develop IELTS online course			
		4. Ensure the financial viability of the new range of IELTS preparation courses	All IELTS preparation courses break even All IELTS preparation courses are profit centres	IEP Director	– end 2008 end 2010
		5. Ensure appropriate staffing levels to support NCELTR's growth as an IELTS teaching and test centre			

6. Explore the feasibility of providing access to IELTS materials for non-Macquarie University students.
7. Explore opportunities to co-publish current and/or new materials with local and international publishers

Organizational capability

Building relationships and partnerships

Business management

Conclusion

Porter has noted that a key role of leaders is strategy, which, he says, includes "defining and communicating the company's unique position, making trade-offs, and forging fit among activities" (1996, p. 77). In this chapter, we have provided a number of tools and theoretical perspectives that will equip leaders to plan strategically. For such a strategic planning process to be successful requires leadership—both soft skills and technical skills. Many of the soft skills of leadership are discussed in other chapters of this book (for example, Chapters 1–7). The chapters on building a communicative toolkit (Chapter 12) and building teams (Chapter 13) are also useful for managing the group session needed in the strategic planning process. If the process we have described is undertaken flexibly, depending on the culture of the organization and its context (see Chapter 1), it "will provide for both the business interests of the organization to be catered for, in parallel to the professional educational values being nurtured—a win/win outcome" (Lewis & Stegemann, 2003, p. 6).

Note

1 Note that TESOL defines vision and mission in reverse.

References

AMES Victoria. (2006). Retrieved February 12, 2007, from http://www.ames. vic.edu.au

Ansoff, H. (1979). *Strategic management*. London: Macmillan.

Bennis, W., & Nanus, B. (1997). *Leaders: The strategies for taking charge* (2nd edn.). New York: HarperBusiness.

Bruce, R. (2000). *Creating your strategic future*. Sydney: HarperCollins.

CATESOL. (1998). *Mission statement*. Retrieved Feburary 12, 2007, from http://www.catesol. org

Cope, R.G. (1989). *High involvement strategic planning*. London: Basil Blackwell.

Covey, S.R. (1990). *Principle-centered leadership*. Provo, UT: IPCL.

Drucker, P. (1993). *Post-capitalist society*. New York: Harper.

Kanter, R.M. (1983). *The change masters: Innovation and entrepreneurship in the American corporation*. New York: Simon and Schuster, Inc.

Kim, W.C., & Mauborgne, R. (2002). Charting your company's future. *Harvard Business Review* (June), 77–83.

Klinghammer, S. (1997). The strategic planner. In M.A. Christison & F.L. Stoller (Eds.), *A handbook for language program administrators*. Burlingame, CA: Alta Book Center Publishers.

Kouzes, J.M., & Posner, B.Z. (1987). *The leadership challenge: How to get extraordinary things done in organizations*. San Francisco: Jossey-Bass.

Lewis, M.J., & Stegemann, L. (2003). The relevance of strategic planning for ESL teaching institutions. *Australian Language Matters, Jan/Feb/Mar*, 5, 6, 8.

Luther, D.B. (1995). Put strategic planning to work. *Leadership*, 73–77.

NCELTR. (2007). Retrieved Feburary 12, 2007, from http://www.nceltr.mq.edu.au

Porter, M.E. (1996). What is strategy? *Harvard Business Review, November–December*, 61–78.

TESOL Inc. (2007). Retrieved February 12, 2007, from http://www.tesol.org

Wiltbank, R., Dew, N., Read, S., & Sarasvathy, S.D. (2006). What to do next? The case for non-predictive strategy. *Strategic Management Journal, 27*, 981–998.

Chapter 10

Ensuring Quality Programs

Colin McNaught

Introduction

In this chapter we look at the notion of quality and how educational organizations define the term, what motivates them to focus on quality standards and how they go about establishing systems to ensure the quality of their teaching programs and other services.

While the quality movement has its origins in the manufacturing industry, there are few educational organizations today that will not have taken some initiatives in an effort to satisfy themselves, or external agencies, of the quality of the programs they offer. Some may have embraced quality assurance in a comprehensive manner and sought external certification through ISO 9001, the international standard for quality management systems. Some may be subject to external accreditation schemes, government-mandated or industry-based, or they may have adopted quality standards associated with membership of a particular industry body. Program providers located within larger institutions, such as universities, may be subject to the quality assurance requirements and processes that apply to those institutions. Others still, notably independent English language schools in non-regulated environments, will have implemented quality assurance processes of their own design, in at least some aspects of their operations, as a means of securing their position in the marketplace.

Sallis (1996) traces the origins of the quality movement from the advent of industrialization when new production methods removed from individual workers the responsibility for the quality of a product and gave rise to the need for a system of inspection known as quality control. In time, quality control and inspection came to be seen as wasteful and expensive processes, and companies sought to replace these methods with methods of quality assurance and quality improvement which build quality into production by returning the responsibility for quality to the workforce.

Sallis goes on to describe the development of interest in quality improvement and quality assurance after the Second World War and the important influence of the ideas of Deming and Juran, particularly in Japan. By the late 1970s as American and other Western manufacturers began to lose markets and market share to Japanese companies and products, they began to take the quality message seriously:

The quest for the answer to Japanese competition was highlighted in one of the most influential of management texts of the 1980's: Peters and Waterman's *In Search of Excellence*, published in 1982. Peters and Waterman analysed the essential features of the 'excellent' company based on the best practice then existing in the USA. Their research showed that those companies which have excellent relationships with their customers are often those which are the most competitive and profitable. Excellence goes hand in hand with simple, but crucial notions, of being "close to the customers" and with an obsession with quality. The excellent organizations have simple and non-bureaucratic structures based on active and enthusiastic teams. These features can be part of any organization whatever its national and cultural origins, but they are ones which many Japanese companies have enthusiastically embraced.

(Sallis, 1996, p. 9)

Quality Assurance in Education

The interest in quality assurance in education is of more recent origin and the motivation somewhat different from that which faced Western manufacturers. While there has been a long tradition within universities of internal program review for faculties and departments (involving both internal and external reviewers) and professional bodies have a role in accrediting professional courses such as law, medicine, and accounting, public interest in the quality assurance processes of universities has really only developed in the past 20 years or so. Pressure upon publicly-funded institutions for greater accountability, reductions in real funding levels, greater competition domestically, involvement in the competitive international education marketplace, changes in academic employment patterns, and developments in information technology have all contributed to a heightened awareness of quality issues within the education sector (Skilbeck & Connell, 2000).

In the field of English language education, there has been considerable growth in the USA, the UK, Australia, and other English-speaking countries in demand from international students enrolling in pathway programs that lead to school, college, or university entry, as well as from those pursuing English language study for personal and professional reasons. The advent of working-holiday agreements, tourism and study packages, home tuition schemes, and school group study tours have added to the diversity of offerings but also brought challenges for governments to ensure that international students and visitors comply with the terms of their visas and receive with reasonable assurance the educational services they purchased. Newly arrived students with limited English skills are not easily able to exercise their consumer rights and demand redress from ineffective or unscrupulous language providers.

There is, in addition, intense competition between language schools, and indeed between countries, for a share of this international market, and professional associations and governments are rightly concerned that national reputations are at stake if students cannot be assured of the quality of programs and services being offered to them.

As a result, external accreditation schemes for English language schools and programs have become increasingly important and prominent. In the UK, the British Council, which has long provided a recognition scheme for language schools, now manages Accreditation UK in partnership with the industry association, English UK. This is a voluntary scheme open to UK-based public and private sector language schools of all persuasions (year-round schools, summer schools, university entry programs, home tuition providers, to name a few) provided they have been in operation for a certain period of time. There are several benefits for schools in being accredited, not least of which are the approval to carry the mark of accreditation on its promotional material and to be included in British Council promotions overseas. In Australia, the National ELT Accreditation Scheme (NEAS), an industry-based body, administers an accreditation scheme that is mandatory for all providers that wish to recruit full-time international students. The situation in the USA is similar in that the professional association, in this case TESOL Inc., has fostered the establishment of an accreditation agency, the Commission on English Language Program Accreditation (CEA) for intensive English programs. As with the UK model, this is a voluntary scheme and institutions and programs must have been operating for at least one year before they can seek accreditation. There is a parallel with the Australian model too in that accreditation enables the program provider to accept international students on a full-time student (F-1) visa.

Other models of external quality assurance operate in countries such as Canada, New Zealand, and Ireland, which also attract international students for English language programs. Our aim here is to explore the options for English language providers which are not subject to (or choose not to participate in) external accreditation schemes and also those that seek a quality standard over and above the external benchmark.

A close examination of the three schemes described above would reveal more similarities than differences in the way that they set out the standards to which language program providers must adhere. Typically these standards address areas such as management and administrative practices, premises and facilities, staffing, curriculum, teaching and learning arrangements, student services, resources, marketing, and recruitment. In many respects these will be expressed as fixed minimum standards (e.g. in relation to size of classrooms or number of students in classes, or qualifications of teaching staff) and in other respects they will be related to the objects and purposes of the organization, or program, (e.g. material resources are aimed at enhancing the achievement of course objectives (NEAS Standards, Section G); admissions policies *are consistent with* program objectives and with the mission of the program or institution (CEA, Student Services Standard 1).

The various requirements for reporting, audit, or inspection that are built into external accreditation models all impose an obligation upon providers to ensure that they continue to meet the accreditation standards, but they vary somewhat in the extent to which they require organizations to improve upon those standards, to strive for higher benchmarks, or to review regularly the manner in which they deliver their services. In other words, external accreditation schemes do not generally require organizations to establish processes for continuous quality improvement in the broad sense. This, then, is the essence of what we mean by quality assurance—all the policies and processes that are directed to ensuring the maintenance and *enhancement* of quality (Lim, 2001).

Task 10.1

Consider your own workplace and those of some competitors with which you are familiar. How do you rate each in terms of the quality of programs or services they provide? On what evidence or assumptions do you base your judgment?

Quality—What is it?

> Quality . . . you know what it is, yet you don't know what it is. But that's self-contradictory. But some things are better than others, that is, they have more quality. But when you try to say what quality is, apart from the things that have it, it all goes poof! There's nothing to talk about. But if you can't say what quality is, how do you know what it is, or how do you know that it even exists? If no one knows what it is, then for all practical purposes, it doesn't exist at all. But for all practical purposes it really does exist. What else are grades based on? Why else would people pay fortunes for some things and throw others in the trash pile? Obviously some things are better than others . . . But what's "betterness"? . . . So round and round you go, spinning mental wheels and nowhere finding anyplace to get traction. What the hell is Quality? What is it?
>
> (Pirsig, 1974, p. 187)

This is not a very encouraging start, but references to Robert Pirsig's ruminations on quality in *Zen and the art of motorcycle maintenance* appear quite often in the literature. To illustrate the difficulty of defining the essence of what quality is itself, Sallis reports on a review he conducted of a range of quality schemes of colleges and local education authorities in the UK in 1991. Some colleges saw quality as a matter of meeting internally set standards, others saw it in terms of the customer. Some viewed it only in terms of the core activities of teaching and learning while others saw it as something which concerns the whole college. Among the definitions offered up, he lists (in Doherty, 1994, p. 232):

- Delighting the customer;
- The elimination of errors and the prevention of waste;
- The complete service provided by the institution and its staff;
- Fitness for purpose;
- Improving the teaching and learning of our students;
- Excellence, customer focus, flexibility, relevance, effectiveness, efficiency, conformance to standards;

- The ability to satisfy the stated or implied needs of our students and their sponsors;
- Conformance to specification;
- Improved client satisfaction;
- Ensuring the accessibility, effectiveness and validity of our programmes.

The variety of responses suggests the question must also be looked at from the perspective of a stakeholder analysis. Whose quality? No doubt different stakeholders will hold different perceptions. While the notion of the primacy of the customer might seem straightforward from a manufacturer's viewpoint, the question is more complex in the context of education. As Hanson notes:

> Identifying the customer in higher education is difficult. Who are the customers? Are they the students, their parents, taxpayers, prospective employers, the public at large? . . . While the immediate customers are students, the real customers comprise two groups with quite similar interests. One is employers who want to draw on the knowledge and skills of new college graduates after their entry into the labour market. The other is the community of taxpayers who want to be assured that the subsidies provided to college students were well spent. These customers want to see evidence that graduating economics majors acquire a substantive knowledge of economics, are proficient in using that knowledge, and display the attributes of educated people through their contributions to their organisations, communities and to society.
>
> (Doherty, 1994, p. 154)

The example here deals with publicly funded higher education. But an exercise in stakeholder analysis for a language education program could yield quite different results, depending on the source of funding for the program, the location of the program, the institutional setting, and the educational or other goals of the students themselves and their families.

Another dimension to be considered, which some teachers will be familiar with, is the sense that students are not necessarily in the best position to judge the quality of programs they undertake. As Parsons puts it, "Professional and specialist training may mean that the customer is not the overriding judge of what constitutes quality" (1994, p. 8). He proposes three dimensions of quality for education services:

1   *Client quality*: what customers (pupils and parents) and clients (employers, community) want from the service.
2   *Professional quality*: whether the service meets needs as defined by professional providers and whether it correctly carries out techniques and procedures which are believed to be necessary to meet client needs.
3   *Management quality*: the most efficient and productive use of resources within limits and directives set by higher authorities.

We see this tension between the notion of professional quality and client quality some-times in schools where the management places great store on the results of student evaluations—perhaps offering bonus payments or renewed contracts based upon the results of student satisfaction surveys—while the teachers perceive the surveys as little more than a popularity poll.

The consensus in the literature is, however, that for all practical purposes, quality can only be defined in relation to the articulated values and purposes and the desired processes and outcomes of a particular program or service, that is to say "fitness for purpose" (Boyle & Bowden, 1997). In other words, if the education provided fulfils its purpose, whatever that may be, then it is said to be one of quality, provided that it accords with publicly accepted standards of accountability and integrity. This is the definition most widely accepted by government and higher education institutions where quality assurance schemes have been established and perhaps the one approach—an instrumental approach—which allows quality assurance programs to become operational (Lim, 2001).

Task 10.2

Who are the stakeholders in your place of work? Would they hold different views or expectations of the programs or services offered? Can you identify, for each individual or stakeholder group, what their perceptions of quality would be?

Approaches to Quality Assurance

We have looked briefly at the role played by accreditation schemes in the field of English language education and seen that while they provide a level of quality assurance that customers may take comfort in, they generally aim to ensure that institutions comply with a certain minimum standard rather than place an obligation upon those institutions to strive for continuous quality improvement.

This is in contrast with the approaches taken in the accreditation and monitoring of higher education institutions. The Australian Universities Quality Agency, for instance, administers a regular cycle of audits of Australian higher education institutions. The audits do not, however, seek to confirm compliance with some external standard. Rather, they focus on verifying that the institution has established standards of per-formance for itself and that it has appropriate and effective processes in place for monitoring whether it meets those standards, and for taking action when it does not.

Where English language programs are situated within larger higher education institutions, it is likely that the quality assurance processes of those larger institutions will have an impact on the language centers or programs as well.

On the other hand, university-based English language providers generally operate on a commercial basis, very much like their colleagues in the private sector. They do not receive public funding (unless perhaps in relation to specific programs for domestic non-

English-speaking students) and they compete in the highly competitive international marketplace with the private sector colleges. Even if they are externally accredited (and the schemes described above do cater for both public sector and private sector institutions) the question arises—what can a single organization do to distinguish itself in the marketplace from others—to stand apart from, or indeed above, the ranks of all those that are similarly accredited? One option is to strive to position oneself at the top of the market in terms of quality.

Doherty, in a wide-ranging review of quality assurance practices in the UK, suggested three main options for educational organizations that wish to adopt a comprehensive internal system of quality assurance: BS 5750 Quality Systems, Total Quality Management (TQM), or a system of the college's own devising (1994, p. 12).

BS 5750 (ISO 9001)

The first of these, BS 5750, is the British Standard for quality systems, developed in the 1980s. This has now been integrated with similar international standards under the banner of the International Standards Organisation (ISO) into ISO 9000, the name given to a family of standards which relate to Quality Management and which address topics including the vocabulary of quality management, guidelines for performance improvement, measurement of management systems, quality documentation, and statistical techniques. The most recent version of the Standard for Quality Management Systems is designated ISO 9001:2000.

While the previous 1994 Standards heavily emphasized process documentation, and did not appear to lend themselves so readily to educational contexts, the central focus of the 2000 Standard is on achieving customer satisfaction and continuous quality improvement. The organization defines the level of quality (service quality in respect of education) which will satisfy its customers' needs—explicit or implicit—and then establishes a system which will demonstrate how it will deliver and document its delivery of the product or service. In other words, the Standard is about the management of a quality system which will deliver the institution's own specified quality standards which are sufficient to meet the needs of its customers (Doherty, 1994, p. 14).

The key features of the Standard are grouped into five major categories, viz:

1   *Quality management system.* The structure and documentation requirements of a system to manage all the processes that contribute to the delivery of a service or product.
2   *Management responsibility.* The role that senior management should play in leading the development of the quality management system, ensuring customer focus, establishing quality policies and objectives, communicating the quality message throughout the organization and reviewing the system at regular intervals.
3   *Resource management.* The need to provide resources to implement and maintain the quality management system and enhance customer satisfaction, including training

and skill development of staff, provision of equipment and facilities, and an appropriate work environment to achieve conformity to product requirements.

4 *Product realization.* The processes involved in planning for new products or services, ensuring conformance to customer needs and expectations, designing and developing, and ultimately delivering those products and services.

5 *Measurement, analysis and improvement.* The mechanisms to be used in monitoring and measuring the effectiveness of processes, analysing data, and taking corrective action where necessary to achieve the goal of continual improvement (Standards Australia, 2001).

The approach described is a self-regulatory, self-improving one and ISO 9001 offers organizations the opportunity to have their quality assurance system approved by an internationally recognized certifying authority. This is done through application to the national body responsible for administering the ISO Standard and will involve having the system assessed by an approved assessor. If the outcome is successful, the organization can use the approved ISO logo for marketing and publicity purposes. This is known as a third-party certification scheme.

For those organizations that achieve ISO certification and, as Doherty shows, examples can be found in every sector of education, the benefits of certification include:

• The creation of documentation that informs staff about the organization, its processes, and mechanisms for checking and maintaining quality. This can be very useful for inducting new members of staff.
• It highlights areas where there are gaps or shortcomings in the system and drives continuous improvement in organizational efficiency and effectiveness.
• It provides a sense of control and focus, a sense that the organization is operating according to plan.
• It can offer a distinct marketing edge over competitors.
• It is well regarded by government and public funding agencies and may influence their purchasing decisions.
• It will lead to increased customer satisfaction.
• Recognition as a quality endorsed organization may attract new business opportunities.

On the other hand, there are drawbacks—in the eyes of some at least—in the time and expense that can be involved in setting up and maintaining the system and in the fact that the language of ISO 9001 does not apply all that easily to education. As we noted above, as well, achieving ISO 9001 does not of itself guarantee excellence, but it confirms that the organization meets the quality standards it has set for itself.

Total Quality Management

Total Quality Management (TQM) is an approach to quality assurance, also originally developed for corporations and the manufacturing sector, built upon the work of W. Edwards Deming (Bogue, 1998; Sallis, 1996). TQM focuses on the ideal of continuous improvement and on customer satisfaction, but is much more people-oriented than the process-oriented approach of the ISO Standard. Doherty presents a comprehensive overview of the origins of TQM, the "missionary zeal" with which it is promoted in some quarters, and the experience of a range of educational organizations which have applied the methodology. While not all are positive, he concludes that "TQM, despite its pluralistic, customer-driven definition of quality, is generally recognised as having much to offer educational organisations committed to developing some form of quality improvement" (1994, p. 21).

In discussing its application to educational organizations, Taylor and Hill give a very strong sense of the employee-oriented flavour of TQM:

> Essentially, it is concerned with customer-focused organisational improvement, achieved through the activities of groupings of employees at various levels in the structure. The employees identify problems and opportunities for improvement and engage in endeavours which determine root causes of these problems, generate and choose solutions and implement improvements. These activities are usually supported by the development of teams and a focus on corporate goals. The teams primarily identify with matters of specific relevance to their own functions in order to engender a sense of involvement in organisational affairs. TQM proposes that all employees can make an impact on the quality of goods and services provided, thus the organisation's systems and processes are regarded as highly as its products and outputs.
>
> (1997, p. 162)

They describe the essential elements of TQM as follows:

- Quality is conceptualized as customers' perceptions.
- A customer is defined as anyone who receives a product or service, whether inside or outside the organization.
- The aim is to identify and meet the customer requirement through the design, development, and management of processes that are error-free, that is, by concentrating on prevention to eliminate waste and reduce costs.
- By utilizing the internal customer concept, the result of each process is viewed as a product; consequently evaluation takes place immediately, possibly by the immediate customer but preferably by the processor.
- Central to TQM theory is the idea of continuous self-improvement, therefore TQM systems are essentially learning systems.
- TQM requires the involvement and commitment of all organizational members in quality matters and continuous improvement.

• TQM requires superior quality information systems to provide timely measures of and feedback on performance (Taylor & Hill, 1997, p. 164).

This does appear to be in sharp contrast to ISO 9001 with its focus on systems, processes, and documentation. Yet Doherty, citing his own institution, the University of Wolverhampton, as an example, regards gaining the Standard as a basis from which to achieve a TQM culture (Storey, 1994). Taylor and Hill argue it is not so much about which approach is better, but which approach is most suited to the organizational environment (1997, p. 168). They do see some potential problems with TQM in education (higher education in particular) arising, for example, from the natural tendency among academics towards individualism and the pursuit of individual knowledge as a key to personal recognition and advancement within the system. This might appear to run counter to the team ethos promoted by TQM, however, there is also, in higher education, a long tradition of committee-based consensus and collegiality. There is also the need to acknowledge the interests and expectations of external customers beyond the student—government, research councils, accreditation bodies, academic peers, employers, and society at large. Bogue adds a note of caution on the concept of student as customer as well, commenting on the tension between caring for students and caring for standards: "It is not an exaggeration to say that it is possible for some students to be highly satisfied yet remain relatively uneducated" (in Gaither, 1998, p. 12).

Nonetheless, the potential benefits, according to Taylor and Hill, of TQM in education are significant:

• Continuous and sustained organizational improvement;
• Increased levels of external customer satisfaction;
• Tangible and significant cost savings of the order of 5–10 per cent of operating costs;
• A focus on the importance of interdisciplinary teams with combinations of academic and administrative staff;
• Improvements in employee morale commitment and motivation;
• A new way of managing the organization which promotes company-wide goal congruence, accountability and involvement. (1997, p. 168)

It is apparent that Doherty's rather simplified proposition that organizations need to choose between the BS5750 (now ISO 9001) Standard, or Total Quality Management, or a system of their own design is misleading. Rather it seems that all roads, faithfully followed, will lead to Rome. As Taylor and Hill put it: "TQM should not be contemplated until an organization has basic management systems and procedures in place" (1997, p. 168).

In exploring the links between ISO 9000 and TQM, Sallis (1996) suggests there are four potential models that might be adopted. Three of these position ISO 9000 as the source of procedural infrastructure and operational consistency within a larger organization-wide total quality framework. The difference between each of these is a matter of degree—the extent to which the Standard underpins the TQM framework. His fourth model, however, takes a different view, regarding ISO 9000 as

a bureaucratic intrusion into the world of education . . . a costly distraction . . .
and counterproductive in occupations with professional and well-educated
workforces, like teaching. The concern is whether the extra workload and the need
to work strictly to systems and procedures, albeit internally generated, could
damage staff morale and creativity.

(1996, p. 58)

The reality is that each organization needs to consider the options carefully and clarify
for itself why it wants to pursue quality, whether it wishes to establish a formal system
and seek external certification, or whether it wishes to focus more on cultural change
and constant, even if incremental, improvement. Certainly, for smaller organizations,
the costs of ISO 9000 may be prohibitive and the benefits long-term.

In the next section, as we look at some practical guidance on the implementation
of quality assurance systems, equally applicable to large and small language colleges,
we will see the similarities are many, even if the primary orientation of the approach
differs.

Task 10.3

From what you have read of the ISO and TQM approaches to quality systems, which
could be applied more readily in your working or teaching context? Would the
existing educational culture of the organization affect your choice? Do you think the
kind of cultural change proposed by a total quality approach is an achievable goal?
What are your reasons?

Implementing Quality Assurance

We have now looked at how the notion of quality assurance applies to education, the
role of external accreditation schemes, alternative approaches to implementing internal
quality assurance systems, the benefits that accrue from implementing them, and the
problems that might be encountered in the implementation.

Organizations which set out to meet the external certification standard of ISO 9001
will find a wealth of material to guide them through the process—the structures to put
in place, the processes to develop, the documents to produce, etc.—but they still need
to work out how to establish a quality culture that will, ideally, pervade the workplace.
Those that follow a TQM philosophy will need to devise effective systems for recording
and documenting their organizational performance and activities to underpin the work
of quality teams.

In Preedy et al. (1997), the Further Education (FE) Unit of the UK Department of
Education presents a practical guide to a methodology for establishing continuous
quality improvement within an educational organization. The principal requirements

focus on means of organizing people—staff and faculty—and engaging them with the quality agenda:

- Establish continuous quality improvement within the mission statement and strategic and operational plans of the organization.
- Establish a shared culture of improvement across the organization. Cultural change of this nature is easier said than done. It is a long-term goal, but can be accomplished through:

  - A change in attitude and behavior from the very top of the organization;
  - Senior managers leading by example and being seen to be genuine in their endeavor to improve quality;
  - Communicating and listening with respect to others' views—whoever they are;
  - Being open to praise and criticism;
  - Encouraging people to identify difficulties/barriers and suggest solutions.

- Train senior managers in the principles and practice of managing for quality, and, later, cascade the training to other members of staff.
- Create a quality infrastructure—a body or bodies responsible for promoting quality throughout the college.

On this last point, the FE Unit suggests two levels of infrastructure—a quality council or board, and a number of quality improvement groups. The role of the quality council is to support the college mission by establishing a quality policy and developing implementation strategies to ensure the policy is translated into practice. Among other things, this means keeping the quality agenda running separate from, but alongside, normal business operations. One of the most important functions of the quality council will be to organize and set up quality improvement groups (QIGs) and ensure they are adequately resourced. QIGs are short-term activity groups set up to improve a particular service. Broadly speaking, their job is to follow a structured process to review current practice, set standards, analyse difficulties in reaching the required standards, suggest improvements, trial and implement improvements, and report back to the Quality Council upon completion (adapted from Preedy et al., 1997, pp. 38–44).

The real appeal of the methodology suggested above is that the work can be staged and undertaken in manageable chunks. QIGs, for instance, might be set up initially to focus on the most obvious areas in need of improvement, and when they have been addressed, other less pressing areas may be tackled. What is critical is that there is continuity of purpose through the active involvement of the quality council or the designated body overseeing the process.

Sallis' *Total Quality Management in Education* (1996) sets out a framework for educational quality management, drawing on the principles of TQM. The term "framework" is used intentionally, rather than "model" or "system" because what is discussed here is a guide and not a prescription. The starting premise has always been that each and every institution has to find its own route to quality, and that externally prescribed approaches are usually the least effective.

(ibid., p. 122)

The components of his framework are:

- *Developing leadership and strategy*: a commitment from senior management for quality initiatives to succeed and clear strategic direction for the organization.
- *Delighting the customers*: this is the purpose of TQM and so there must be effective methods for establishing, and reviewing periodically, both internal and external customers' needs.
- *Designating quality champions*: the person who will lead the quality steering group and publicize the quality program internally.
- *Ensuring that the senior management team monitor progress*: through training in the philosophy and methods of quality management itself and in the appropriate evaluation strategies. The commitment of senior managers to the process is essential.
- *Initiate staff quality for training*: staff development is an essential tool for building the awareness and knowledge of quality, and it can be a key agent for developing cultural change.
- *Monitoring the delivery of the curriculum*: putting in place methods for collecting information about each program delivered: the level of student demand, documented aims and objectives, level of resourcing, syllabuses, assessment methods, etc.
- *Verifying the assessment of student performance*: the results of student assessments, systems for verifying grades and the award of qualifications all should be documented as evidence of the quality of the management of learning.
- *Communicating the quality message*: putting in place a clear and positive communications strategy for the whole organization alongside the staff development arrangements, keeping people informed and celebrating achievements.
- *Measuring the costs of quality*: devise methods for measuring the costs of implementing the quality program, and the costs of not undertaking it—an important means of highlighting the reasons for staying with the program.
- *Supporting teams*: perhaps the most important element of all, as teams are the engine of quality improvement and of innovation. Recognition of the internal customer chain is also important—the mutual recognition of other people's roles in the organization and the need to deliver services internally to agreed standards.
- *Applying quality tools and techniques*: focus on getting things done and achieving initial successes, identifying areas that need to be improved, and selecting the right teams and tools to tackle them.
- *Developing a self-assessment culture*: the organization needs to establish means of evaluating its overall performance, whether through a system of internal audit, where, for example, staff assess areas other than their own, or by drawing upon

external auditors. The results of these processes need to feed back into strategic planning, as should the monitoring and review activities of the quality steering group and senior management.

(Adapted from Sallis, 1996, pp. 126–130)

There are evident parallels between Sallis' framework, the guiding principles outlined by the FE Unit, and the key features of the ISO 9001 Standard presented earlier, even though the fundamental orientation of approaches might differ. Perhaps we should view these as part of a continuum rather than opposites, with each organization free to choose an approach to quality assurance that aligns with the educational culture of the organization itself and its surrounding environment.

It should also be clear that we are not talking about approaches that only apply to the teaching and learning process. There are arguments for a staged introduction of the quality assurance system, focusing on certain areas of activity first and then moving on to others, but the goal should be to embrace every aspect of the organization's activity that affects the customer experience—and since we define customers as internal as well as external, that means everything the organization does that goes towards the achievement of mission and objectives. In the context of English language organizations, the following list, by no means exhaustive, identifies other functions or services that should be subject to evaluation for quality:

*   Procedures for managing enquiries and enrolments;
*   Induction arrangements—both for students and for new staff;
*   Guidance and counselling services;
*   The management of staff performance;
*   Extra-curricular and activity programs;
*   Administrative arrangements for record keeping and document control;
*   Marketing and publicity materials;
*   Financial management and reporting systems;
*   Equal opportunity and other institutional policies—how these are implemented and their aims achieved.

Task 10.4

Think about your working/teaching context, or one that is familiar to you.

*   Does the organization have a policy on quality and practices that aim to maintain or improve the quality of its programs or services?
*   Is there room for improvement? In what areas?
*   If you were asked to take on the role of "quality champion," what would be your first steps?

Conclusion

In concluding this chapter, it is perhaps worthwhile to reiterate the importance of keeping focus and perspective in planning for, and implementing, quality assurance. It is not hard to see how easily an institution might find itself entrapped in a paper bureaucracy or bound up in procedures whose purpose and relevance have long been lost or forgotten. The importance of planning and putting *workable* structures in place, and of maintaining the commitment and momentum, cannot be overstated. As Sallis concludes:

> Quality already exists in educational institutions. What TQM does is to build on to existing quality and develop it into continuous quality improvement. Industrial models can be drawn upon to provide useful pointers and examples. However, it is important to ensure that any approach used is realistic, workable and affordable. TQM is not something that can be introduced overnight. Nor is it a miracle cure. It will throw up new difficulties and challenges. It's a slow process and the benefits are long-term.
>
> (1996, p. 132)

References

Anderson, D., Johnson, R., & Milligan, B. (2000). *Quality assurance and accreditation in Australian higher education: An assessment of Australian and international practice.* Canberra: Department of Education, Training and Youth Affairs.

Bogue, E.G. (1998). Quality assurance in higher education: The evolution of systems and design ideals. *New Directions for Institutional Research*, (99), 7.

Boyle, P., & Bowden, J.A. (1997). Educational quality assurance in universities: An enhanced model. *Assessment & Evaluation in Higher Education*, (111–121), *22*, 2.

Brown, R. (2004). *Quality assurance in higher education: The UK experience since 1992.* Abingdon: RoutledgeFalmer.

Brown, S., Race, P., & Smith, B. 1997. *500 tips for quality enhancement in universities and colleges.* London: Kogan Page.

Doherty, G.D. (Ed.) (1994). *Developing quality systems in education.* London: Routledge.

Freeman, R. (1993). *Quality assurance in training and education: How to apply BS5750 (ISO9000) Standards.* London: Kogan Page.

Further Education Unit (1997). Continuous improvement and quality standards. In M. Preedy, R. Glatter & R. Levacic (Eds.), *Educational management: Strategy, quality and resources.* Buckingham: Open University Press.

Gaither, G.H. (Ed.) (1998). *Quality assurance in higher education: An international perspective.* New Directions for Institutional Research, Number 99. San Francisco: Jossey-Bass Publishers.

Lim, D. (2001). *Quality assurance in higher education: A study of developing countries.* Aldershot: Ashgate.

Mackay, R., Wellesley, S., Tasman, S., & Bazergan, E. (1998). Using institutional self-evaluation to promote the quality of language and communication training programmes. In P. Rea-Dickens, & K. Germaine (Eds.), *Managing evaluation and innovation in language teaching.* Harlow: Addison-Wesley, Longman.

Parsons, C. (1994). The politics and practice of quality. In *Quality improvement in education: Case studies in schools, colleges and universities*. London: David Fulton Publishers.

Pickering, G. (1999). Roads to quality street: Perspectives on quality. *ELT Management*, 28, December.

Pirsig, R. (1974). *Zen and the art of motorcycle maintenance: An enquiry into values*. New York: Morrow.

Preedy, M., Glatter, R. & Levacic, R. (1997). *Educational Management, Strategy, Quality and Resources*. Buckingham: Open University Press.

Sallis, E. (1994). From systems to leadership: the development of the quality movement in further education. In Doherty, G.D. (Ed.), *Developing quality systems in education*. London: Routledge.

Sallis, E. (1996). *Total quality management in education*. 2nd edn. London: Kogan Page.

Skilbeck, M., & Connell, H. (2000). *Quality assurance and accreditation in Australian higher education: A national seminar on future arrangements*. Canberra: Department of Education, Training and Youth Affairs.

Standards Australia International (2001). *Education and training guide to ISO 9001:2000*. Sydney: Standards Australia International.

Storey, S. (1994). Doing total quality management the hard way: Installing BS5750/ ISO9000 at the University of Wolverhampton. In G.D. Doherty (Ed.), *Developing quality systems in education*. London: Routledge.

Taylor, A., & Hill, F. (1997). Quality management in education. In A. Harris, N. Bennett, & M. Preedy (Eds.), *Organizational effectiveness and improvement in education*. Buckingham: Open University Press.

Chapter 11

Managing Performance

Colin McNaught

Introduction

One of the most important dimensions of leadership is, of course, the leadership of people. Great leaders inspire loyalty, commitment and enthusiasm from their staff while poor or ineffective leaders run the risk of presiding over organizational decline, a dispirited workforce and fragmentation of purpose. We saw in Chapter 1 in Covey's depiction of the attributes of transformational leaders, some examples of leadership behavior that seek to draw out the best from individual staff and teams. The transformational leader "makes full use of human resources; recognises and rewards significant contributions; designs and redesigns jobs to make them meaningful and challenging; releases human potential." (Covey, 1990, p. 254).

It is clear as well, from the discussion in Chapter 10, that communication and staff motivation are key requirements for the successful implementation of quality assurance systems. Leaders need to be able to convey the quality message effectively to staff at all levels and engage them in the processes of continuous quality improvement. This applies just as much to those processes that deal with the performance of staff as it does to processes for curriculum review or assessment and grading or student counselling. In small organizations, the management of performance often happens informally because of the frequent and close contact between managers and their staff, but as organizations grow it becomes increasingly important, in the interests of fairness, objectivity, and efficiency, to introduce systematic practices for managing staff performance.

Perhaps the most common practice found in English language organizations where there is continuity of employment is the annual interview, often linked to a pay increment that has become due. At their worst, such interviews are poorly directed, perfunctory, and superficial in character and somewhat uncomfortable for both interviewer and interviewee. At their best they can be a productive and motivating opportunity for a manager and a staff member to reflect on the work that has been done in the preceding period, the goals and directions of the organization, how those goals bear upon the local work unit, and what this means for the future, in terms of the staff member's performance objectives and personal or professional development needs.

Even so, it is doubtful that an interview that takes place just once a year can contribute very much to the organizational goal of *continuous* quality improvement. There is a great deal more to human resource management than the annual review, and language teaching organizations, being highly labour-intensive, need to have a very clear understanding of this.

In this chapter we start by looking at the many sub-processes that are part of human resource management in a typical language teaching context. We will attempt to situate these within a broad framework of performance management and identify the processes required to establish an effective framework for performance management. We will then relate theory back to practice by focusing on one key part of the cycle—the performance review—and how this can be most effectively structured and carried out. Finally, we will look at a case study where staff and management worked closely together to design and implement a new approach to performance management.

Personnel Matters

Geddes and Marks (1997) provide a very thorough account of key human resource issues for language program managers and administrators, and they include recommended procedures for dealing with the processes of establishing positions, recruiting and screening applicants, interviewing and making appointments, inducting and supervising staff, and providing for professional enrichment. They note that, while work styles, personalities and commitment to the program will differ dramatically among faculty, "it is the administrator's responsibility to oversee and assess objectively the job performance of each employee in a manner that will promote personal and program growth" (ibid.: p. 206).

They draw upon literature from the field of clinical supervision to outline different approaches to supervision that might be taken in the language teaching context and they discuss the importance of formative and summative evaluations. There is a range of measures and sources of information for this purpose: "supervisor and peer classroom observations, structured observations by trained observers, student evaluations, self-assessment reports, student achievement results, and documentation of scholarship and program contributions" (ibid., p. 210). As to the conduct of an evaluation session itself, however, their advice is limited. While they place great importance on the need for "proper documentation and meaningful feedback during all stages of the process" (ibid., p. 210) and allowing employees the opportunity for response, there remains a strong sense that this is a carefully controlled, rather "top-down" approach to personnel management, more directive than nurturing.

White et al. (1991), in contrast, devote a chapter to many of the same personnel processes—training, induction, performance reviews, observation, and career counselling—under the heading of "Staff Development," an indication of a rather different, more forward-looking, orientation to the complex matter of managing staff, especially teaching staff, in English language schools:

> Successful organisations are learning organisations, and the potential to learn is present in all who work therein. Staff development is a way of ensuring that people learn and develop and that the organisation can grow and respond to a changing environment.
>
> (1991, p. 61)

Performance review, seen from this perspective, is an opportunity for managers to encourage staff and give feedback on the work undertaken and, with sensitive handling, deal with poor performance and look at avenues for repair—whether through change of behavior, training, or reorganization of tasks in the job. What is most important, argue White et al., is that, regardless of the size of the organization, some formal and regular processes are put in place, with clear objectives established and records maintained for future reference (ibid., p. 68).

The reality in many English language centres, it has to be said, is far from this. English language teachers work in such a variety of contexts all around the world, they are witness to widely varying approaches to the management and reward of staff. The extent of variation reflects, among other things, the different educational cultures within which they work, the sources and amount of funds available for the teaching program, the competitive climate and the degree of involvement of host organizations (such as universities) or government in regulating their activities. In one place it will seem that staffing decisions and contract renewals are guided very much by the latest set of student satisfaction statistics while in another there might be a rigorous process of recruitment and selection of teachers but little evidence of performance review on an ongoing basis. In other, less privileged, circumstances, the difficulty of recruiting appropriately qualified staff leads program managers to control and direct staff performance very closely, while in an opposite context, a large public institution, the teachers observe a comprehensive framework of planning, reporting and inspection that seems to provide little individual help or feedback at all.

One thing comes through, however, quite clearly from the reports of teachers who have made it their profession—that teachers want feedback on their performance, they want to know how they are doing, and they are keen to learn and develop their skills. As one insightful student put it, "Excellence is possible without feedback. Sustained excellence isn't." What concerns them, however, is just how that feedback is presented, on what evidence or information it is based and to what purpose will it be put. This is where it becomes helpful to regard performance review, as White et al. suggest, not as an element in a linear sequence of human resources activities, but as an integral part of a self-renewing performance management framework.

Defining Performance Management

In its most general sense, performance management can be regarded as "the arrangements organisations use to get the right things done successfully" or "the organisation of work to achieve optimum results" (Lawson, 1995, p. 2). However, to understand how this translates meaningfully to management practice, we should go back a few steps and review the background to what has become the management discipline of Performance Management.

In his overview to *The performance management handbook*, Lawson discerns two approaches to management thinking that have developed, more or less in parallel, over the last few decades—a scientific school of thought and a humanistic school of thought.

The scientific approach focused on work processes and was based on the notion that improved performance could be achieved by analysing work processes closely and designing the most effective sequences of activities for the workforce to follow. This line of thinking gave rise to management techniques such as critical path analysis, operational research, cost–benefit analysis, job evaluation, and management by objectives.

The humanistic approach was more interested in people-focused techniques of management and was based on the notion that if you have the right people in the right jobs and the right environment, people will work out the best ways to approach the work that has to be done. This gave rise to such approaches as training needs analysis, merit rating, quality circles, and performance-related pay (Lawson, 1995, p. 4).

There are, of course, elements of truth in both approaches, but none of the many management tools and techniques based on one or other of these approaches has had a lasting impact on management practice. As Lawson notes: "people-based approaches to performance management must be underpinned by some supporting process" (ibid., p. 6). Equally, "process-based approaches must take into account the changes in attitude and skill required to make them operate effectively, and the issue of ownership". He notes, too, that neither approach will succeed if it is incompatible with the organization's culture and way of doing things:

> Informal and flexible organisations reject highly structured approaches just as surely as command and control organisations reject collaborative or team-based approaches. The cultural implications of any approach must be taken into account as part of the implementation process of any initiative.

Lawson's analysis of past trends leads him to conclude that "each function, department or work centre must understand, manage and improve those aspects of its performance that best enable the company or organisation to achieve its aims, goals and objectives"(ibid., p. 8). He sees performance management addressing "not only the internally focused financial and productivity performance, but also externally focused performance in such areas as market share, customer satisfaction, flexibility, quality and the delivery of products and services".

Armstrong characterizes performance management as "a shared process between managers and the individuals and teams they manage . . . based on the principle of management by contract rather than command" (2000, p. 4). He rejects the notion that only managers are accountable for the performance of their teams, arguing instead that "responsibility is shared between managers and team members". Armstrong offers this definition: "Performance Management is a strategic and integrated process that delivers sustained success to organisations by improving the performance of the people who work in them and by developing the capabilities of individual contributors and teams" (ibid., p. 1).

If we unpack the key words, we get a more complete sense of Armstrong's view. Performance Management is a *strategic* process because it is focused on the organization's direction and long-term goals. It is *integrated* in two senses, vertically in that it links the objectives of the organization with those of individuals and teams, and horizontally in that it links the different aspects of human resource management, such as pay policies, appraisal systems, and planning for professional development. The goal is to deliver *sustained success*, that is, an orientation towards continuous improvement, by improving *individual performance*—not only the outcomes or the results achieved, but also the behavior or the way the work is done—and developing *individual capabilities*, the skills and competencies that people apply to their work.

A similar definition, less formally expressed, is offered by Jones (1999, p. 3):

> Performance management is about getting results. It is concerned with getting the best from people and helping them to achieve their potential. It is an approach to achieving a shared vision of the purpose and aims of the organisation. It is concerned with helping individuals and teams achieve their potential and recognise their role in contributing to the goals of the organisation.

It is not so difficult to see how these principles can be applied to the types of jobs where outcomes are measured readily and objectively, for instance, in terms of sales targets, billable hours or client enquiries processed, but the measurement of performance in educational contexts is a much more complex issue. Reeves et al. describe it in terms of "the contrast between treating teachers as technicians, whose role is to carry out prescribed tasks, or as professionals, who are trusted to develop practice appropriate to the learners in their care" (2002, p. 3). They characterize the debate as one between a "managerial approach" which draws upon the work of Armstrong and others, and a "professional approach" which sees the management of performance as the responsibility of the individual professional.

The characteristics of an organization which adopts the former approach is that it:

- Communicates a vision of its objectives to all its employees;
- Sets departmental and individual performance targets that are related to wider objectives;
- Conducts a formal review process to identify training, development and reward outcomes;
- Evaluates the whole process in order to improve effectiveness (ibid., p. 5).

In contrast, Reeves et al., whose focus is specifically on the teaching profession, see the professional approach being grounded in the notion of professionalism, "the sense of duty to perform to a level necessary to ensure the well-being of the client" (ibid., p. 5). This notion includes, as well as the sense of moral obligation to the client, a commitment to professional development, "a self-directed commitment to review the effectiveness of one's practice, expand one's repertoire and develop one's expertise" (ibid., p. 6 quoting Eraut, 1994). This is, in effect, an argument for the teacher as reflective practitioner, recognizing that teacher learning and performance improvement are far more the result of teachers reflecting upon and responding to the changes in their teaching environment, and testing their beliefs and assumptions than they are a simple process of filling in gaps in skills or knowledge.

While they initially suggest that the managerialist and professional approaches might be seen as two ends of a spectrum, Reeves et al. acknowledge there is perhaps a growing congruence between the two, "with an emphasis on self-evaluation, growth and par- ticipation, 'democratic' decision making and shared values" (ibid., p. 6), a position which brings together the notion of professional responsibility on the part of individual teachers with the requirement of accountability —to students, employer organizations, and the community.

Task 11.1

Think about your place of work. What are the processes for managing staff performance? How would you characterize them?

- systematic or ad hoc?
- formal or informal?
- top-down or bottom-up?
- subjective or objective?
- forward-looking or backward-looking?

If you work in an educational environment, do the processes for faculty or teaching staff differ from those in administrative roles?

The Performance Management Process

In the typical English language program, if there is not congruence, there is almost surely a degree of tension between the individual teacher's sense of professionalism and the program manager's need to be accountable to stakeholders—owners, directors, faculty heads, accreditation bodies—for the performance of the program and the efficient management of the resources at his or her disposal. The approach taken to management of both program and staff performance will undoubtedly have a profound impact upon the attitudes, motivation, and commitment of the staff themselves.

While Armstrong's approach may be characterized as managerial by some, he goes to some lengths to reject "imposed, top-down and rigid systems" of performance management in favor of an approach where "performance management is a flexible and evolutionary process applied by managers working with their staff in accordance with the circumstances in which they are working" (2000, p. 16). He suggests the conceptual framework of a continuous self-renewing cycle within which the appropriate processes can be developed to assist both managers and individual staff to play an appropriate part (Figure 11.1).

The starting point is *role definition* where the duties, required capabilities and key result areas associated with each position are clearly stated. This then enables the negotiation of the *performance agreement (or contract)* that defines expectations: what each individual has to achieve and how their performance will be measured. Linked to this is the negotiation of a *personal development plan* in which the individuals set out the actions they intend to take to extend their knowledge or skills or improve their performance in specified areas. The next stage in the cycle, *managing performance*, is an ongoing process in which the individual implements their side of the performance agreement and the manager provides support and guidance where necessary, perhaps updating objectives along the way, conducting a progress review or offering informal feedback, and dealing with any performance problems. Finally, the *performance review* is the formal evaluation stage, when a review of performance takes place, covering achievements, progress, and problems. This forms the basis of a revised performance agreement and personal development plan and a further iteration of the cycle.

The importance of personal and professional development planning is clear in this framework, an opportunity for manager and staff member collaboratively to map out

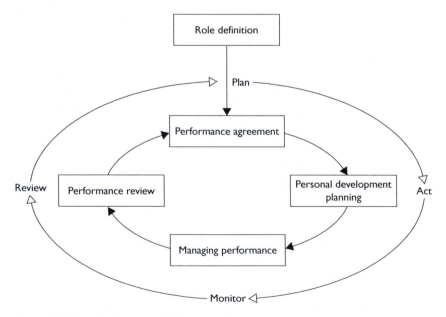

Figure 11.1 The Performance Management Cycle
Source: Armstrong (2000, p. 17).

the actions that the staff member will take to develop themselves, extend their knowledge and skills, and, possibly, improve performance in specified areas.

The skills the manager needs to bring to bear to foster confidence and faith in the performance management process are well articulated by Jones (1999, p. 24), who notes the importance of leadership skills and being able to develop a "sunny" work climate in which:

- People are allowed to take initiative.
- Team work flourishes.
- People understand their contribution.
- There is a clear direction and good communication.
- Workload is distributed evenly, taking account of individuals' skills and abilities.
- Skills, abilities, and motivation of team members are recognised.
- The physical work environment is conducive to good performance.

Armstrong emphasizes the forward-looking and continuous nature of the process and the flexibility that his framework offers managers, individuals, and teams to work together in ways that best suit them. The performance review is, admittedly, a more formal stage in the cycle, yet he is keen to play down the formality and encourage "free-flowing, open meetings where views are exchanged so that agreed conclusions can be reached . . . a conversation with a purpose" (ibid., p. 20).

This is perhaps, as was noted at the beginning of this chapter, in somewhat stark contrast to the manner in which periodic reviews or appraisals are conducted in many language programs across the world. For this reason, and because such reviews are very often linked to classroom observation of teacher performance, it is worth us taking some time to focus on this particular aspect of the performance management cycle.

Conducting the Performance Review

We have seen above that the process of performance management entails far more than the conduct of an annual appraisal meeting. Armstrong sees the annual meeting—he uses the term "performance review"—as part of a continuous self-renewing cycle that involves managers working with their staff. Lawson views performance management as a wider process by which an organization monitors and reviews its overall performance, with the appraisal scheme being that part which focuses on the performance of individuals. Reeves et al. note (2002, p. 49) that the term "appraisal" is less often used in industry these days as it carries associations with backward-looking judgmental schemes. Teachers in English language programs will undoubtedly be familiar with a very wide range of approaches to performance management that reflect the differing orientations described above.

Lawson offers a very thorough and practical analysis of the performance review meeting—though he uses the term "appraisal meeting"—and draws attention to the importance of careful preparation by the manager, transparency of process, active listening, and systematic follow through on actions that are agreed. He notes, importantly

> the value and impact of this discussion is limited by its very infrequency. Full advantage is gained by making performance an issue for discussion as frequently as possible—perhaps even on a daily basis if it is possible and appropriate.
>
> (1995, p. 71)

Armstrong makes the same point (2000, p. 62): "a formal, often annual, review is still an important part of a performance management framework but it is not the most important part. Of equal, if not greater prominence, is the performance agreement and the continuous process of performance management" through which progress can be reviewed and plans and objectives revised and updated. He does not underestimate the challenge for managers in conducting effective reviews. While the underlying objectives of the performance review appear straightforward—motivation, development, establishing a channel of communication—the problems that can be encountered, for example in identifying performance measures and criteria for evaluation, collecting appropriate evidence, handling negative feedback, and dealing with defensive behavior are very real:

> It is wise never to underestimate how hard it is for even experienced and effective managers to conduct productive performance review meetings. It is the facile assumption that this is a natural and not too difficult process that has bedevilled many performance appraisal schemes over the years. This assumption has certainly resulted in neglecting to provide adequate guidance and training for reviewing managers and, importantly, those whom they review.
>
> (2000, p. 71)

In a similar way to Lawson, Armstrong sets out in detail the approach that managers need to take in setting up and conducting effective performance reviews. He summarizes these in terms of ten golden rules (ibid., p. 84):

1   Be prepared.
2   Create the right atmosphere.
3   Work to a clear structure.
4   Use praise.
5   Let individuals do most of the talking.
6   Invite self-appraisal.
7   Discuss performance, not personality.
8   Encourage analysis of performance.
9   Don't deliver unexpected criticism.
10   Agree measurable objectives and a plan of action.

In the context of teaching, as we have noted earlier, the task of identifying performance objectives and outcomes that are measurable, valid, and informative is a very difficult one. Reeves et al. take up this question in a discussion of the quality of value judgments. Can program managers who may well be less expert (in some areas at least) than the teachers they are responsible for, make judgments on the performance of those teachers? Evidence from industry, in areas where high level professional expertise is required, suggests this may not be a serious problem:

> Appraisal judgements can be carried out very effectively by managers whose training, management style and relationship with their staff are based on observations, questioning and monitoring of outputs rather than on "I know the right way to do your job."
>
> (Reeves et al., 2002, p. 44)

The evidence further suggests that courses and training programs offered in industry place far greater emphasis on management style and interpersonal skills than on the mechanics of "schemes," leading Reeves et al. to speculate that there is far too much focus in education on the "what" of performance management, rather than on "the complex human skills of making judgements and of communicating them constructively – the how" (ibid., p. 45).

This theme, concerning the role and impact of performance appraisal schemes in education, is taken up forcefully by Jones and Mathias in considering the introduction in 1991 of a national framework for teacher appraisal in UK schools. They argue strongly for appraisal to be seen as a positive and forward-looking process which can only be meaningful and workable if it "stems from and leads to the professional development of teachers" and is seen as "a right of all teachers, something which is done with people rather than to them" (1994, p. 122).

Their interest is in establishing the basis for a relationship between staff appraisal and the development of total quality management cultures within educational institutions; hence the important need for appropriate training in the concept and implementation of appraisal in institutions developing a quality culture.

The essence of their argument is contained simply in two words—entitlement and involvement (ibid., p. 130):

> a "quality" appraisal programme can enhance both individual and institutional development, particularly when it is based upon a concept of staff entitlement and active involvement – in other words, a model which demonstrates trust and which provides some sense of ownership to participants may be the best way of satisfying the sometimes conflicting demands of individual development, institutional growth and public accountability.

The theme of placing individual development at the heart of the performance management framework is consistent with the underlying argument presented by Reeves et al.

in their consideration of the state of teaching in the UK. In their view, the morale and status of the teaching profession can only be raised if the relationship between performance management and professional development is handled with care and sensitivity at national, local area, and school level. Reward is part of this equation as well:

> The emergence of the morale and status of the teaching profession as a policy concern has given rise to an alternative, which is to look to more tangible rewards for individual teachers through schemes of performance-related pay or progression-related pay, both to raise the morale overall and to create a view of the teaching profession as attractive to new entrants (as well as to maintain and improve the practice of serving teachers).
>
> (ibid., p. 38)

Performance-Related Pay

Schemes and arrangements for payment of English language teachers vary considerably depending on whether one is employed in an English-speaking country or overseas, in the public sector or private sector, in an environment of fixed industry-wide awards, enterprise-based agreements, or individual contracts. For a lot of teachers, continuity of employment and progression along a structured pay scale are not guaranteed and even where there is a structured progression, it is more likely to be linked to years of service or experience than to an evaluation of skills and performance in the job. In such cases teachers can find themselves at the top of the pay scale within a few years, but with little prospect of any further pay increases, no matter how well they perform or what their students achieve. Pay based on length of service fails to differentiate between the most and the least effective teacher, and provides no incentive to improve teaching practices. It may even cause some good teachers to leave the profession in search of alternative career and financial progression.

Performance-related pay, then, might be seen as a logical and desirable complement to an effective performance management scheme. As Armstrong says, it can motivate people to perform better, develop their skills and competence and should allow a fair and equitable means of rewarding people differentially according to their performance, competence, or contribution (2000, p. 165).

The quality of the performance management process is of fundamental importance. Managers need to be highly skilled and well trained for their part in the process to ensure that the credibility of the process is maintained and performance assessment is fair and consistent, and seen to be so. In employment contexts where performance ratings are used as a part of the performance review process, the subjective nature of the assessment can present difficult problems. Lawson outlines (1995, p. 74) some steps that organizations can take to monitor the quality of assessment data, and try to reduce inconsistency in the performance appraisal processes. However, he points out that inherent problems of human judgment are likely to be made worse if financial incentives or rewards are directly linked to the review process. Individual staff may be reluctant to speak openly about weaknesses in their own performances, and managers may be uncomfortable about highlighting problem areas if they know that will adversely affect a staff member's pay. He concludes: "The received wisdom, therefore, is that as far as possible the *developmental* aspects of performance appraisal should be kept separate from any assessment for payment purposes" (ibid., p. 75; original emphasis).

Instances of the use of ratings systems, performance-related pay and standardization of performance assessments are much less common in educational organizations than in other types of enterprise, but there is anecdotal evidence, at least, from teachers working abroad whose end-of-term bonuses (or even their re-appointment) are dependent upon the apparently arbitrary judgment of school principals, or on post-course evaluations provided by students. In the schools sector, it is sometimes proposed that teacher evaluations be based upon a combination of factors, such as student grades, classroom performance, student or parent feedback, involvement in professional learning, or contribution to extra-curricular programs, but the challenge of devising meaningful and efficient models is considerable.

Reeves et al. (2002, p. 46) note the concern that performance-related pay can become "the tail that wags the dog" and acknowledge, too, the evidence from industry that separation of performance reviews from pay reviews can help to avoid a conflict of aims. Their concern for ways of raising the morale and status of teaching in the UK leads them also to look to the USA where there has been more progress with developing models for performance assessment that could be linked to an appropriate pay structure. In particular, they cite the work that has gone into developing national standards for the assessment of the knowledge and skills levels of beginning and experienced teachers and other tools that have been developed for assessing teacher competence (ibid., p. 52).

Task 11.2

1 How useful do you think classroom observation is as a tool of performance appraisal?
2 Have you seen it work effectively in practice in a place where you have taught? What were the factors that contributed to that result?
3 What other types of data or evidence could contribute, in your teaching context, to the assessment of teacher performance—student grades or assessment results, student evaluations, peer assessments, portfolios?

A Case Study—Performance Management in Practice

A paper by Renwick and Thomas (2000) presents an account of a system of performance appraisal introduced at a university college in Australia. The authors assert that performance appraisal is a "beneficial process for both employees and employers in an English language college that is concerned with best practice in both teaching and organisational management" (ibid., p. 175). Yet their account of the planning and implementation of the process at the college reveals what sensitive ground this is, both for appraisers and appraisees, and the anxieties it can generate.

In this case the motivation for introducing the performance management system was that it was a requirement of a recently agreed college-wide enterprise agreement. It became the responsibility of a management group comprising the Directors of Studies and program coordinators to devise and implement the new system. Preparations took several months during which the management group worked on articulating their objectives for the performance management system, how those objectives could be achieved by teaching staff, the aspects of performance that would be measured, and the tools of measurement.

After much discussion the management group concluded that the key areas to be measured for performance were:

- *Teaching preparation*: including the place of the lesson in the overall course/unit documentation of lessons and programs, appropriacy of lesson content;
- *Classroom teaching*: interaction with students, giving of instructions, use of questioning and response to students' questions, providing appropriate feedback, conveying interest in and enthusiasm for the lesson content;
- *Record-keeping*: attendance rolls, course outlines, student results;
- *Consultation with students*: formal consultation time, informal consultation time;
- *Contribution to course development*: participation in faculty meetings, generation/creation of new/updated teaching resources, cooperation with colleagues;
- *Professional development*: attendance at courses, further study, dissemination of ideas and material among colleagues;
- *Self-assessment*: reflective teaching, ongoing assessment of own performance, seeking feedback from students.

(Renwick & Thomas, 2000, p. 177)

To measure the above criteria, tools including student surveys, classroom observations, self-assessment, and reflection and goal-setting would be adopted.

Together with an external consultant, the management group at the college formulated a process for the performance review which is not unlike the performance management cycle depicted by Armstrong. The following steps were involved:

- An initial discussion between the supervising coordinator and staff member during which arrangements would be made for a classroom observation and the staff member would be provided with relevant review documentation including information on the observation criteria, a feedback form and teacher self-assessment.
- A classroom observation of approximately one hour.
- A post-observation discussion at which the coordinator and teacher would discuss

the observed lesson, feedback from other sources such as student surveys and general observation, and also the teacher's wider role within the organization.

- Discussion of goals and objectives with the staff member.
- Self-assessment by the teacher of own teaching performance.

Renwick and Thomas' subsequent analysis of the reaction of both supervisors and staff members to the process provides interesting reading. On the management side there were mixed feelings initially with some apprehension about how time-consuming the process would be, but most seemed to agree that it was a valuable process overall, particularly the post-observation discussion.

Teaching staff were, similarly, apprehensive about the process and concerned that too much of the focus would be on the single observed lesson. With the experience of appraisals behind them, teachers seemed also to agree that it was a valuable process overall, although some felt the observed lesson was rather artificial and some aspects of the goal setting and self-assessment exercises were felt to be more suitable for inexperienced teachers than those with many years of experience, or those nearer to retirement. Interestingly, both supervisors and teaching staff seemed to feel that a process of ongoing, less-formal appraisals throughout the year would be the ideal approach to assessing staff performance. It was acknowledged, however, that the opportunity, valued by most teachers, to reflect upon one's own teaching and to discuss goals and directions would be less likely to take place in an informal process.

This attitude would seem to reinforce strongly the view of performance management as an ongoing process, not an annual event, as is expressed in Armstrong's diagram of the performance management cycle (Figure 11.1). An important stage in the process— that of managing performance throughout the year—requires supervisors to keep in touch with their teaching staff along the way, offer feedback and praise when the opportunity arises, conduct informal reviews or discuss updates to goals and objectives. If these practices are followed conscientiously, the annual formal review will seem a far less daunting prospect to staff and might even be regarded by all parties as a welcome opportunity to sit down and have an open discussion about progress and directions.

Conclusion

In this chapter we have only been able to provide an overview of what is a rather complex subject. It is clear that performance management is very much more than being able to conduct an annual incremental interview successfully. It is a comprehensive process, forward-looking, developmentally oriented, and focused on the alignment of organizational goals with those of the individual. It is also clear that much can be gained—or lost—depending on the approach that is taken to implementing performance management processes. A process that is consultative and inclusive, one which is sensitive to the culture of the organization and which encourages the trust of staff by engaging them in planning and implementation, and developing the skills of the reflective practitioner, is surely best placed to achieve the goal of mutual benefit and long-term success.

References

Armstrong, M. (2000). *Performance management: Key strategies and practical guidelines,* 2nd edn. London: Kogan Page.

Covey, S.R. (1990). *Principle-centered leadership.* Provo, UT: IPCL.

Edge, J. (Ed.) (2002). *Continuing professional development: Some of our perspectives.* Kent: IATEFL.

Geddes, J.M. & Marks, D.R. (1997). Personnel matters. In M.A. Christison, & F.L. Stoller (Eds.), *A handbook for language program administrators.* Burlingame, CA: Alta Book Center Publishers.

Impey, G., & Underhill, A. (1994). *The ELT manager's handbook.* London: Heinemann.

Jones, J., & Mathias, J. (1994). Staff appraisal, training and total quality management. In G.D. Doherty (Ed.), *Developing quality systems in education.* London: Routledge.

Jones, P. (1999). *The performance management pocketbook.* Hampshire: Management Pocketbooks Ltd.

Lawson, P. (1995). The appraisal process. In M. Walters (Ed.), *The performance management handbook.* London: Institute of Personnel and Development.

Reeves, J., Forde, C., O'Brien, J., Smith, P., & Tomlinson, H. (2002). *Performance management in education: Improving practice.* London: Paul Chapman Publishing.

Renwick, J., & Thomas, H. (2000). Executing performance appraisal. Paper from the 13th Educational Conference of the ELICOS Association, Fremantle, October.

White, R.V., Martin, M., Stimson, M., & Hodge, R. (1991). *Management in English language teaching.* Cambridge: Cambridge University Press.

Chapter 12

Building a Communicative Toolkit for Leadership

Mark A. Clarke and Julian Edge

Introduction

In this chapter, we examine leadership as a function of communication. While other chapters in this volume illustrate the wide range of definitions of leadership available these days, each with its particular contribution, our stance is best understood in a very mundane, pragmatic way: If you act and people follow your lead, you are a leader, if only for a brief period or on a seemingly unimportant issue. This idea of leading from behind is also taken up by Anderson in Chapter 7.

We do not, therefore, begin from the assumption that leaders are in named positions of power in organizations. We take a slightly different approach. Following a perspective on leadership provided by Harvard psychologist Robert Kegan and his colleagues (Kegan, 1994; Wagner et al., 2006) and influenced by arguments developed by scholars of modernity (Berger & Luckmann 1966; Berger et al., 1973) and globalization (Diamond, 2005; Friedman, 2005), we believe that the world is too complex and the risks too great to yield the territory of "leadership" to politically and organizationally designated individuals. All professionals must assume leadership responsibility at different times in their careers.

One upshot of this position is that leadership must always be considered a function of human relationships. Leading is a matter of constructing an environment that increases the likelihood of people acting in concert. Thus, the importance of communication. Only through communication is understanding possible; only through understanding is communication possible. Inside this circle of possibility, we seek acts of leadership based on understanding and driven by communication.

But we go further. It is not merely a matter of communicating with others. One must also improve one's ability to communicate with oneself (see also Chapter 5 on emotional intelligence, which makes this same point). We assert that an important aspect of leadership in today's complex and risky world is to develop an approach that emphasizes learning about oneself and talking oneself through difficult situations. In the process, one improves one's ability to communicate effectively with others, as well as developing routines of rehearsing one's participation in the predictable (and unpredictable but expectable) situations that may arise. This unpredictable nature of open systems is discussed in Chapter 1 on the ecology of leadership.

So, while we take a socio-cultural-historical view of education (Cole, 1996; Wertsch, 1998) and write with an awareness of the political nature of teaching and learning (Freire, 1985), and while we acknowledge the contribution of organizational perspectives (Senge, 2000; Bolman & Deal, 2003; Fullan, 2003, 2006a, 2006b; Senge et al., 2005) as well as those of established scholars of leadership (Burns, 1978), the primary foundations for our work come from Bateson (Bateson, 1999), Kegan (Kegan, 1994; Kegan & Lahey, 2001), and Rogers (1969).

We are working out for ourselves how to negotiate the complex territory of modern professional life and we offer our insights to others who are similarly bewildered by the onslaught of demands and expectations that assail them. Consider, for example, the following vignette (adapted from Clarke, 2007).

A middle school teacher steps into the hall during passing period just in time to see two boys square off. Faces contorted in anger, books and ugly epithets flying, kids pushing back against the lockers to give them room to fight. One boy pulls a long key chain from his pocket and rears back in gladiator fashion when the teacher pushes him up against the lockers and brings the fight to a halt. The question is, "What to do next?"

School policy states that fights are to be handled by the Assistant Principal, and teachers are to fill out a disciplinary sheet describing the incident. Any involvement of weapons requires an immediate three-day expulsion from school and key chains are explicitly listed as weapons. Three expulsions and the student is expelled for good. Failure to act in strict accordance to the rules could result in disciplinary action for the teacher.

Put yourself in the teacher's position. The policy makes sense in these times of increased violence. Fighting should not be tolerated, repeat offenders and their families need to be sent clear messages about inappropriate behavior, and disciplinary action needs to be consistent within the school. Your job is to teach, not keep the peace; the Assistant Principal presumably has the training and experience to handle such situations. On the other hand, you know the boys and have some insight into the causes of the altercation. You are also aware of the problems they have had as immigrants to a new land and of the adjustments they are making as they struggle to learn English and to survive in a strange culture. You may have had them in class and you know that they are making significant progress in both academic and social adjustments, in spite of the fact that they are still noticeably behind their English-speaking peers. You also know that one of them has at least two referrals and writing them up will result in expulsion, putting them permanently out of the reach of the education they so obviously need.

We see this as the archetypical dilemma of the times—you find yourself in a situation where rules and regulations that make sense in the abstract pose difficulties for you in the moment. You feel pressured to resolve a tension between cultural and organizational expectations and personal and professional instincts. You do not want simply to pass this pressure on to those for whom you are responsible. Both with regard to your own options for action and with regard to the environment that you create for others, you are looking for creative ways to respond.

In what follows, we return repeatedly to the above vignette in order to ground our observations and suggestions. At the same time, however, we ask you, the reader, to see the more general dilemma as it is realized throughout our educational systems, in the work of teacher educators, of administrators, of kindergarten assistants, and of doctoral supervisors. Most importantly, we ask you to evaluate our ideas against the criterion of their relevance to your own situation.

Task 12.1

Think back through your own experience to identify a dilemma of this kind. Take a little time to clarify the details and construct a vignette of your own to work with as you read on.

A Conceptual Framework

In developing a conceptual framework, we draw on the work of philosopher Steven Toulmin (2001) for two insights. First, that large-scale historical and cultural conditions shape the philosophical, political, and professional contexts in which we operate. We see ourselves in a time of hardening absolutes, where individuals and groups seek security in the certainty of their convictions and the fixedness of their procedures. This may be an inevitable consequence of the complexity of the era we live in, as discussed in the Introduction: we all seek ways of achieving some modicum of certainty in uncertain times. Second, and as a result of this phenomenon, that an increasing centralization of power and decision-making has reduced the professional discretion of educational practitioners, who are often called upon to act more as technicians in a delivery system than as professionals in a creative environment for learning. Increasingly frustrated and sometimes demoralized in the face of mounting demands, educators are reduced to individual reactions to incoherent situations. We find it useful to represent this overall situation as a pressure continuum between two poles that we call the Rational and the Reactive.

The Rational ————————————————— **The Reactive**

The Rational represents decisions one might make with ample time in a utopian world where matters can be logically organized to the best possible ends. These are decisions made at a distance in time and space from where the action is. They are usually experienced as mandates handed down from above as policies or "best practices" to be implemented.

The Reactive represents our scramble under everyday pressure, where one attempts to do the best one can, given scarce time, resources, and support. We see our Middle School teacher above as living at some point along this pressure continuum. Into this continuum, following Toulmin, we attempt to introduce the Reasonable.

The Rational ——————— The Reasonable ——————— The Reactive

The Reasonable represents an elusive goal: an attempt to balance an understanding of the pressures that everyone is under when crafting responses to authority, while simultaneously promoting healthy learning for one's charges and for oneself.

We begin with the assumption that practitioner knowledge is the primary source of insight for the strategies required. One cannot defer to authorities merely because they are the authority. We are inspired by Toulmin's assertion:

> The future belongs not so much to the pure thinkers who are content – at best – with optimistic or pessimistic slogans; it is a province, rather, for reflective practitioners who are ready to act on their ideals. Warm hearts allied with cool heads seek a middle way between the extremes of abstract theory and personal impulse.
> (Toulmin, 2001, p. 214)

And in this assertion we hear echoes of our own experience in TESOL and teacher education regarding the dysfunctions of a theory/application discourse (Clarke, 1994) and the need to augment such an approach with a discourse of exploration and articulation (Edge, 2003).

In Table 12.1, we move to a level of abstraction that we find helpful in trying to clarify further our understanding of how this continuum affects us, and how we might make it useful to us in trying to craft responses to the pressurised situations in which we work.

In the first column, we have listed a series of fundamental concepts, beginning with reality and truth, that we think are in play as the Middle School teacher above faces up to the moment of conflict in the school corridor, or as each of us engages with whatever challenging incident confronts us.

In the second column, we look at how we might see those concepts operating if we enjoy the luxury provided by distance from actual practice. Seduced by our insulation, we base our Rational claims on the objective assessment of how things *really* are. Once we have established the nature of this single reality, we can predict the outcomes and consequences of different actions and thus establish a sound base for policy. Just as objective reality is predictable, truth, once we have established what it is, becomes an absolute concept and thus generalizable across different situations. The key value is objectivity, on the basis of which we can act with as much certainty as we can muster. And while we may not deceive ourselves into thinking that perfection is achievable, we

Table 12.1 The Characteristics of the Rationality–Reaction Continuum

	Rationality	Reaction	Reasonableness
Reality	single, predictable	atomized, uncontrollable	multiple, emergent
Truth	absolute, generalizable	unclear, threatening	relative, situated
Key values	objectivity, certainty	control, fear	openness, respect, fairness
Goal	perfection, clarity, explicitness	escape, suppression	understanding, learning
Procedures	precise, standardized	one-shot, erratic	intuitive, improvised
Decisions	long-term cycles	moment by moment	short-term cycles
Outcomes	seeking permanence	transitory	seeking flexibility

behave as if it were the only worthwhile goal, coupled with the clarity and explicitness that will help everyone move along together using precise and standardized procedures. Once we have committed to a particular set of policy structures, we favor decisions that operate over long-term cycles as we move toward outcomes that would be, in the best of all possible worlds, permanent, arising as they do from the optimal arrangements possible. This position is the standard one taken in strategic planning (see Chapter 9).

In the third column, we look at how our basic concepts might play out for the individual on the ground, under pressure, trying to cope. This occurs against a background of deep dissatisfaction with mandates from authorities, based on the conviction that such regulations have been drawn up by people who have no real understanding of the situation "in the trenches." In this Reactive mode, we suggest, there is a sense of trying to deal with a reality made up of unendingly separate, atomized incidents, out of control, and uncontrollable. Exactly what is true in this, or any, particular situation is unclear, which makes the prospect of establishing truth, or of proceeding without it, threatening. The key value in such situations is the desire to exert control, accompanied by fear of not being able to do so. The most attractive goal, were it available, would be to escape from this situation altogether or to find a way to suppress it. Our responses in such an environment are made on a one-shot basis, arising erratically from moment-by-moment decision-making. The outcomes are transitory, leaving the overall situation feeling as uncontrollable and threatening as ever.

In the fourth column, we offer a conceptual underpinning for what we have already described as an elusive goal, a position of Reasonableness that can free us from the worst extremes of the rational and the reactive. Here, we claim that the reality with which we have to deal is neither single nor hopelessly fractured. It is multiple, in the sense that different people have different, honest perceptions of what is going on. Reality is also emergent, in the sense that people's perceptions of what is happening develop as they become more aware. In similar fashion, many important elements of truth are relative to a particular situation and a particular perception. Our key value here is to be open to the multiple possibilities with which we are presented, to respect the different truths that people hold dear, and to be fair in our dealings with difference. It is not simply that we do not believe that we can attain perfection; it is rather the case that we do not acknowledge perfection as an appropriate goal. Our goals are to increase our understanding, to continue learning, and to create an environment in which these values and goals come to be shared. We require some freedom to improvise our procedures and to invest our intuitions as this enables us to bring our professional expertise to bear. In an emergent reality of increasing understanding, we want our decisions to operate over short cycles and to be available for constant review over longer cycles of time as we seek a dynamic state of flexibility.

Let us now re-examine the vignette from the perspective we have created to see if we can credibly locate these abstractions in it.

Hallway scuffles between students are predictable occurrences and teachers need guidelines for dealing with the individuals involved in ways that are fair to them and that maintain the general order and safety of the school. But in the heat of the moment it is difficult to act decisively if you have not developed a frame of mind that takes into account all the conflicting pressures that come into play.

Our young Middle School teacher, whom we'll call Maria, understands the situation (reality, as she experiences it) and knows that the school policy was developed to provide her with a single, predictable response to student altercations. She balances the automatic reaction that the fight provokes with an awareness that there are several points of view about the fight that she might want to take into account (truth). Viewed from a distance, of course, there is only one interpretation that she should apply, but at the moment she wants merely to dampen her anxiety and control the situation. At the same time, she wants to respond to the students with a sense of respect and fairness (values). The goal of the policy is to establish a perfectly clear solution to the problem, which contrasts dramatically with her desire to escape or suppress it so she doesn't have to deal with it. She believes, however, that if she can understand all the factors that contributed to the fight, she will be able to come up with a more productive stance (goal). Rather than either following standardized procedures to the letter, or reacting in a one-shot effort at dealing with the boys, she wants to improvise an intuitive, but reasonable and justifiable response (procedures), one that takes into account both immediate and longer-term consequences in the light of her professional judgment (decisions). She hopes to afford herself and the boys a certain amount of flexibility and autonomy (outcome), a happy medium between the illusion of a permanent resolution envisioned by those who developed the policy and the temporary stop-gap solutions that a reactive response produces.

Of course, it is one thing to work all this out in the abstract, and quite another to behave consistently in pressurized situations, but we contend that this is precisely what is required of leaders—that they approach problem-solving in a way that permits them to avoid merely passing the pressure on to their charges. In the following section we develop tools that facilitate this effort.

Task 12.2

Think again about the vignette your created in Task 12.1. Do you find the conceptual framework we provide useful in understanding it? Which elements seem most helpful?

Tools for Reasonable Responses

The tools are provided as a list, but we do not mean to suggest that this list represents a sequence in which they should be used. We illustrate them using Maria's dilemma, but we assume readers will shift from her context to theirs as they check for relevance. We do so in full awareness of how easy it is to write about such issues rather than live them. We hope, in the process, to avoid becoming an example of the lines attributed to Harrison Ford about a script he was given, "OK, so somebody can write this stuff, but nobody can *say* it!"

As we elaborate on the tools in our toolkit we will discuss Maria's reactions in the moment to the boys in the hallway and we will project her responses in other contexts where she might display leadership qualities around issues relating to the fight.

1   *Avoid simply reacting*. Don't panic. Use any ritual or discipline that helps you create space to formulate a response. Psychologist Robert Kegan (1994, pp. 32–34) refers to shifting what we might call the "you-in-action" from subject to object position. That is to say, step back from being totally embedded in the turmoil of the moment where you cannot separate yourself from events, to a point psychologically where you can analyze your feelings and gather your wits. The "I" who has stepped back then has a chance to observe the "me" who is a part of the situation. Leadership theorist Ronald Heifetz uses the metaphor of stepping up to the balcony to observe events (Heifetz, 1994). This little space that you create also gives you time to focus on your core values. We realize how Pollyanna-ish this sounds, but in fact the single most distinguishing feature of leaders is the clarity with which they see who they are and what they stand for. We also contend that the approach we are advocating, which is consistent with recent applications of ecological principles to teaching and teacher education (van Lier, 2004; Clarke, 2007; Larsen-Freeman & Cameron, forthcoming), requires us to think of the development of core values as an ongoing task, one that occurs precisely in situations such as these. The essential point is to develop strategies that remind you to pause before you speak, to think before you act, to gather yourself. Your mother may have told you, "Count to ten." If you can't think of a better trick, use that. Whatever else Maria does at that moment in the corridor, she needs to create a moment to think. This may be achieved by saying something like, "OK, guys, let's just step into this empty classroom here and take a breath." Later, in a meeting with administrators and colleagues, during heated discussions about fighting and referrals and suspensions, Maria will bite her tongue

when others make comments she considers racist or ill-informed generalizations. Her goal in that context is to help fashion policies and procedures that both reduce violence and keep students in school and she realizes that outbursts that polarize faculty are not going to be helpful.

2   *Focus on now.* Whatever you decide to do, do just that. The present, passing moment, is really the only time that we have available for action. The nature of that action will differ. You may be analyzing the past, or planning for the future, but whatever you are doing now, give it your full attention (Tolle, 1999). Our ability to deal with the pressures we face is seriously compromised by fragmented attention and the rising sense of panic that accompanies the scramble from one task to another. Once you have committed yourself to do something—it may be so mundane as washing the dishes or clearing your emails—put your whole attention to it. If it is a small-scale task, you will hope to complete it. With something larger, you may have to break off. If you do, then do break off and shift your full concentration to what you are doing *now*. Maria has engaged with the boys in the corridor and this situation will need her full attention. If she was on her way to another appointment, she will try to send a message on ahead to say that she will be a few minutes late, before tuning in completely to the situation in hand.

3   *Assume good will.* Act as if everyone is doing the best they can according to their own perceptions of what is important, or true, or good. This applies to all situations, until one receives evidence to the contrary. A fundamental hypothesis of Carl Rogers' was that the main obstacle to communication among people is our rush to evaluate others from our own perspective (Rogers, 1951). A helpful aphorism from Peter Elbow runs, "In order to understand what another person is saying, you must assume it is true and try to imagine what it might be true of" (Elbow, 1986, p. 154). This is the kind of environment that Maria wants to create. In her work to construct better discipline policies she understands that everyone in the building got into teaching in order to contribute to a better world, and although she may consider some of her colleagues and administrators to be woefully uninformed about cultural and linguistic differences, immigrant communities, and English language learners in general, she works to understand their world and the motivations for their contributions to the conversations.

4   *Establish clear expectations and strategies.* This applies both to yourself and others as you attempt to shape the environment in which you do your work. Speak in a way that gives you the best possible chance of framing the topic and working toward a desired outcome (Bolman & Deal, 2003; Lakoff, 2004). Maria might say to the boys, "I believe that you two were about to get involved in a disagreement and I want us all to understand what that disagreement would have been about." The topic-shift from breaking up a fight to investigating a hypothetical disagreement may be crucial to what follows. The same applies to possible conversations with the Assistant Principal. Maria realizes it is not enough to critique the current disciplinary policy; she needs to have a proposal and steps for reaching a more equitable approach to the problems the school faces. The Assistant Principal is under

pressures of his own and will need help in understanding her point of view and in devising strategies for making changes. Maria realizes that she must come to the table with a structure and a goal. If she wants people to get on board in a direction that she favors, she needs to have at least a rough outline of what it is she wants them to do. They are going to want to proceed in their comfortable routines, but if she can promise them an equally promising replacement, she will have a chance of nudging them toward her point of view.

5 *Identify your spheres of responsibility and influence.* Do not take responsibility for problems for which you do not have the resources or authority to solve. Avoid augmenting your difficulties by taking on more work than you are able to do. Do not fall into the over-simple diagnosis of being "stressed" (Patmore, 2006). You may be overworked, tired, unhappy, worried about something, or all of these. Talk to yourself and try to identify where real problems lie. And listen. Martyrdom is not a requirement. Nor is it a helpful leadership strategy for most people. It restricts your capacity for effective action. It is not Maria's duty to put herself in the firing line. She may decide that she needs to refer the boys to the Assistant Principal after all, but this does not mean she has conceded the legitimacy of the policy or that she will not pursue action to ameliorate its impact on the boys. At the moment, however, direct action to challenge the policy would set her on a path that removes her from her spheres of responsibility. We cannot solve all problems at the moment they occur, and Maria realizes her credibility with both the boys and the Assistant Principal requires her to act consistently and thoughtfully. She may have to settle for doing what she can on this occasion to soften what she considers to be the misguided elements of the policy, and she will press for the changes through appropriate channels.

6 *Identify your options, and the consequences of each one.* This will lead you to an awareness of the patterns or cycles of the problems that you are likely to face, and help you identify the ramifications of your actions. You do not face a random or haphazard world; each school day brings with it a range of predictable events. You can anticipate them and develop strategies for dealing with them. As corny as it sounds, this is a learning opportunity for Maria to the extent that she decides to make it one. In fact, she cannot avoid learning from what happens next. The issue is the extent to which she will have this experience, or the experience will have her (Kegan & Lahey, 2001, pp. 149–186). In either case, similar situations will come around again.

7 *Learn to see how your problem is part of larger patterns.* Significant problems cannot be solved at the level they are encountered. Study the patterns and adjust your responses for the next time. Identify leverage points for action—events and situations that come around as part of the daily routine during which you can nudge the system toward your goals. The fight in the hallway could be explained in a variety of ways—racial tensions, gang influences, youthful romantic rivalries, for example. But it may also be the case that the bell schedule contributes to the problem by putting all the students into the hallway at the same time. Or district policy

concerning pupil attendance areas may have increased the number of students in the building. In any case, calming the boys down and helping them focus on productive academic activities is only the most immediate requirement of the situation. Maria may have to become more involved in school decision-making or district policy development if she is to make a significant difference in the problems she has been dealing with. If a problem is important, we cannot be content with fixing it every time it occurs; we need to work on making it less likely to occur.

8   *Rehearse your role in the situations you have identified as likely to occur.* Use your understanding of events and people to predict what you will hear and to formulate what you will need to say. This is just as important in the hallway as you are pulling pugilists apart as it is in the faculty meeting where you argue for more flexibility in the disciplinary policy. Life is cyclical; it comes at us in waves of fairly predictable events, so it is not unreasonable to anticipate the need for language that will calm combatants as well as language that will appeal to the best instincts of our colleagues and administrators. And it is also the case that attempting to find the right words to defuse a fight or to placate a colleague is easier when you are not actually facing your protagonist. It now becomes invidious for us to pursue Maria's options further. To do so would be to fabricate a response from afar that would not, by definition, be based in her embodied, contextualized knowledge and professional expertise. What we are trying to do is assemble a toolkit that will enable her to establish a place to stand in these dangerous times. These are extensions of efforts we have been working on for some time (Edge, 2002; Clarke, 2003).

9   *Celebrate how far you have come, rather than agonizing over how far you have to go.* Remind yourself of what is good and give yourself time to enjoy the noticing. Recognize that life is dynamic, complex, and demanding and that it cannot be "solved." Nurture a tolerance of ambiguity and imperfection. We do well to remember Caleb Gattegno's insight that to require perfection is the greatest imperfection (Gattegno, 1976). This is a stance which your students and subordinates will find affirming and energizing and which you must remember to extend to yourself and your superiors as you work toward common solutions to complex problems.

Task 12.3

Returning once more to your vignette. Do you find these tools, singly, in groups, or in concert, potentially useful to you in your own development? Or do they perhaps motivate you to formulate your own tools?

Moving On

We have not set out to identify the characteristics of *a leader*. Rather, we have attempted to identify some ways in which people in various situations might offer leadership. We can now define this leadership more precisely as a way of behaving that demonstrates congruence between what one says and what one does, such that those set above you and those for whom you are taking on some element of responsibility see you as adding to the quality of their experience both by the ways in which you work toward sustaining their perceived interests and the ways in which you influence them to develop (or change) those interests.

This is tender territory and it requires a delicate touch. Your colleagues and administrators, or you yourself, may find our suggestions inappropriate or officious, disingenuous or Machiavellian or contrary to the norms of your culture.

In the search for the reasonable, we have ranged from a view on fundamental philosophical stances to the provision of practical mental and communicative tools for use on Monday morning. We remain convinced of the necessity to try to deal coherently with the broad sweep as well as the specific detail, against a background of critical values. We have foregrounded the need to create space for thought under pressure, so that reason, embodied and situated beyond arid rationality or impulsive reaction, may inform word and deed. We have been dealing with issues of communication, including communication with oneself, and issues of action, almost always actions by oneself, which also communicate. In interim conclusion, then, we pause on two reflections:

- Everything that we communicate is framed in some way (Goffman, 1974; Lakoff & Johnson, 1980; Lakoff, 2004). If the director accepts your going your way while I go mine, we may interpret this as a sign of weakness or as a sign of strength. And from that framing interpretation many more actions and meanings will flow. The more we understand the frames that are operating in any given context and can influence them, the greater chance we have of being understood as we intend, and of drawing others into the frames that we believe conducive to productive communication.
- Our systems of, and possibilities for, action are similarly nested. Important problems are unlikely to be solved, or significant opportunities taken, only by action at the same systemic level on which they are met (Bateson, 1999). The constant litter along the corridor requires picking up, but it may also signal a need for better training or supervision of the custodians. Just as likely, it may indicate the need for an educational campaign and sensitivity training for those who litter.

We have also tried to exemplify what we mean by our suggested "tools" through the use of a vignette based on a true story, while also inviting readers to consider the more general relevance of our analysis to situations and dilemmas with which they are familiar. In this connection, and during the finalization of this chapter, one of us (Edge) was sitting on a school committee considering new regulations on the circumstances under which part-time doctoral students would be allowed to suspend their registration for a period. In other words, when, for one reason and another, they needed some time out. Mindful of the fact that overall research funding is tied in with PhD completion rates, the new regulations from the center stipulated that only medical reasons were now acceptable as grounds for a suspension of registration. Other reasons, such as a change in work responsibilities, were no longer permissable. "That is to say," a committee member noted, "that if someone gets a promotion and has to take on a whole range of new responsibilities, that is not acceptable grounds. First, they have to work themselves into a state of certifiable ill-health, then they have grounds to ask us for a break from their studies."

This we see as analogous to Maria's moment in the corridor. The university seeks rational procedures in order to improve figures and cut out malingering. Another committee member voiced almost word for word our characterization of the rational position: "It's alright for the people who write these regulations, they don't have to deal with the students." The individual doctoral supervisor looks to protect and further the interests of his or her student, but an impulsive, unilateral granting of time out might lead only to serious consequences down the line, perhaps most of all for the student. Once again, the search is on for the reasonable position.

As with all other aspects of modern life, issues of leadership remain an emergent phenomenon. This chapter represents a first effort at bringing together elements of our work in English language teaching, teacher education, action research, and collaborative decision-making (Edge, 2001, 2002; Clarke, 2003, 2007) and at applying them to the topic of leadership. As such, it is tentative and incomplete; we welcome all feedback.

References

Bateson, G. (1999). *Steps to an ecology of mind*. Chicago: The University of Chicago Press.

Berger, P., Berger, B. et al. (1973). *The homeless mind: Modernization and consciousness*. New York: Vintage Books.

Berger, P., & Luckmann, T. (1966). *The social construction of reality*. Garden City, NY: Doubleday.

Bolman, L.G., & Deal, T.E. (2003). *Reframing organizations: Artistry, choice, and leadership*. San Francisco: Jossey-Bass.

Burns, J.M. (1978). *Leadership*. New York: Harper.

Clarke, M.A. (1994). The dysfunctions of the theory/practice discourse. *TESOL Quarterly* 28(1), 9–26.

Clarke, M.A. (2003). *A place to stand: Essays for educators in troubled times*. Ann Arbor, MI: University of Michigan Press.

Clarke, M.A. (2007). *Common ground, contested territory: English language teaching in troubled times*. Ann Arbor, MI: University of Michigan Press.

Cole, M. (1996). *Cultural psychology: A once and future discipline*. Cambridge, MA: Harvard University Press.

Diamond, J. (2005). *Collapse: How societies choose to fail or succeed*. New York: Viking.

Edge, J. (Ed.) (2001). *Case studies in TESOL: Action research*. Alexandria, VA: TESOL Inc.

Edge, J. (2002). *Continuing cooperative development: A discourse framework for individuals as colleagues*. Ann Arbor, MI: University of Michigan Press.

Edge, J. (2003). Alternative discourses in teacher education. Interview in *ELT Journal 57*(4): 386–394.

Elbow, P. (1986). *Embracing contraries: Explorations in learning and teaching*. New York: Oxford University Press.

Freire, P. (1985). *The politics of education*. Granby, MA: Bergin and Garvey.

Friedman, T.L. (2005). *The world is flat: A brief history of the twenty-first century*. New York: Farrar: Straus and Giroux.

Fullan, M.G. (2003). *Change forces with a vengeance*. New York: RoutledgeFalmer.

Fullan, M.G. (2006a). *Breakthrough*. Thousand Oaks, CA: Corwin Press.

Fullan, M.G. (2006b). *Turnaround leadership*. San Francisco: Jossey-Bass.

Gattegno, C. (1976). *The common sense of teaching foreign languages*. New York: Educational Solutions.

Goffman, E. (1974). *Frame analysis*. New York: Harper & Row.

Heifetz, R.A. (1994). *Leadership without easy answers*. Cambridge, MA: Belknap Press.

Kegan, R. (1994). *In over our heads: The mental demands of modern life*. Cambridge, MA: Belknap Press.

Kegan, R., & Lahey, L.L. (2001). *How the way we talk can change the way we work: Seven languages for transformation*. San Francisco: Jossey-Bass.

Lakoff, G. (2004). *Don't think of an elephant: Know your values and frame the debate*. White River Junction, VT: Chelsea Green Publishing.

Lakoff, G., & Johnson, M. (1980). *Metaphors we live by*. Chicago: The University of Chicago Press.

Larsen-Freeman, D., & Cameron, L. (forthcoming). *Complex systems and applied linguistics*. New York: Oxford University Press.

Patmore, A. (2006). *The truth about stress*. Ocala, FL: Atlantic Publishing CO.

Rogers, C. (1951). Communication: Its blocking and its facilitation. In Teich, N. (Ed.), *Rogerian perspectives: Collaborative rhetoric for oral and written communication*. Norwood, NJ: Ablex.

Rogers, C. (1969). *Freedom to learn*. Columbus, OH: Charles E. Merrill.

Senge, P. (2000). *Schools that learn*. New York: Doubleday.

Senge, P., Scharmer, C.O. et al. (2005). *Presence: Exploring profound change in people, organizations, and society*. New York: Currency Doubleday.

Tolle, E. (1999). *The power of now: A guide to spiritual enlightenment*. Novato, CA: Namaste Publishing.

Toulmin, S. (2001). *Return to reason*. Cambridge, MA: Harvard University Press.

van Lier, L. (2004). *The ecology and semiotics of language learning: A sociocultural perspective*. Dordrecht: Kluwer.

Wagner, T., Kegan, R. et al. (2006). *Change leadership: A practical guide to transforming our schools*. San Francisco: Jossey-Bass.

Wertsch, J.V. (1998). *Mind as action*. New York: Oxford University Press.

Chapter 13

Building Effective Teams

MaryAnn Christison and Denise E. Murray

Introduction

One would be hard pressed these days to find an English language teacher who has not been part of a team in some way. In the last half of the twentieth century, the concept of building effective teams was recognized in the business world as an integral factor in a company's ability to remain both productive and competitive (see online sources, such as www.teamtechnology.co.uk, www.corplearning.com, www.business.com, and www.teambuildinginc.com). Teams are serious business and much time and considerable effort are placed on building effective teams in order to create greater employee involvement, leverage human resources, foster innovation, and shore up the bottom line (Cole, 2001). According to the Center for the Study of Work Teams at the University of North Texas, the number of companies using self-directed teams in 1987 was 27 percent. The number increased to 68 percent in 1993, and the numbers continue to increase (Cole, 2001).

The concept of team building has also spread to educational contexts. We have teams that work on developing new courses, on redesigning curriculum, on creating alternative assessments, on revising admission policies, on implementing new teaching methodologies, and on finding solutions to student retention. Teamwork is popular, and it is common knowledge that most English language program leaders use teams in the day-to-day running of English language education programs throughout the world.

Although teamwork is a popular approach for solving problems and increasing effectiveness and productivity in the twenty-first century, it remains a vague and nebulous concept for many leaders—even for those who are creating teams and working on teams. As a result of the lack of clarity about the critical components of teamwork, teams are sometimes overused or used in contexts where they are inappropriate. In this chapter, we will offer some guidelines on building effective teams and some guidance for leaders who are in charge of teams. We will focus on defining teams and team building, motivating teams, critical factors in developing effective teams, including roles and responsibilities of leaders and team members, and qualities of effective teams.

Defining Teams and Teambuilding

What is a *team?* In the workplace, a *team* can be defined in many different ways. For example, some people define a team as simply a group of people. Others define a team in terms of the person to whom the team reports. You can become a member of a team by virtue of the person to whom you report—your department chair, program administrator, or simply the unit to which you belong. Other ways of defining a team are related to solving problems. You may be considered a member of a team even if you are at cross purposes with other individuals who have been assigned to solve the same problem. Teams are also defined in terms of people who are working on similar tasks, such as selecting texts or revising the entrance exam. In order to discuss the concept of building effective teams, we believe that it is important to define the concept of a *team*. For the purposes of this chapter a *team* will be defined as *a group of people who are working together to achieve a common goal*. If we define a *team* as a group of people who are working together to achieve a common goal, then building effective teams is *the process of enabling a group of people to reach their goal*.

Task 13.1

Work with a partner if you can. Make a list of at least five different things that groups are good at doing (as opposed to individuals).

What is a Team Good at Doing?

The first step in the process of building effective teams is to determine what teams are good at doing. Working in a team can be both efficient and effective, but like any dynamic it can also be overused or misused. In order to use teamwork effectively, we must be very clear about the contexts in which group work is useful and about the ways in which group work and individual work differ. Douglas (1983) provides a list of 15 advantages associated with working in a team. His initial work was situated in business contexts; therefore, the list we offer you has been adapted from Douglas to fit the contexts of education and specifically the contexts of English language education. This list of advantages for working in teams can help us develop a more complete understanding of what teams are good at doing:

1 Teams are good at tasks that require more than one person. If you are working on a project that must be done quickly or one in which several things must be done at one time, it is advantageous to work with a team.
2 Teams are good at tasks requiring a division of labor. If you are working on a project that requires different kinds of expertise, then a team is often advantageous.
3 Teams are good at reducing the risk of error in completing a task. We have all heard

the phrase, "The more eyes, the better," used in the workplace in reference to the need to reduce the risk of errors in written work. The more people you have look at a document, test, paper, or letter, the less likely the risk will be that the item in question will be submitted, printed, or circulated with errors. The concept extends to other projects as well.

4   Teams produce more solutions to a problem. Individual members on a team seldom see the world in quite the same way. If you are working on solving a problem, it is beneficial to work with a team who can brainstorm a number of potential solutions.

5   Teams produce "better" solutions to a problem. The term "better" can best be described in terms of a phenomenon that Murphy (1996) refers to as a "synergistic kick." A "synergistic kick" means that collectively a group of people can perform at a higher level together than they can separately as individuals. The concept also actualizes itself in the *Apollo Syndrome* (Belbin, 2004). Belbin noticed that highly intelligent people often performed worse individually than teams made up of "less-able" individuals. Putting a team together with the cleverest or smartest individuals does not necessarily produce the best results.

6   Teams can make more efficient use of resources. Teams are less likely to re-invent the wheel because they have a broader knowledge base on which to draw. They make use of existing resources and resources within the team rather than plan to outsource work related to the teams goals.

7   Teams are more motivated because social motivation is higher when working with others. We often hear the adage that "a rotten potato spoils the bag," but the same power to influence can also be true for a highly enthusiastic and influential person. This person has the potential to motivate productive and positive change in a team.

8   Teams learn faster. Individuals who work on a team receive more stimulation than people who work alone; consequently, they have many more opportunities to learn. More opportunities for learning result in a steeper trajectory for the acquisition of new concepts and ideas.

9   Inferior ideas are eliminated more effectively when working in teams. When you are working in a team, you can get immediate feedback on your ideas. In addition, the relevance and appropriateness of ideas can be examined with the benefit of different backgrounds and points of view; consequently, inferior ideas are rejected much more quickly.

10   Individual members tend to increase output when working in teams. The "synergistic kick" (Murphy, 1996) is not only about the quality of teamwork, but about the quantity of teamwork as well.

11   Teams minimize the sense of workload for any one member. Any project can seem daunting when you are the only person working on it; however, when you divide a project into different tasks and assign the tasks to different members, the sense of workload diminishes.

12   Feedback on performance is likely to be more accurate since the feedback is from multiple sources. When there is only one person giving feedback, there is always a risk that something has been missed or misinterpreted. Different people see

different pieces of the puzzle. The more people involved in giving feedback, the more opportunity there is for seeing different points of view.

When can Individuals be More Effective Than Teams?

1   When it is difficult to demonstrate the solution to others, individuals are generally more effective than teams. When a group has found a solution to a very complex problem, it may be better for the person in the group who best understands the solution to demonstrate it to others so that the solution can be presented in a clear and succinct manner.

2   When the status hierarchy or conformity pressures of a team hinder the freedom of the individuals on the team, it may be better to find a solution outside the context of the team. For example, an English language program for which we have worked adopted new textbooks for their advanced level and needed new training materials for teachers. The adoption was not fully supported by the senior level teachers who wanted to maintain the status quo. The teachers thought that the director should appoint a team of senior teachers to create the new training materials. However, the director appointed a more junior person to work on the project because she had a better understanding of the new textbooks and the concepts associated with them.

3   When the speed of response is crucial, individuals may be better than teams. There are often tasks that come to a leader's attention that are time-sensitive. The task must be completed on time. Assigning an individual to complete the task is faster because this person doesn't have to consider other people's opinions and has more flexibility in scheduling and more time to work on the task.

4   When an individual's skill is crucial, an individual is better suited to the task. For example, if you need someone to review the budget and determine where cuts could be made, you will want to work with one person who is very good in both building and understanding budgets rather than a team whose members may not have this important skill.

5   When an individual's style or creativity is important in the completion of a task or project, you may want to use an individual rather than a team. For example, perhaps you are working on a development project in order to raise money for student scholarships. A highly creative person with a certain style and panache may be able to create a development plan to attract potential donors far better than a team of individuals without these qualities.

6   When the cost of training and the time to get up and running exceeds the organization's resources. While training in team work should be an essential part of professional development, in some instances, for some tasks, it may be better to postpone such training for a more appropriate task.

Effective leaders understand what teams and individuals are good at doing and make decisions about when to use teams based on this understanding.

Task 13.2

Why do you think people agree to serve on teams? Have you ever served on a team? If yes, what was your reason?

Motivation

What Motivates Individuals to Join Teams?

We often hear the term *motivation* used in educational literature. Its common and frequent use lead many educators to believe they know what motivation is. In terms of a technical definition, motivation is simply *a state of mind that moves a person to action*. Yet, defining the state of mind is difficult. As leaders, we have found it useful to try to put ourselves in the state of mind of individuals being asked to join a team. In order to do this, we focus on possible questions that might accompany an individual's decision-making process. In addition, we focus on the questions that might be part of this process. What are the reasons a person might want to become part of a team? Here is a list of questions that are associated with why individuals might want to be part of a team. Thinking about possible answers to these questions can prepare a leader for working more efficiently and effectively with potential team members.

- What is the purpose of the team?
- What will the team try to accomplish?
- Is it a topic that interests me?
- Who will be on the team?
- What roles will team members play?
- Who will lead the team?
- What kind of authority will the team have?
- How accountable is the team?
- Is there a realistic timeline for it to accomplish its goals?
- What non-human resources will be made available to the team?
- Is the team important to the leaders of the program?
- What is the reward for participating on the team?
- What are the risks for not participating?
- How long will it take to achieve the goal?
- Will I be better off if I participate?

What Motivates Individuals to Stay on a Team?

Understanding the intricacies of motivation is not an easy task. We believe that leaders can benefit from learning about some general principles related to motivation and that these principles can guide a person's actions. Grazier (1998) states that motivation for working on a team can increase or decrease depending on the presence of six key principles:

1 *Purpose*. If we were asked to describe the characteristics of our most successful and rewarding team experiences, we would both have to say that clearly articulated purposes and goals would be at the top of our list. If the purpose for working on the team is clear from the beginning, a team will be able to maintain enthusiasm and motivation for the task.
2 *Challenge*. Challenge is a motivator. Many people say that their most rewarding team experience resulted from some sort of challenge. Challenge has much to do with the match between the level of difficulty of the task and the skills of the team members. If a challenge is too difficult, team members will not be motivated to finish the task or they may give up before they start. If the task is too easy, team members may have little energy or excitement for completing the task. An appropriate level of challenge can create high levels of motivation and a sense of accomplishment for the team.
3 *Camaraderie*. Positive relationships among team members are also powerful motivators. If one studies the literature on highly effective groups, one finds that the most successful groups over the long haul address both the technical needs associated with accomplishing a task or achieving the goal and the human needs associated with fellowship and loyalty among members of the team.
4 *Responsibility*. Teams are motivated when they are given responsibility and when they have ownership over the process of completing the work. Teams that are given responsibility maintain motivation over longer periods of time.
5 *Growth*. Most people feel motivated when they believe they are learning new concepts, developing their skills, and improving their minds. When members of a team believe they are growing and developing, motivation remains high.
6 *Leadership*. A leader can be the catalyst for motivation, but, more importantly, a leader works to create the conditions for a team to motivate itself.

Task 13.3

Imagine that you are a team leader. What qualities do you look for in selecting members of your team? As a team member what do you believe are your strengths?

Developing Teams

Developing teams include selection of team members as well as the stages teams go through as they develop, each of which is discussed below.

What Factors are Important in Selecting Team Members?

The responsibility of a leader is to establish a team or appoint new team members. In Chapter 2, we provided Murphy's roles for leadership. One of the roles he identified was that of selector. We would like to suggest that you re-read this section on the selector in Chapter 2 to remind yourself of the importance of that role. Sometimes the task of selection can be accomplished through internal promotion. At other times, external recruitment is involved (Heller, 1999). In addition, there can be instances when both internal and external recruitment are necessary. Whether a team is comprised of members internal to a program or a combination of members both internal and external to the program, it is critical that a leader find the right combination of individuals for the make-up of the team.

In selecting team members, we have found that it is best to take as much time as needed in the selection process. However, our experience has also been that it is quite difficult to do this consistently. In English language programs, the need for a team to work on something often arises quite unexpectedly. As leaders, we often fall into the habit of appointing the more vocal and involved teachers and staff or the ones that have done something well in the past. In addition, we are often under pressure to make appointments on the spot so that the team can get to work quickly. While we understand that these pressures exist and that, sometimes, we have to respond to the immediacy of a given situation, we also believe that teams work better if leaders can take time to think about the individual appointments and follow a list of procedures.

The first step in appointing a team is to create a description of what the team is to accomplish and what the goal or outcome of their work will be. Articulating the goal for a team and describing the task(s) that the team must accomplish to achieve the goal are ultimately important for the team itself, but are critical for the leader as well. It is through this process that a leader develops clarity on exactly what qualities and skills the team members must possess in order to achieve the goal. At the same time, the leader needs to develop a realistic timeline and level of responsibility. Again, these are vital for the team to accomplish its goals. Deciding on these issues is also a self-checking mechanism for the leaders to determine whether the tasks can be accomplished in the given time frame and the extent of the leader's involvement. "Empowerment means managers identifying areas where they can relinquish power in favor of others—and then actually giving up those areas" (Hargie et al., 1999, p. 62).

The next step in the process is to use the carefully articulated goal as a springboard for establishing criteria for membership on the team. By looking carefully at the goal, leaders can draw up a list of essential skills and characteristics that collectively the team members must have. Individuals who fulfill all criteria will be rare, but because the individuals comprise a team, the focus should be on how the team members collectively meet the necessary criteria. Below is a discussion about different roles team members may play.

The final step in the process is to cast the widest possible net. It is important for everyone to feel included. No one wants to feel that they have been passed over. Ask for volunteers or interested parties to review the necessary criteria, to let you know if they are interested in joining a specific team, and to indicate what expertise or skills they bring to the task. Or, you can send out a detailed expression of interest (EOI) to all staff and have them apply. As well as casting a wide net, it also involves all staff in thinking about the team and their own skills. The final decision lies with the leader (or a management team). In some cultural groups, sending out an EOI is not part of the cultural norms; however, we have found that leaders who only choose from amongst their coterie often miss choosing the people best suited to the task. The job of the leader is to make the best possible match and to be on the lookout for individuals with the requisite skills that can be exploited in helping teams achieve their goals. One of the most important skills that a leader can have is to appoint competent individuals to a team who have the potential to meet the expected goal. The leader also needs to choose who will lead the team. Again, the criteria for this choice need to be transparent. Some scholars (e.g., Fogg, 1999) recommend training of team members because not everyone necessarily has the skills, but some staff may want to acquire the skills.

What are the Stages in Team Development?

All people who work together go through a number of different stages as they work to achieve their goals (Handy, 1985; Peck, 1998; Tuckman, 1965). The amount of time that teams spend at each stage changes as does the sequencing of the stages. Also, the fact that a group has passed through a particular stage once does not mean that it will not, as some point, pass through the stage again. Effective leaders will want to become familiar with the different stages of team development so that they know when to leave the team alone to work out its own process or when to intercede to offer some guidance. Effective leaders should consider educating teams about these stages so that they can learn more about the process they are going through and, thus, become more productive. Different researchers have characterized these stages in different ways. Tuckman (1965) proposed four states (forming, storming, norming, and performing). Handy (1985) proposes seven and Peck (1998) offers six stages. We have adapted these models for English language educational contexts and propose the stages shown in Table 13.1.

Individuals who have worked together for a long period of time, such as in a program or department with a stable faculty and staff, may begin a new task at the *maturity* stage and be able to come to solution fairly quickly. However, it is also possible that individuals who have worked together for a long period of time may begin a new task at the *bliss* stage and have to go through a number of different stages in order to come to solution. Different tasks produce different challenges for groups, even for groups who have a long history of working together effectively.

Table 13.1 Stages in Team Development

Stage	Description
Bliss	Everyone in the group seems happy, and everyone gets along. All of the members are committed to a peaceful co-existence. No one disagrees or voices a contrary opinion.
Breakdown	Individuals begin to feel they need to say what is true for them. Getting along becomes less important.
Confusion	Nobody is sure where they stand in relation to the others or how to move forward without conflict. There may also be confusion about what is required. Group members are looking for a structure or framework in which to function.
Dependence	The group feels inadequate about its ability to achieve the goal. Individuals begin to look for support or direction from a source outside of the group on which to depend. Authority may be embodied as an influential person outside of the group or as a set of procedures or rules. The group begins to function as a group of individuals rather than as a group.
Conflict	There is conflict among the group members and the group withdraws from the problem or task in order to focus on the individual conflicts.
Opposition	Individuals take sides and different points of views form. The members of the group begin to recognize themselves as a group with different ideas and opinions.
Maturity	The group begins to focus on the task and on reaching a solution rather than on individuals' differences.

Source: Adapted from Handy (1985) and Peck (1998).

Team Responsibilities

What are the Responsibilities of Team Leaders?

A team leader is a person who presides over the team and coordinates its efforts. The team leader is responsible for monitoring the team's activities and making certain that everyone is working toward agreed upon goals and objectives. A team leader needs to be able to work competently with three different types of responsibilities. There are responsibilities related to the task, towards the group, and for the individuals on the team (Adair, 1985). In terms of responsibilities for the task, a group leader must be able to do the following: (1) engage individuals; (2) define the task; (3) make a plan for completing the task; (4) allocate work relating to the task; (5) control the quality of the work done related to the task; (6) control for the pace and tempo of the work; (7) check performances against the plan; and (8) adjust the plan accordingly.

A team leader also has responsibilities towards the group. These responsibilities include the following: (1) setting standards; (2) maintaining discipline; (3) building team spirit; (4) encouraging and motivating members of the team; and (5) ensuring effective communication within the group.

The third area of responsibility for a team leader is for the individual members of the team. Team leaders must be able: (1) to give honest praise when appropriate; (2) to recognize the strengths of individual team members; (3) to use the strengths to help the team achieve its goal; and (4) to help individuals develop new skills if necessary. In order to maintain a focus on these different responsibilities, some leaders find it useful to post the responsibilities in their offices or work areas and review the list each day.

An informed team leader keeps all three responsibilities—task, group, and individuals—in balance. When task, team, and individual needs coincide, a team will be able to create its optimum performance level and achieve its goal. In most teams, it is not possible to satisfy all individual and group objectives simultaneously. There has to be a trade-off or a balance among the three responsibilities, and achieving this balance is one of the greatest challenges for team leaders.

What are the Roles and Responsibilities of Team Members?

In order for a team to work well, it is important for leaders to be aware of different personality types that can affect team interaction as well as possible roles and responsibilities that need to be assumed within the team. In an effective, high performance team, team members are aware they are playing important key roles. The role of the team leader is to help them do this effectively. We have found a useful taxonomy for this purpose. In Table 13.2 team member roles are matched to team member responsibilities. It provides a succinct and clear outline of the specific tasks that the group may need to accomplish. If a team has only a few members, tasks may need to be doubled or tripled in order to make sure that the team's needs are covered. These member roles can also be used when selecting team members.

Belbin (1993, p. 98) contrasts two different leadership styles that are possible for leaders: the solo leader with the team leader. These two different leadership styles can be characterized as outlined in Table 13.3.

Belbin and his associates analyzed two world leaders to exemplify these two styles of leadership—Margaret Thatcher and Ronald Reagan. They found that "Thatcher's natural team role was that of Shaper; . . . she was not seen as consultative or diplomatic or interested in others, but as hard-driving and aggressive. The team role for which she has the least affinity is that of Team Worker" (1993, p. 102). Reagan, on the other hand, scored strongly "on all the social team roles, with his lead role being Resource Investigator . . . His weakest team roles [were] the cerebral ones, Plan and Monitor Evaluator." How did these leadership styles affect their leadership? Thatcher's downfall came about from rejection from her own team. Reagan, on the other hand, survived tests of his leadership (e.g. Irangate) so that when he left office, because of the US two-term limit for Presidents, he "had lost little of his personal popularity and the American public forgave all" (ibid., p. 103).

Table 13.2 Team Roles and Responsibilities

Team Member Roles	Team Member Responsibilities
Task master	This is the person who has the drive and passion for the task and the person who spurs the team to move ahead and take action. This person keeps the team focused on the task.
Idea person	This person is intellectually the dominant person in the group and is the person who has the most original and imaginative ideas. However, this person may not take criticism well or be good at hammering out the details of the ideas s/he generates.
Critic	This person is analytical and is able to carefully dissect ideas and find flaws in ideas and arguments. This person can sometimes be tactless and aloof.
Resource person	This person has a good sense of humor and is sociable and relaxed. The resource person thinks out of the box and has many contacts and resources. This is a person who can help the group maintain a sense of balance.
Implementer	This person is the practical organizer who turns ideas into manageable tasks. This person is good at making schedules, charts, and plans. While this person is not a vision person and is not very exciting in terms of unusual ideas, s/he gets things done.
Supporter	This person holds the team together, offering supportive comments, listening carefully, and encouraging all group members. This person is likeable and non-competitive.
Closer	This person checks the details and is relentless in following up with the team members and following through on assigned tasks that s/he may have. This is the person that makes certain the goal is accomplished and the group members follow through on their individual commitments. The closer in a group is not always popular with the other group members.
Coordinator	This person clarifies goals, promotes decision-making, and delegates well. This person is also mature, confident, and a good chairperson. The coordinator can be seen as manipulative.

Source: Adapted from Belbin (2004) and Heller (1999).

Although leadership styles can be a result of personality, one can learn different styles. As you lead teams, you can choose your style of leadership—at the ends of the Solo Leader–Team Leader range or you can choose somewhere in the middle. However, whichever you choose, has its own consequences. You need to carefully examine your particular context, the task for which the team is being put together, and the types of relationships your team members expect in a team leader before you decide your own style.

Table 13.3 Team Leader Styles

Solo Leader	Team Leader
Plays unlimited role: the Solo Leader interferes in everything.	**Chooses to limit role** to preferred team roles—delegates roles to others.
Strives for conformity: the Solo Leader tries to mould people to particular standards.	**Builds on diversity:** the Team Leader values differences between people.
Collects acolytes: the Solo Leader collects admirers and sycophants.	**Seeks talent:** the Team Leader is not threatened by people with special abilities.
Directs subordinates: subordinates take their leads and cues from the Solo Leader.	**Develops colleagues:** the Team Leader encourages growth of personal strengths.
Projects objectives: the Solo Leader makes it plain what everyone is expected to do.	**Creates mission:** the Team Leader projects the vision which others can act on as they see fit.

Source: Belbin (1993).

Qualities of Effective Teams

What are the Factors that Affect Team Quality?

In order to implement effective teams, leaders need to understand the factors that make teams successful. Zoglio (1993, 2002) presents a clear picture of the factors that high-performance teams have in common. We have found these factors useful in educational environments in creating effective teams and in identifying potential team problems:

- *Commitment*. In order to be successful, a team needs a clear sense of direction. When the team is committed to the purpose and goals of a program, they understand how their work interfaces with the overall mission and goals of the program. They see how the work they do in their team benefits the program as a whole. In order to enhance team commitment, leaders must connect the team's work to the mission and purpose of the program. The time spent up front making certain that all team members are on the same track will improve commitment and reduce the number of derailments that can occur later on.

- *Contribution*. The effectiveness of a team is in direct proportion to the skills of its members. Teams need people with different skills and abilities. An affective leader understands this concept and appoints members to teams that have the requisite technical skills and interpersonal skills (see Chapter 5 on emotional intelligence for further information) so that all members of the team can make a contribution. If only a few team members shoulder the workload burden, then the team runs the risk of member burnout and resentment and, ultimately, will not be able to achieve its goal. In order to enhance team member contributions, team members need to be informed. Leaders also need to solicit input from members and support an atmosphere of collegiality. For example, if members are not offering suggestions, invite them to do so. If members miss team meetings, follow up with an email and let them know they are missed. Team leaders should always show appreciation for individual member initiative and contribution. Hargie et al. (1999) recognize the importance of celebrating individual and team achievements in strengthening relationships among team members and in motivating them.

• *Communication*. In order for a team to work well together, the team members need to be able to say what they think. Most teams do not begin at this stage of development (see What are the stages in team development?, pp. 207–208; Handy, 1985; Peck, 1998). Rather, they begin to work together by saying things they think others want to hear. However, in order for a team to work effectively together to achieve the intended goal, individual members must be able to say what they think, share unpopular ideas, and risk making others upset. When there is an atmosphere of concern and trust, communication can be honest even if the ideas being offered are not popular. Zoglio (1993, 2002) focuses on the notion of positive communication. Positive communication is characterized as individuals talking about what they like, need, or want relative to the intended goal. This type of communication is quite different from individuals venting about anything that annoys them. In order to develop team communication, leaders can both model effective communication strategies and help facilitise these strategies in other team members (see Chapter 12 on communicative tools for effective leadership).

• *Cooperation*. The success for a team to a large degree depends on the degree of interdependence within the team. In order to encourage cooperation, leaders must highlight the impact that each individual's work has on the overall outcome of the team. We have found the F.A.C.T.S. model (Zoglio, 2002) to be an effective guide in identifying behaviors that are important to support the work of the team. F.A.C.T.S. stands for *follow-through* (Team members do what they say they will do), *accuracy* (Team members do it right the first time), *creativity* (Team members think out of the box and are supported by their colleagues for taking risks even when the ideas are rejected), *timeliness* (Team members respect their own time and the time of others), and *spirit* (Team members are a family).

• *Conflict management*. It is inevitable that teams experience conflict from time to time. In fact, conflict is a necessary stage in the process of team development (Handy, 1985; Peck, 1998). The problem is not that differences exist among team members; it is rather in how the differences are managed. There are many strategies that leaders can employ to help teams deal with differences that result in conflict. For specific information on strategies, see Chapter 12 in this volume and Palmer and Christison (2007).

• *Change management*. Tom Peters, author of *Thriving on chaos* (1988), believes that teams must not only respond to change, they must actually initiate it. In order to help teams manage change, leaders must be clear on the inherent threats they see on the horizon and balance these threats by assisting teams in identifying inherent opportunities. For a more complete discussion of these concepts, see Chapter 11, and Chapter 7 in this volume, for a more in-depth discussion of opportunities and threats within the concept of developing personal mission statements and strategic plans.

- *Connections*. Effective teams need to form connections in three important ways. The team needs to connect to the larger program or organization, to each other, and to the goal or purpose for the team. Teams that are able to connect in these three important ways are primed to accomplish their goals and find satisfaction in the process.

- *Feedback*. Another factor we have found essential for teams to be effective is feedback. Teams need to constantly evaluate their progress towards their goal, as well as their communications. For example, at the end of meetings, we have often circulated a brief evaluation, in which team members can evaluate both the communication during the meeting and what was achieved. Given that many people find meetings unproductive, this focuses team members on the goals of the meeting and on their own communication style.

Conducting Team Meetings

Meetings are very important if they are conducted and managed well. Through meetings, team members can stay informed about a project. Meetings also help develop and maintain a sense of solidarity and a spirit of cooperation in a shared mission. In meetings, everyone gets the same message, at the same time, removing some of the possibility for miscommunication when information is repeated. In addition, leaders can read non-verbal cues (e.g., head nodding, folded arms, etc.) to determine the level of support for particular ideas.

Determining When to Call a Meeting

Conducting team meetings is an important responsibility of team leaders. Before a leader calls a meeting, it is important to determine whether a face-to-face meeting is required. In order to do this, it is important to ask the following questions:

1   What is the purpose of the meeting? Meetings have six basic purposes. If a meeting does not meet one of these six purposes, then perhaps a face-to-face meeting is not needed.

    (a)   Informational—to disseminate information that must be given in a face-to-face format or conduct training sessions on new information.

    (b)   Identification—to identify problems and to determine what is working and what it not working.

    (c)   Discussion—to gather information and to find out what people know, to determine the strengths of individual members on the team.

    (d) Solution—to discuss complex problems that require extensive information; to share information; to reach agreements.

    (e) Community building—to build commitment among group members.

    (f) Planning—to plan for the future or to chart a course of action.

2   What information do you want to convey or collect?

    (a) Could the information be conveyed in another format, such as a memo, email message, or phone call?

    (b) What is the time frame? Phone calls or memos take much less time and are sometimes preferred to meetings.

    (c) What information do team members need in advance of the meeting in order to be prepared?

3   What should the team leader do to prepare for the meeting?

    (a) Do you understand the issues?

    (b) Is there an agenda?

    (c) Have you distributed the agenda to the team members?

    (d) Have necessary assignments been made for the meeting?

    (e) Have the necessary arrangements been made for the meeting?

    (f) Have a date, place, and time for the meeting been set? Has this information been communicated to the team members?

4   Can all team members attend the meeting?

    (a) Be patient and flexible in trying to set up meeting times.

    (b) Schedule well in advance of the meeting date.

5   How much will the meeting cost? Consider both financial and human resources. Meeting on a holiday or in the evening may not have a heavy financial cost, but it may weigh heavily on human resources.

6   What is the anticipated outcome of the meeting?

    (a) Think about what the meeting is to accomplish; a leader needs to know how to guide the meeting.

    (b) Anticipated outcomes are different from solutions.

7   What group processes or decision-making formats will be used?

    (a) Plan the content and what will be discussed.

    (b) Plan for the processes that will be used, e.g., brainstorming, open discussion, structured discussion, individual reports.

8   How will you keep a record of the meeting? Make sure minutes are taken and that the minutes are disseminated.

Steps in Planning and Managing

Managing and planning meetings are also the responsibility of a team leader. We outline some important steps in planning and managing below:

1   Decide on the purpose of the meeting (see item 1 under "Determining when to call a meeting" above).

2   Plan the meeting's content and format (i.e., What will be discussed? Will a large or small group format work best?).

3   Prepare yourself:

   (a)   Review your reasons for holding the meeting.
   (b)   Know the information.
   (c)   Picture the meeting running smoothly.

4   Prepare others:

   (a)   Create an agenda.
   (b)   Determine what will be on the consent agenda. These are items that are non-controversial and routine actions. Avoid consent agendas that contain items that are too time-consuming, highly controversial, and non-action items. Purely informational items are not included on a consent agenda.
   (c)   Review the goals of the meeting.
   (d)   Determine who will keep a record of the meeting and let them know in advance.

5   Invite the right number and mix of participants. Is this a meeting for the entire team or part of the team? Who are the cooperators? Competitors? What is the best mix of team members?

6   Decide on the format for the team meeting. Who will introduce the topic of the meeting and focus members on the purpose? How long will discussion last?

7   Decide on the processes that will be used. How will decisions be reached? By majority vote? Consensus?

8   Think about how to manage the meeting's process effectively. What will you do to keep the meeting running smoothly? What will you do to ensure that decisions are reached?

9   Establish ground rules for the meeting:

   (a)   Use "I" statement.
   (b)   Address issues rather than people.
   (c)   Come prepared to contribute.
   (d)   Listen to others' concerns.
   (e)   Do not interrupt.

(f)   Avoid abusive language.

(g)   Do not raise your voice.

(h)   Stay flexible.

10   Follow up. See that a record of the meeting is given to all individuals present at the meeting. The record should include a list of persons who will do what, when, and how. Contact each person and make certain they understand their assignment or obtain this clarification during the actual meeting and let each person know that you will not be contacting them later and what your expectations are for the completion of the tasks.

Planning for and managing meetings are not easy tasks for a team leader. The best rule of leadership for team meetings is this: *Never waste people's time.* Do not just meet to meet. Do not have a meeting if you do not have a specific reason to meet and a goal that you want to accomplish. When people have a reason to meet, they will perform better as individuals and as a team. When teams work together to achieve a common goal, they discover many reasons for regular meetings.

Virtual teams

What is a Virtual Team?

When most educators think about teams, we do so in terms of conventional teams—teams that meet face-to-face and have routine contact. Because the world of English language teaching and learning is continually expanding and changing with programs and teachers in different countries and continents forging partnerships, it may also be important for a leader to think about virtual teams. A virtual team is *a team whose members share a common goal or purpose but are separated by distance, time, and, sometimes, organizational boundaries* (Duarte & Snyder, 1999). In such a team, members are linked only by communication technologies.

In the past few years, we have been involved in both research and materials development projects with individuals from different English language programs and from different English language programs in different countries. In one case, the team of researchers collected data from six different locations and stored it in a common database which automatically identified the location source and, then, integrated it into the already existing data that all team members could access. In another case, four teachers from four different countries contributed to a materials development project by accessing a secure website. All teachers were able to respond to and update information on a daily basis, and participate in both synchronous and asynchronous discussions. Without these virtual teams, the work could not have been achieved.

What Challenges do Virtual Teams Face?

Virtual team members face a unique set of challenges; yet, as with conventional teams, leaders must follow a set of principles in order to build a strong team foundation for the team and its work. Most of the principles for virtual teams are the same ones that guide conventional teams and have been covered in this chapter, such as establishing a purpose and goal for the team, understanding roles and responsibilities, and establishing effective communication practices (Jude-York et al., 2000; Lipnack & Stamps, 1997). There are no easy answers or foolproof ways to launch a virtual team. Just as with a conventional team, a leader needs to pay attention to the basic principles that support successful performance and achievement of team goals.

Conclusion

In order to work effectively with either face-to-face or virtual teams, leaders must understand the types of activities that teams are good at doing so that they can create an ideal match between the task and how to accomplish the task. In addition, leaders must also understand how to motivate teams and select team members. Teams go through stages in their development. Effective leaders are able to recognize these stages and work with teams accordingly. Knowing group and leader responsibilities and recognizing the qualities of effective teams are also important skills for leaders. In this chapter, we have presented information that we believe is essential for leaders in English language education to have as they develop skills in building effective teams.

References

Adair, J. (1985). *Effective leadership*. Aldershot: Gower Press.

Belbin, R.M. (2004). *Management teams: Why they succeed or fail*, 2nd edn. Burlington, MA: Elsevier Butterworth-Heinemann.

Cole, B. (2001). When you're in charge: Tips for leading teams. *Kiwanis Magazine*. March.

Douglas, T. (1983). *Groups: Understanding people gathered together*. London: Tavistock.

Duarte, D.L. & Snyder, N.T. (1999). Mastering virtual teams: Strategies, tools, and techniques that succeed. San Francisco: Jossey-Bass Publishers.

Fogg, D. (1999). *Implementing your strategic plan*. New York: American Management Association.

Grazier, P. (1998). Team motivation. *Employee Involvement Network*. January.

Handy, C.B. (1985). *Understanding organizations*, 3rd edn. Harmondsworth: Penguin Press.

Hargie, O.D.W., Dickson, D., & Tourish, D. (1999). *Communication in management*. Aldershot: Gower.

Heller, R. (1999). *Learning to lead*. New York: DK Publishing, Inc.

Jude-York, D., Davis, L., & Wise S. (2000). *Mastering virtual teams*. San Francisco: Jossey-Bass.

Lipnack, J., & Stamps, J. (1997). *Virtual teams: Reaching across space, time, and organizations with technology*. New York: John Wiley & Sons, Ltd.

Murphy, E.C. (1996). *Leadership IQ*. New York: John Wiley & Sons, Ltd.

Palmer, A., & Christison, M.A. (2007). *Seeking the heart of teaching*. Ann Arbor, MI: The University of Michigan Press.

Peck, M.S. (1998). *The different drum: Community making and peace.* New York: Simon and Schuster.

Peters, T. (1988). *Thriving on chaos: Handbook for a management revolution.* New York: HarperCollins.

Tuckman, B.W. (1965). *Psychological Bulletin. 63,* 384–399.

Zoglio, S.W. (1993). *Teams at work: Seven keys to success.* Doylestown, PA: Tower Hill Press.

Zoglio, S.W. (2002). Seven keys to building great workteams. Available at: http://www.team buildinginc.com/article_7keys_zopgko.htm. Accessed March 5, 2007.

Part III

ELT Leadership in Practice

Introduction

Parts I and II of this volume focused on the leader—on the roles and responsibilities of leaders and on the development of leadership skills. Part III of this volume takes on a different focus. In this part of the book, we turn our attention to looking at ELT leadership in practice. We offer three examples of how ELT professionals are working with leadership models and concepts in their teaching and research. In Chapter 14, MaryAnn Christison and Denise E. Murray present the results of a research study they conducted with ELT leaders using Murphy's model for leadership IQ. The aim of the research was to see how effective ELT leaders were in implementing the eight different roles that constitute the concept of leadership IQ.

Kathleen M. Bailey, David Nunan, and Jaala A. Thibault discuss their research in Chapter 15. In this study the three researchers surveyed former TESOL Presidents in order to determine how positions of leadership change leaders. Since TESOL is such a large and diverse association that serves a broad constituency, the position of TESOL President is considered by most ELT professionals to be one of the most challenging and difficult for leaders. How does such an experience change an individual? Are these changes positive or negative? What did these leaders learn from this challenging leadership opportunity?

Teachers often have negative attitudes and experiences with supervision. In Chapter 16, Juliet Padernal discusses her experience in developing servant-leadership skills through a cooperative development approach to teacher supervision. Padernal wanted to know what academic leaders, such as department heads, might do to greatly minimize, if not totally eliminate, the pervading negative thoughts and feelings towards supervisory visits that have great potential for professional benefit. She also wanted to know how to help academic leaders, whose responsibilities include teacher supervision and evaluation, deepen and expand the processes of accountability, as well as how teachers can be empowered for their own professional growth. What tools or strategies are available?

Chapter 14

Developing Leadership IQ in ELT

MaryAnn Christison and Denise E. Murray

Introduction

In Chapter 2, Christison and Murray provide an introduction to Murphy's model of Leadership IQ (1996) and offer ideas about its application to English language education. The concept of Leadership IQ has its roots in the personal intelligences (i.e., interpersonal and intrapersonal intelligences) in Howard Gardner's model of Multiple Intelligences (Gardner, 1983 1985, 1993) and more specifically in the concept of Emotional Intelligence (EI) (Goleman, 1998; Mayer et al., 2000). More specifically, Murray and Christison discuss the importance of emotional intelligence in the development of effective leadership in English language education in Chapter 5 of this volume. The model of Leadership IQ has been most prominent in leadership development in the business world. Nevertheless, we believe that the model of Leadership IQ can be very useful in understanding leadership development in English language education.

Except in K-12 environments (e.g., school leaders and principals) (Marzano et al., 2005), there has been little research on educational leadership. In addition, there has been only minimal research on leadership across cultures (Hofstede, 1990, 2001; Mead, 1994; Murphy, 1996). Determining possible cultural influences on leadership and management styles in English language education is a key factor in understanding effective leadership in this discipline.

The aim of this research was to investigate the cultural dimensions of the management and leadership styles of English language program leaders by describing how ELT leaders responded to a Leadership IQ survey. By conducting this preliminary research we hope to add to the body of educational research and the research in English language education on leadership. The study is based on the theoretical framework for Leadership IQ (see Table 14.1).

In this model for Leadership IQ (see Chapter 2 in this volume for a more detailed account of Murphy's research and model), Murphy identified eight roles associated with effective workleaders, *individuals who demonstrated leadership excellence and were considered by both their peers and superiors to have a high leadership IQ.* These eight roles along with their purposes are listed in Table 14.1. The main premise of this model is that effective

Table 14.1 Theoretical Framework for Leadership IQ

Workleader Roles	Purposes of the Roles
• **The selector** selects the right people	• Select for the customer
• **The connector** connects them to the right cause	• Build and enhance relationships
• **The problem solver** solves problems as they arise	• Produce results
• **The evaluator** evaluates progress towards objectives	• Enhance individual performance
• **The negotiator** negotiates resolutions to conflicts	• Achieve consensus on what needs to be done
• **The healer** heals the wounds inflicted by changes	• Mend the fabric of organizational life
• **The protector** protects their cultures from the perils of crisis	• Diagnose and respond to threats to the organizational well being
• **The synergizer** synergizes all stakeholders in a way that enables them to achieve improvement together	• Create a whole greater than the sum of its parts

leadership is a measure of how well and how consistently leaders are able to apply the basic theoretical framework and the principles of leadership in the workplace, in this case, in English language education.

Methodology

Subjects

There were 92 subjects in this study. At the time they responded to the Leadership IQ Questionnaire, they were all employed as English language program leaders and none of the subjects had received training or information about leadership IQ or Murphy's model. They were working in 21 different countries. The largest pool of subjects came from Australia, with the U.S.A. ranking second. The data for non-English-speaking countries was aggregated. Data on subject and country are presented in Table 14.2. The 92 respondents were employed in English language education in 21 different countries, not necessarily their countries of origin (see Table 14.3).

Four different subject profiles emerged relative to country of origin and country of employment. These three profiles and the frequency of the profile among participants appear in Table 14.4. The largest category of subjects was those who were born in and were working in an English-speaking country. The smallest category of subjects was those who were born in a non-English-speaking country and were working in an English-

Table 14.2 Country of Origin

	Frequency	(%)	Valid (%)	Cumulative (%)
Australia	23	25.0	25.0	27.2
Canada	3	3.3	3.3	25.6
New Zealand	2	2.2	2.2	31.1
South Africa	2	2.2	2.2	33.3
the UK	4	4.3	4.4	37.8
the USA	28	30.4	31.1	68.9
Non-English-speaking[1]	28	30.4	31.1	100.0
Missing information	2	2.2		
Total	90	97.8	100.0	

Note: [1] The countries represented in this sample were: Austria, Brazil, Costa Rica, Guatemala, India, Iran, Japan, Mexico, Peru, Poland, Russia, Singapore, South Africa, Thailand. Non-English-speaking is simply a cover term used for countries with fewer than five respondents.

Table 14.3 Country of Employment

	Frequency	(%)	Valid (%)	Cumulative (%)
Australia	25	27.2	27.5	27.5
Canada	3	3.3	3.3	30.8
New Zealand	1	1.1	1.1	31.9
the USA	21	22.8	23.1	54.9
Non-English-speaking[1]	41	44.6	45.1	100.0
Respondents not answering	1	1.1		
Total	92	100.0	100.0	

Note: [1] The countries represented in this sample were: Cambodia, China, Costa Rica, Guatemala, Hong Kong, Japan, Korea, Malaysia, Mexico, Peru, Russia, Singapore, the Slovak Republic, Taiwan, Thailand, UAE. Non-English-speaking is simply a cover term used for countries with fewer than five respondents.

speaking country. The total number of subjects working in non-English-speaking countries was 40 with 50 subjects working in English-speaking countries.

There were 69 females and 23 males, ranging in age from under 30 to over 60, with the largest number of leaders in the age range of 40-50 years of age and following with a close second in the age range of 50 to 60 years of age (see Table 14.5).

The highest level of education obtained among the respondents varied greatly. Seven respondents had a post-secondary diploma of some sort. Seventeen respondents had an undergraduate college education. Fifty-one had done graduate work and 50 had

Table 14.4 Country of Birth and Currently Working

	Frequency	(%)	Valid (%)	Cumulative (%)
Born and working in ESC	44	47.8	48.9	48.9
Born in ESC but working in non-ESC	18	19.8	20.0	68.9
Born and working in non-ESC	22	23.9	24.4	93.3
Born in non-ESC and working in ESC	6	6.5	6.7	100.0
		2.2		
Respondents not answering	2			
Total	92	100	100	

Notes: ESC = English-speaking country
Non-ESC = non-English-speaking country

Table 14.5 Age of Respondents

	Frequency	(%)	Valid (%)	Cumulative (%)
Fewer than 30 years	7	7.6	7.8	7.8
30 to < 40 years	17	18.5	18.9	27.8
40 to < 50 years	32	34.8	35.6	60.0
50 to < 60 years	31	33.7	34.4	94.4
60 years and above	3	3.3	3.3	100.0
Missing responses	2	2		
Total	92	100.0	100.0	

completed a Masters degree. Fifteen leaders had completed the PhD degree and another one was working towards a PhD degree.

The subjects held many different positions of leadership. There were 34 program directors, 10 deputy directors, 15 coordinators, and 10 managers. The other subjects who responded categorized themselves into 14 other leadership positions that varied from program to program.

The number of years spent teaching was between five and 30 or more years (see Table 14.6). Thirty-one subjects had between 20 and <30 years of teaching with 29 subjects with 10 to <20 years teaching comprising the second largest group of respondents.

The number of years of experience in administration was less than five years to more than 30 years, with the largest number of respondents falling into the category of fewer than 5 years of administrative experience (see Table 14.7).

The programs in which the subjects participated varied greatly in size, operating budgets, number of faculty, number of office staff, number of English language learners in the program, number of employees for which they were responsible, and number of teachers (see Table 14.8). Programs ranged in operating budgets from US$54,000 to US$40,000,000. The total number of students ranged from 61 to 12,000 and the number of teachers from 23 to 1,500. The total number of employees that subjects were responsible for ranged from 64 to 200 and the total number of English language learners from 61 to 100,000.

Instrumentation

We used a management and leadership questionnaire (see Appendix 14.1) in order to investigate leader practices in relationship to the leadership IQ model. The questionnaire

Table 14.6 Years of Teaching Experience

	Frequency	(%)	Valid (%)	Cumulative (%)
< 5 years teaching	7	7.6	7.8	7.8
5 to < 10 years teaching	18	19.6	20.0	26.7
10 to < 20 years teaching	29	31.5	32.2	62.2
20 to < 30 years teaching	31	33.7	34.4	96.7
30 or more years teaching	5	5.4	5.6	100.0
Missing respondents	2	2.2		
Total	92	100.0	100.0	

Table 14.7 Years of Administrative Experience

	Frequency	(%)	Valid (%)	Cumulative (%)
Fewer than 5 years	35	38.0	42.7	42.7
5 to < 10 years	20	21.7	24.4	67.1
10 to < 20 years	20	21.7	24.4	91.5
20 to < 30 years	7	7.6	8.5	100.0
Missing respondents	10	10.9		
Total	92	100.0	100.0	

Table 14.8 Program Data

	N	Minimum	Maximum
Program size—USD	21	$54,000	$40,000,000
Program size—office staff	47	2	280
Program size—faculty	2	10	16
Program size—teachers	17	4	125
Program size—students	61	20	12,000
No. of employees responsible for	64	1	200
No. of teachers responsible for	23	4	1,500
No. of students responsible for	61		100,000

was based on Murphy's original research and adapted from his original questionnaire. Since Murphy's original questionnaire contained scenarios for business, it was not appropriate to use in conducting research on leadership practices in education. For this study, we created a similar questionnaire with scenarios appropriate for English language education (see Appendix 2.1). There were 27 questions presented in a multiple-choice format with a, b, and c options. The 27 questions presented were based on 23 language education scenarios across different sectors. Each question was related to one of the workleader roles (i.e., Selector, Connector, Problem Solver, Evaluator, Negotiator, Healer, Protector, or Synergizer) presented in Murphy's leadership IQ model.

Data Collection

The sample was not random or representative but rather an opportunity sample. Since the authors both work broadly in international education and with English education programs around the world, we asked each program administrator with whom we worked during an 18-month period to complete the questionnaire. In addition, we circulated the questionnaire among program administrators with whom we were acquainted and with whom we had worked previously. We used both hard copy and electronic versions of the questionnaires. Respondents were asked to take as much time as they wished to complete the personal data portion and the leadership IQ questionnaire. There was no time limit. We specifically asked the subjects not to consult anyone else in determining how to respond to the various questions and scenarios.

For each question, respondents were asked to circle the answer for the action they would most likely perform in the situation. We asked respondents to think about how they would act in that role if they had to make the decision. For example, consider the scenario below which appears as item #1 in the leadership questionnaire.

One of your staff who has always been effective in her job shows negative signs such as tiredness, loss of a sense of humor, and general malaise.

1. It's best to:

    a.   Discuss the situation with her as soon as you notice the changes

    b.   Discuss the situation with her as soon as possible after you witness a specific incident

    c.   Wait and only discuss it with her after you have several specific examples or other staff members mention the signs, too

2. When you discuss these changes in your staff, it's best to:

    a.   Discuss these signs only as they relate to her performance of her job

    b.   Discuss these signs as they might affect all aspects of her life

    c.   Avoid discussing the causes of the problem, focusing instead on how she can change

In order to encourage subjects to respond to the questionnaire, we scored each response and provided an analysis based on the Leadership IQ model for those who requested it.

Data Analysis

Each of the questions on the Leadership IQ survey was analyzed and (see Appendix 2.2, p. 44 for a complete analysis of the questionnaire) and aligned with the theoretical framework for Leadership IQ (see Table 14.9).

Once we had analyzed the survey questions, using the Statistical Package for the Social Sciences (SPSS), we did a frequency count of the number of most appropriate responses given by the subjects for each question on the survey and calculated the percentage. The analysis appears in Figure 14.1.

These rankings were then compared to the theoretical model for leadership IQ and rank ordered, with the highest ranking going to the question that received the greatest number of correct answers and the lowest to the question with the fewest correct answers. The results of this analysis appear in Table 14.10. A summary table of workleader roles in relation to survey questions appears in Table 14.11.

Results

Survey Questions

Percentages for number of correct answers for this group of leaders in English language education ranged from 6.52 percent of respondents giving the correct answer to

Table 14.9 Correct Answers to Questions and Workleader Roles

Correct Answers for Questions	Demonstrated Workleader Role
1. Discuss the situation with her as soon as possible after you witness a specific incident.	(b) Healer
2. Discuss these signs only as they related to her performance of her job.	(a) Healer
3. Listen to her problems and tell her several places where she might get help.	(b) Healer
4. Tell her that since this affects students, she has put you in a very awkward position.	(a) Protector
5. "Can you work on that web page later? There are a number of students who need help. When the student assistant comes back from lunch, let her deal with the front office and let's talk about the web page then."	(c) Problem Solver
6. To draw specific information from both faculty, but also give them opportunity to discuss freely between themselves.	(c) Protector
7. Adjourn the meeting for a couple of days.	(a) Protector
8. "You've clearly been an excellent instructor here for many years, so your last two semester student evaluations really seem odd. But, I don't want to talk about them first—let's talk about you. How do you feel about the program? About the students and your job?"	(a) Selector
9. "Laura, I've asked you in to discuss your separation from our program. We've discussed your evaluations and performance many times over the past year and there's been no improvement. So, it would be best for all of us if we went our separate ways. You'll need to go to the director of administration to arrange for our final check, turning in the keys and so on. She's expecting you."	(a) Selector
10. Do an adequate needs analysis and then mobilize for action.	(b) Synergizer
11. Invite them to participate, but don't use a lot of effort to get them to participate; instead, focus on the faculty who are excited about this change.	(c) Synergizer

Table 14.9 Continued

Correct Answers for Questions	Demonstrated Workleader Role
12. What are you doing?	(b) Problem Solver
13. The way work is organized.	(a) Problem Solver
14. "I understand that you're angry. Your job is to coordinate your program and tell me if you have problems. You've done that, so now it's my problem, not yours. Let me do my job and you do yours, okay?"	(a) Protector
15. Admit your mistake and try to remedy it immediately.	(c) Healer
16. Talk with each person individually so you can assess the issues for yourself.	(b) Protector
17. "I can understand the faculty's concerns here. What I hear you say is that they can't see the point in agreeing to a three-year contract when they don't know whether there will even be the same district next year. Do I understand this correctly?"	(a) Negotiator
18. Give him a few days off to sort out his problems, but remind him that the purpose is for him to get back to his usual high level of performance.	(a) Healer
19. A very specific form with few written notes from the evaluator.	(b) Evaluator
20. Arrange two meetings with her. In the first, explain the review process and review with her the draft of goals she is to work towards in the first quarter.	(b) Evaluator
21. You thank her for her input and enthusiasm. You tell her that you look forward to her playing a major role on the committee.	(c) Connector
22. You tell him you understand his concern, but are pleased he wants to be on the committee. You tell him that you're sure with him and Deanna as core people in the committee, the recommendations will be excellent.	(c) Connector
23. You tell her you value her opinion and that it's important to build a team that can work well together. So, you ask her to think about all the potential problems and prepare a list that you can use later with the whole committee. You tell her that it's important for the committee to address all of the real issues.	(c) Connector

continued

Table 14.9 Continued

Correct Answers for Questions	Demonstrated Workleader Role
24. You and the staff member together fill out the evaluation form rating her performance.	(a) Evaluator
25. You thank the Dean for his confidence in your program and tell him you know you could develop a quality program for these students. However, you need his assurance that you'd be granted additional resources, not just to run that program, but to support all the important work you do.	(b) Negotiator
26. In an office or conference room with the interviewers and applicant sitting side by side.	(b) Selector
27. Ask questions so the candidate will tell you their work history.	(b) Selector

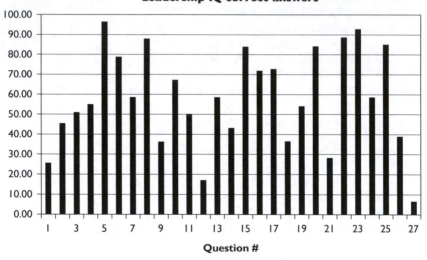

Figure 14.1 Questionnaire Rankings

question 27, to 96.74 percent of the respondents giving the correct answer to question 5. Clearly there was a difficulty level present for the questions on the survey. Fifty percent or higher percentages were realized for 18 of the questions on the survey, with 50 percent or lower percentages realized for 9 of the questions on the survey. Two-thirds of the questions ranked 50 percent or higher in terms of difficulty rankings.

Table 14.10 Rankings for Survey Questions and Workleader Roles

Survey Question	Percentage Correct	Difficulty Ranking	Workleader Role
5	96.74	1	Problem Solver
23	92.39	2	Connector
8	88.04	3	Selector
22	88.04	3	Connector
25	84.78	4	Negotiator
15	83.70	5	Healer
20	83.70	5	Evaluator
6	79.35	6	Protector
17	72.83	7	Negotiator
16	71.74	8	Protector
10	67.39	9	Synergizer
7	58.70	10	Protector
13	58.70	10	Problem Solver
24	58.70	10	Evaluator
4	55.43	11	Protector
19	54.35	12	Evaluator
3	51.09	13	Healer
11	50.00	14	Synergizer
2	45.65	15	Healer
14	43.48	16	Protector
26	39.13	17	Selector
9	36.96	18	Selector
18	36.96	18	Healer
21	28.26	19	Connector
1	26.09	20	Healer
12	17.39	21	Problem Solver
27	6.52	22	Selector

Workleaders Roles

The workleader role associated with the highest ranked question was Problem Solver. The workleader role associated with the lowest ranked questions was Selector. The workleader roles associated with the five highest ranked questions were Connector, Healer, Negotiator, Problem Solver, and Selector. With the exception of Negotiator,

Table 14.11 Summary of Workleader Roles

Workleader Roles	Survey Questions
Connector	21, 22, 23
Evaluator	19, 20, 24
Healer	2, 3, 15, 18, 20
Negotiator	17, 25
Problem Solver	5, 12, 13
Protector	4, 6, 14, 16
Selector	8, 9, 26, 27
Synergizer	10, 11

these were the same workleader roles associated with the five lowest ranked questions. All eight workleader roles appeared in questions ranked in the top 50 percent. Evaluator, Negotiator, and Synergizer did not appear in questions ranked below 50 percent, but all other workleader roles did.

Discussion

Subjects

Although we relied on an opportunity sample for this study, we were able to collect data from subjects working in 21 different countries and from 20 different countries of origin, mirroring to some extent the situation for English language education programs worldwide. Forty-four percent of the subjects were employed in English language education in non-English-speaking countries. This speaks to the growth of English as a world language and the demand for English language education around the world. However, only six of the subjects were born in a non-English-speaking country and then found employment in an English-speaking country. Since this is a sample of opportunity rather than a representative sample, we do not know if this profile is consistent for leaders in English language education or whether it is an anomaly associated with these data.

The data in Table 14.4 indicate that very few individuals under 30 are working as administrators and leaders in language education programs. Seventy percent of the respondents in leadership positions were between 40–60 years of age. This profile suggests that two factors may be influencing the results. One might be that leaders rise from the ranks of experienced teachers. If this is the case, then it is not surprising that few subjects were under 30. Most individuals do not finish their college undergraduate education or teaching qualification until age 23 or 24. It would be difficult to complete the requirements for the qualification and garner more than four to five years of teaching before age 30. We assume there is some basis for this interpretation since approximately two-thirds of the respondents had between 10 and <30 years of teaching experience.

Many educators consider people who are in the first five years of teaching to be novice teachers. Another factor that could be influencing the age of leaders in English language education is that we make better leaders as we get older because we develop more of the qualities consistent with effective leadership, such as patience and a broader experience base from which to make decisions.

The level of education of leaders varied greatly with some leaders having only a diploma of some kind while other leaders had earned a PhD. It seems that factors other than formal education affect whether a person is in a position of leadership in English language education.

In terms of leadership experience, the profile was quite different from experience teaching. Forty-three percent had fewer than five years of administrative experience. Over two-thirds of the subjects had fewer than 10 years of experience. It would seem that the profile for this group was to come to administration much later in one's career and to come from a teaching position into administration. This profile would also mean that there would be very few administrators with over 20 years of administrative experience. In a sense, one could say that leadership in English language education is constantly re-inventing the wheel.

English language education is big business. English language education programs are diverse and require leaders who have varied skills and abilities. One leader managed a US$40 million budget, and office staff of over 40, 125 teachers, and 12,000 students. This requires a person to be skilled at managing budgets and a staff, able to work with a diverse group of people, develop curriculum, make changes to the curriculum, keep records, and offer support to young leaders. As Christison and Lindahl point out in Chapter 3, we expect a great deal from our leaders.

Leadership IQ Questionnaire

There was definitely a difficulty level associated with the various questions on the survey since the percentages of correct responses ranged from 6.52 percent to 96.74 percent. However, given that four of the five workleader roles associated with the questions ranked in the top five are also in the bottom five (i.e., Connector, Healer, Problem Solver, Selector), it is impossible to say that some workleader roles were more challenging for these subjects than others or that some workleader roles were less developed in these subjects. If it is true that workleader roles are comprised of different sets of behaviors, then it may also be true that some of the questions or scenarios spoke to different skills within the workleader role. This may help to explain why the workleader role of Problem Solver could be associated with questions ranked #1 and #21 (out of 22 rankings).

The easiest question was #5 and is associated with Problem Solver. The most important issue for the Problem Solver is the customer or, in this scenario, the student. An effective workleader in English language education solves problems by attending to the needs of the students. An effective workleader makes certain to talk with staff later on, out of earshot of others. Solving student-related problems was the easiest role to fulfill for this group of subjects. We speculate that this is, in part, the result of the competitive nature of English language education. Students are similar to clients in the business world and other programs are seen as competition for these "clients." Consequently, putting students first is seen as a prime motivator for leaders in English language programs.

What then, makes question #12, which is also related to the workleader role of Problem Solver so much more difficult than question #5? In question #12, we asked:

When addressing productivity problems with your staff, the best way to start is by asking:

a.   How do you feel?

b.   What are you doing?

c.   Where's the problem?

Sixty-one percent of the respondents answered (a) *How do you feel?* as the correct response. There are two reasons that this response does not surprise us. First, leaders in English language education are humanists and most generally come from humanities and education backgrounds rather than from business or science backgrounds. We are concerned about other people, students, and staff. To focus on the individual and how they feel seems perfectly logical to us. In addition, Christison and Stoller (1997) have pointed out that most administrators in English language education learned to do their jobs much like apprentices in a twelfth-century craft guild. We learned on the job, through trial and error, with very little formal training. Without formal training and principles (e.g., a specific model such as Murphy's Leadership IQ) to guide us in the situation outlined in question #12, we fall back on our focus on individuals, feelings, and our concern for the well-being of students and staff. A basic principle for the Problem Solver in Murphy's leadership IQ model, is that an effective workleader focuses on the business, in this case, the program and on how to collect data to understand the issue, in this case productivity. In order to solve the problem, a leader needs to understand what the employee is doing because that is at the core of the issue of productivity. The data that are discovered become the basis for action the workleader takes to solve the problem. Therefore, the correct answer for #12 is (b) *What are you doing?*

The fact that workleader roles were quite evenly distributed throughout the rankings (i.e., Problem Solver is ranked both #1 and #21; Connector #2 and 19, and Healer #5 and #20) combined with the fact that a difficulty level was also apparent (i.e., there is a range in percentages all the way from 96.74 to 6.52), was unexpected. We had anticipated that workleader rankings and the difficulty rankings would be similar. In other words, we believed that it would be the skills related to workleader roles that would motivate the difficulty of the question. We expected to see some workleader roles ranked more difficult than others. This seems not to have been the result.

Murphy's Leadership IQ model seems deceptively simple at first glance. It is centered on eight roles that effective leaders play, and these roles are associated with a very clear set of skills and principles for each role. However, there are multiple behaviors and skills associated with each workleader role, so the model is more complex than one may expect it to be. It may be necessary to master several skills for each workleader role. It is possible for a leader or new administrator to develop competence in one skill associated with a workleader role but not with all of the skills associated with that role. Given that most of the leaders in this sample were new at their jobs with fewer than five years of experience, this explanation makes sense to us.

The second explanation has to do with how much the culture of educational practices most likely governed many of the answers given by these administrators. For example, the workleader role of Selector ranked both high with Question 8 and low with Question 27. Question 8 reads as follows:

You have just been hired as the director of an intensive English program. One of the instructors, Carlos, has been teaching in the program for over 15 years. In reading the personnel files, you notice that he had always received excellent student evaluations until the last two quarters. In your first meeting with all the faculty you notice that he seems withdrawn and unenthusiastic. You arrange to have lunch with each instructor to get to know them better. After some general conversation with Carlos, you say:

a. "You've clearly been an excellent instructor here for many years, so your last two semester student evaluations really seem odd. But, I don't want to talk about them first—let's talk about you. How do you feel about the program? About the students and your job?"

b. "You've clearly been an excellent instructor here for many years, so your last two semester student evaluations really seem odd. Let's go over all the students' comments and find out what's going wrong with your teaching."

c. "You've clearly been an excellent instructor here for many years, so your last two semester student evaluations really seem odd. When I see a sudden change like this, I get very worried. Perhaps it's time for you to think about a change. As you know, I do have to ensure the whole program provides excellent instruction for all our students."

The correct answer is (a) and 88.04 percent of the respondents made this choice, so it seemed that the group of respondents understood that some of the basic features of the role of the Selector, choosing the right person for the right job and retaining them in the job were clear. Why, then, did the respondents respond so differently on Question 27, which is also related to the workleader role of Selector? Question 27 reads as follows:

> To gather the most useful information from each applicant,
>
> a.   create a list of core questions to ask each candidate and use the same structure approach for each candidate
>
> b.   ask questions so the candidate will tell you their work history
>
> c.   use a loose format, allowing each applicant to focus on his or her strengths.

The correct answer is (b), but 62 percent of the respondents selected (a). The Leadership IQ model states that to select the best people, workleaders provide opportunities for potential employees to relate as much as possible about their previous experiences and responses to different work situations. Interviews, therefore, should not be intimidating, but they should be formal. While it may be superficially fair to each candidate to have core questions, such as outlined in 27 (a) and use the same structure for each candidate, such a rigid structure often means the interviewers do not learn as much about the candidate. The focus moves away from the main premise of the role of the Selector. This rigid structure is part of what public school and public institutions of higher education require in the U.S. and Australia, where most of the respondents were working. In fact, this type of interview structure has become part of the educational culture in the U.S. The interview becomes more about maintaining a certain process of equity, by asking all candidates the same questions, than about finding the right person for the job. In addition, in many countries and institutions, there are legal requirements to conduct interviews with each candidate in exactly the same manner. If this is the case in the country in which you work, it is important to have at least one question that is sufficiently open-ended for candidates to reveal their work behavior. This can often be achieved through asking a question that asks the candidate how they responded to a particular work event.

Cultural Influences

Since the numbers were small, we were unable to determine whether country of origin and country of work affect responses. With further data collection, we believe we could further untangle what influences leader responses.

Experience and Gender

In these data, we were unable to determine if years spent as an administrator and gender had an effect on questionnaire responses. We believe these two concepts could prove useful in understanding leadership development in English language education. If we use the Leadership IQ Questionnaire to collect additional data in the future, we will code the data in order to make this determination.

Conclusion

Educators have long known that some leaders and administrators are more effective than others. Yet what exactly characterizes effective leadership has been somewhat elusive. We believe that Murphy's Leadership IQ model can be a useful tool in helping us understand more about how leaders develop and what characteristics contribute to overall success. We encourage other researchers to consider the Leadership IQ model in their research and to continue to conduct research on effective leadership to help us understand more about effective leadership in English language education and more about the cultural dimensions of this leadership.

References

Belbin, R.M. (1993). *Team roles at work*. Oxford: Butterworth Heinemann.

Christison, M.A., & Stoller, F.L. (1997). *A handbook for language program administrators*. Burlingame, CA: Alta Book Center Publishers.

Gardner, H. (1985). *Frames of mind: The theory of multiple intelligences*. New York: Basic Books.

Gardner, H. (1985). *The theory of multiple intelligences*. New York: Basic Books.

Gardner, H. (1993). *Multiple intelligences: The theory in practice*. New York: Basic Books.

Goleman, D. (1998). *Working with emotional intelligence*. London: Bloomsbury.

Goleman, D., Cherniss, C., & Cowan, K. (n.d.). *Guidelines for best practice*. Retrieved February 18, 2007, from http://www.eiconsortium.org/research/guidelines_for _best_practice.pdf

Hofstede, G. (1990). *Culture's consequences: International differences in work-related values*. Newbury Park, CA: Sage.

Hofstede, G. (2001). *Culture consequences*. 2nd edn. Thousand Oaks, CA: Sage.

Marzano, R.J., Waters, T., & McNulty, B.A. (2005). *School leadership that works*. Alexandria, VA: ASCD and Aurora, CO: McREL.

Mayer, J.D., Salovey, P., & Caruso, D. (2000). Models of emotional intelligence. In R.J. Sternberg (Ed.), *Handbook of intelligence*. Cambridge: Cambridge University Press.

Mead, R. (1994). *International management*. Oxford: Blackwell.

Murphy, E.C. (1996). *Leadership IQ*. New York: John Wiley & Sons, Inc.

Chapter 15

How the Experience of Leadership Changes Leaders

Kathleen M. Bailey, Jaala A. Thibault, and David Nunan

Introduction

At the end of the 2001 TESOL Convention[1] in St. Louis, where Neil Anderson had just finished his term as President, David Nunan and Kathi Bailey took Neil and three recipients of TESOL Leadership Mentoring Award[2] out to dinner to celebrate the culmination of Neil's presidency. This celebration was a last-minute decision. We had no reservation and had to wait 40 minutes for a table at a crowded and noisy restaurant. We weren't served dinner until nearly 10 pm. The place was very loud and not conducive to quiet conversation. In addition, we all had to catch very early flights the next morning.

We talked through the meal about the experiences the three of us, Neil, David, and Kathi had had while serving as TESOL President. Just as the evening was winding down, Andy Curtis, one of the three Leadership Mentoring Award recipients, asked the following question: "Knowing what you know now, would you run for President again—not for a second term, but would you go through that experience again?" David, Neil and Kathi immediately responded "Yes!" and then burst out laughing and stared at one another in amazement.

We were all tired. It had been a long week and we all had early morning flights to catch. But we sat and talked for another hour about why all three of us would repeat an experience that had been so time-consuming, so taxing, and sometimes downright unpleasant. Being TESOL President is also costly. As members of the Board of Directors of TESOL, officers are expected to speak at numerous TESOL and TESOL affiliate functions, but cannot accept any payment for doing so (due to the association's conflict of interest rules). Likewise, the volunteer service to TESOL takes up so much time that there are few opportunities for consulting, writing, giving workshops, and so on.

Nevertheless, for all three of the Past Presidents at that dinner, the experience of serving as TESOL President had been so powerful and so enriching that we all agreed we would do it again. Why? That conversation is part of what spurred us to write this chapter. We wanted to collect data from other people who had served as TESOL President and see if they had had similar positive experiences. We also wanted to find out whether other Past Presidents felt they had developed as leaders through the experience of service to the organization. For these reasons, we decided to conduct the small-scale investigation reported here.

Research Questions

The research questions we addressed in this investigation are: (1) Does the experience of being TESOL President change the people who hold the office? (2) If so, how? (3) After the fact, how do the Past Presidents view the experience?

There are numerous reports in the literature about being effective leaders, and about how leaders can influence the people they lead. For instance, Christison and Murray (Introduction in this volume) state that "in transformational leadership, individuals are transformed in some way, and they produce results beyond their expectations." This seems to be a statement about the effect of leaders on their followers. However, we have not found many reports in our profession (language teaching) of how the experience of leadership has changed individual leaders.

One exception is Bailey's (2002) discussion of what she learned by being TESOL President. That paper reports on development in her interpersonal skills, management and leadership skills, professional communication skills, and time management.

Data Collection and Analysis Procedures

In order to answer the three research questions posed above, we drafted a brief questionnaire. We piloted the questionnaire ourselves first, amended it and then asked MaryAnn Christison and Denise E. Murray—the editors of this volume and themselves both Past Presidents of TESOL—if they would also complete it. They suggested some changes which we incorporated in the questionnaire before it was sent electronically to the other Past Presidents. See Appendix 15.1 on p. 253 for the revised version of the questionnaire.

The questionnaire consisted of both open-ended items and Likert-scale items, in which respondents indicated the extent to which they agreed or disagreed with four statements. The open-ended items yielded qualitative data and the four Likert-scale items yielded quantitative data.

Part of the questionnaire was influenced by Freeman's model of the constituents of teaching. Freeman's model defines four key constituents (1989, p. 36):

1 *Awareness* serves the function of triggering our attention to attitude, skills and knowledge.
2 *Attitude* is described as a stance toward self, activity, and others.
3 *Skills*, which constitute the "*how* of teaching," include our methods, techniques, activities, materials, and other tools.
4 *Knowledge* embodies "the what of teaching," which includes our subject matter and our knowledge of the students, as well as the sociocultural and institutional context.

Using these concepts, we asked the Past Presidents about their strengths and weaknesses when they began their term of service; about the significant challenges TESOL was facing at the time; about the knowledge and/or skills they had gained by serving as

President; and about any changes they had experienced in their attitudes and/or aware-ness. Finally, we asked each person if the experience of being President had changed him or her as a leader and a person (see Appendix 15.1).

Some literature on leadership (see, e.g., Gibb, 2004; Norman, 1993; Turner, 2002) cites various kinds of skills that leaders need. A distinction is made between "hard skills" or "technical skills" (such as accounting, auditing, and knowledge of business law) and "soft skills" (including communication, problem-solving, and teamwork). Both types of skills were addressed in the questionnaire.

At the time of this writing, there have been 40 Presidents of TESOL, four of whom are deceased. We sent the questionnaire as an email attachment to all the TESOL Past Presidents we could contact via email. For the others for whom we had contact infor-mation, we sent the questionnaire as paper mail, with a self-addressed stamped return enveloped included. A month later, a second request was sent to those who had not yet responded.

Two people declined to participate and 13 did not respond. In the final analysis, we had questionnaire data from 21 of the 36 living Past Presidents (a total of 58 percent). Thus, our data paint only a partial picture.

Self-report data presupposes a certain amount of self-awareness on the part of the respondents. Following Goleman (1998), Murray and Christison (Chapter 5 in this volume), have defined *self-awareness* as "knowing one's own internal states, preferences, resources, and institutions." These authors say self-awareness involves emotional awareness, accurate self-assessment, and self-confidence. The questionnaire elicited information about these issues.

As mentioned above, the questionnaire elicited both qualitative and quantitative responses. Both data sets will be addressed in turn, in the sequence with which they appeared on the survey instrument.

The open-ended data were partitioned into electronically stored data sets corre-sponding to each question on the questionnaire. The following findings emerged in our analyses of the respondents' open-ended comments.

Pre-existing Strengths and Gaps

First, the Past Presidents (the respondents) were asked to identify three strengths they possessed as they entered the office. Among the 21 respondents, leadership experience was the most frequently reported strength. One hundred percent of respondents mentioned that they had had previous leadership experience as they began their role as TESOL President. For instance, one respondent stated, "I had been a designer and planner in corporate structures where my philosophic and organizational knowledge contributed to critical functions and effectiveness."

The least frequently reported strength was experience concerning finance, budgeting, and management—the technical skills required to lead a large organization. Only two respondents said that they had had specific finance, budgeting, and manage-ment experience prior to becoming President. Others may have had such experience but did not report it as being among the three strengths they identified. One respondent stated, "I had extensive administrative and management experience in academic and political settings as department head, institute director, and president of a local political club." However, technical skills are not the primary factor in effective leadership (Goleman, 1998), so the perceived lack of such knowledge and skills may have little impact on the role of the President.

Other perceived strengths the Past Presidents identified included: (1) extensive experience with TESOL either as a member, a board member, or a president of a local chapter; (2) a strong desire and motivation to serve; (3) good organizational skills; (4) exemplary public speaking skills and a sense of humor; (5) knowledge of the field and professional experience; (6) administrative experience; (7) flexibility; and (8) international teaching experience. Items (2) and (4) have been found to be essential competencies for effective leaders (Cooper & Sawaf, 1997; Goleman, 1998). These data then indicate that these respondents had some of the competencies required for effective leadership prior to serving as President of TESOL.

Task 15.1

Think of someone that you respected as a leader. What strengths did that person possess that were qualities of a good leader? Could these strengths apply in any leadership position?

Next, the Past Presidents were asked to describe three gaps or deficiencies they felt they possessed as they entered the office. Among the 21 respondents, dealing with inter-personal relationships among and between board members and affiliates was the most frequently reported gap or deficiency. Nearly half (48 percent) of respondents mentioned that they felt under-prepared to deal with difficult people. One respondent said, "I was afraid of losing my temper when dealing with stupid people." Another wrote, "I was impatient at times with individuals and with the pre-occupation to focus on management issues and not membership issues." Since interpersonal skills have been found to be one of the key components for effective leadership, this finding indicates that TESOL Presidents may need additional on-the-job mentoring and training in such skills.

Another self-assessed deficiency had to do with time management. Nearly half (48 percent) of the respondents said that they were unaware of the extensive time commitment that the role of president required. One Past President wrote, "The job of TESOL President was (and still is) too big for one person to handle along with a full-time professorship and administrative duties."

The least frequently reported initial gap or deficiency that respondents reported was self-awareness. Only two respondents reported that they felt a deficiency in their self-awareness. Other perceived gaps and deficiencies included: (1) knowledge of or experience with finance, budgeting, and management; (2) difficulty saying no to people and not wanting to be the "bearer of bad news;" and—rarely—(3) becoming TESOL President without much experience with the organization. Again, self-awareness, one of the "soft skills," is an essential competence for effective leaders (Goleman, 1998).

From this self-report of strengths and weaknesses, we can see that TESOL Past Presidents overall believed they had many of the skills essential for effective leadership. However, the data also show that some of the Past Presidents felt the need for additional training in technical skills such as budgeting, time management, and running meetings, as well as some of the soft skills related to interpersonal relations.

Significant Challenges Facing TESOL

The Past Presidents were asked to describe one or two of the most significant challenges TESOL was facing at the time of their particular presidency. We posed this question partly to put their other responses in context. This item elicited a range of responses, some more predictable, some less predictable. The themes that emerged were: (1) budget and finances; (2) legal issues, (3) structural issues; (4) professionalization and association growth; (5) relationships; and (6) TESOL's interface with the profession at large. Each of these issues will be addressed in turn.

Budget and Finances

Not surprisingly, money was a major challenge for several Past Presidents. This problem was particularly true for at least two Past Presidents who served in the aftermath of the 9/11 attacks. Predicting how that event would affect the budget and developing contingency plans proved to be very challenging.

In addition to the outside world's effect on the actual budget of TESOL as an organization, some of the Past Presidents' apparent lack of experience with budgeting and finance may have affected their presidencies as well. Only two Past Presidents overtly identified their familiarity with budgeting and managing finances of a large organization as strengths at the beginning of their presidencies. Since financial resources determine (to some extent) what the organization can accomplish, this issue may have influenced other challenges as well.

Legal Issues

Getting the Association's legislative house in order was identified as a major challenge for several Past Presidents. One foregrounded it as THE major challenge facing TESOL during his/her presidency. This person wrote:

> The major issue TESOL faced was revising the constitution and by-laws because we were out of compliance with DC law . . . The revision brought into focus a host of issues around membership, finance, governance, etc., which led to the creation

of the Forward Plan. The key breakthrough in the process was the decision to ask the entire membership to vote on the revision which broadened access and decision-making.

Another Past President also identified the constitutional basis of the organization as a major challenge: "[My presidency] was a time of growth and change. We were in the midst of writing a new constitution while also experiencing rapid growth."

Interestingly, the theme of growth came up a number of times. Some Past Presidents were challenged by declining membership, while others saw expansion as a challenge. One identified numerical growth in the membership as the greatest challenge he/she had to face during his/her presidency.

Professionalization and Association Growth

More than one Past President identified the pressure to grow from a "Mom and Pop" association to a fully professional organization as a major challenge that they had to confront during their presidency. This resulted in tensions, not only between various Presidents and Central Office (CO) staff members,[3] but within the Board itself.

> TESOL continues to experience growing pains as it works through the stage of becoming a professional association with more of a policy orientation. Major progress was made in gearing the Board toward position statements on professional issues; yet the Board, in their understanding of member pressure, wanted to remain at an implementation level that is more appropriately delegated to TESOL's professional staff.

Not all the Past Presidents saw this change as a completely positive development. One reported that while the move to employ full-time, paid professional staff was on balance a good thing, it led to a loss of the "volunteer" spirit which had been a well-spring of potential leaders.

Developing the structural entities was also seen as a challenge by a number of Past Presidents. In particular, the TESOL affiliates (the organization's regionally defined entities) were mentioned by several respondents. For example, one person wrote:

> One of the larger challenges I felt was how we could nurture affiliates and TESOL at the same time . . . Just as we were beginning to make progress in regional conferences and networking, we were caught up in developing an international character and attitude.

Thus, these issues of professionalization and growth of the association proved a range of challenges to the Presidents. The picture that emerges upon reading their comments is one of an organization experiencing profound change.

Relationships

The topic of relationships was the theme that probably preoccupied the most Past Presidents. The theme is multilayered and multileveled, ranging from relationships with the Executive Director (ED) and CO staff members to relationships with the membership and entities within the organization.

The relationship between the President and the Board on the one hand, and the ED, on the other hand, was one of the most frequently mentioned challenges faced by Presidents from the earliest days of the association through to the present day. For several Presidents, the relationship with the ED was particularly challenging, either because of conflicting views over the role and responsibility of the ED, or because the association was transitioning from one ED to another during the President's term in office. As one Past President stated:

> The major challenge was the balance between the decision-making authority of the . . . Board and the Executive Director. As TESOL grew, issues became more complex and there was a feeling that more decisions should be made by the Board rather than the Executive Director.

Relationships with the members and with various TESOL entities also featured in the data. One Past President wrote:

> Several dedicated TESOL leaders had undertaken initiatives they felt were good for TESOL. Some of these initiatives were very costly and some were potentially quite dangerous for TESOL. I had to negotiate the delicate interactions among the Board members, these leaders (who didn't have the full picture), and the ED. Trying to be fiscally and legally responsible to the organization's membership as a whole and not discourage (or enrage) those leaders was often a very skinny tightrope to walk.

Thus, relationships within the Association were frequently perceived as problematic and difficult. This sentiment was expressed by one Past President in this way:

> There was great distrust of the Board of Directors by those below, both the entities and committees, and the general membership. It was perceived that governance was too top down. . . . There was also great distrust on the Board itself . . . Members of the Board felt that they were shut out of decision-making and the Executive Committee/Executive Director had little faith in the rest of the Board.

From these data it is clear that relationships between the full-time Executive Directors of TESOL and the part-time volunteer leaders were sometimes strained. For this reason, we suggest that leadership training programs address the management of this complex partnership.

Interface with the Profession

The interface between the association and the profession, as well as interactions with other professional associations, such as NABE (the National Association of Bilingual Educators in the U.S.) was another theme running through the comments we received in this section of the questionnaire. The following quotes give some idea of the kinds of interface issues that TESOL Presidents faced:

> [A critical area] when I stepped into TESOL roles had to do with certification, licensure, and hiring criteria of those in our profession at all levels.

> [The TESOL] organization has a broad and varied constituency in which it is very difficult to make everyone happy: researchers don't find it academic enough; teachers don't find it practical enough; EFL sees too much ESL; Higher Education sees too much about kids; Elementary Education sees too much about adults.

> We were facing the need to expand the organization to include ESL teachers from all levels, from all countries, and providing them with useful information on a regular basis.

Not surprisingly, the data yielded by the prompt concerning challenges faced by Past Presidents are complex and multifaceted. In this section we have grouped these responses into several themes. These challenges included financial and legal issues, as well as concerns about the professionalization and growth of the organization, relationships within TESOL, and the interface of the association with the profession at large. Of all the challenges identified by the Past Presidents, the one that stands out concerns roles and relationships with Central Office staff in general and with the Executive Directors in particular.

The Past Presidents' self-reports of their own strengths and weaknesses coming into the position (discussed in the previous section) identified both technical and soft skills that were needed. It appears that the issues challenging the association during their presidencies also demanded a mix of the technical and soft skills of leadership.

Task 15.2

Think about an organization in which you have been a leader in the past. Were there any challenges facing that organization? How did you adjust your style of leadership to face those challenges and move the organization forward?

Based on your experience and your reading to date, what types of information or tasks would you suggest to help leaders deal with organizational challenges?

Changes in Skills and Knowledge

The questionnaire also included an item which asked about the knowledge and/or skills the respondents may have gained as President. Some clear patterns emerged from these data as well. For instance, eight of the Past Presidents (38 percent) said they learned about financial and/or legal aspects of leading a large association. In addition, eight of the Past Presidents noted that they had learned about specific issues in organizational management. These included the skills of negotiating, building consensus, getting the best out of Board members, and running effective meetings.

Four people (19 percent) wrote about some aspect of time management, such as prioritizing or delegating tasks. One wrote, "You have to prioritize your goals as a leader; otherwise you can be carried along by others' agendas." Three respondents specifically mentioned learning about strategic planning and/or forward planning.

Some people commented on learning about teachers' lives and needs. For instance, one Past President wrote "Attending many affiliate board meetings and sessions at affiliate meetings made me very knowledgeable about what issues teachers faced and what the professional trends were at the time." Thus traveling to affiliate conferences—both in the U.S. and elsewhere—could be an educational experience in terms of understanding the field better.

Some contrasting viewpoints emerged. For instance, different Past Presidents learned different things about working with the Executive Director (which is not surprising, since there have been various Executive Directors over the years). One person wrote that he or she had learned "ways to work with an organization in which the Executive Director was a very powerful figure and who did a LOT for the organization but for whom the organization was getting too big to handle it all."

Another Past President wrote:

> I found that just as a small city's progress depends more upon the abilities of a trained city manager than on the background of the Mayor, who is there for a short time and should restrict his/her involvement to policy matters, the President of TESOL, who is in that position for only one year, should have the same limitations.

This is an apt analogy since the Presidents serve for a set period of time, but the Executive Director's period of appointment is indefinite.

Changes in Attitudes and Awareness

Next, the respondents were asked if there were any ways that being TESOL President had changed them in terms of their attitude(s) and/or awareness. The responses to this prompt were varied.

While most of the Past Presidents (95 percent of the respondents) stated that the experience had changed their attitudes or awareness in some way, one Past President stated, "I am basically the same person that I was before I became president."

Most frequently, Past Presidents reported that their awareness and attitudes towards volunteerism within the organization had changed for the better. For example, one Past President wrote:

> I also became aware of the incredible dedication of TESOLers around the world, of the strength and depth of commitment to the profession and TESOL, and recognized that I was really a part of an international community of learners and teachers.

The following bullet points summarize other comments concerning changes and shifts in attitudes and awareness:

- One respondent reported that she became aware that leadership skills are learnable.
- Two respondents reported developing better listening skills and having more patience.
- Four respondents said the experience has made them better and more effective leaders in general.
- Three respondents reported the experience forced them to be more aware of time management skills and prioritizing.
- Two respondents reported that they became emotionally stronger.

One of our favorite quotes in the data came from a Past President who wrote that he or she had learned an important lesson: "Take the job seriously, but don't take yourself seriously."

Changes the Past Presidents Experienced as Leaders and People

Finally, the last item asked, "Given your answers to the questions above, how did the experience of being TESOL President change you *as a leader and a person*, if at all? Please write a paragraph or two." Three areas of change emerged from the data: (1) personal/affective issues; (2) procedural/organizational issues; and (3) interpersonal/communication skills.

Personal/Affective Issues

The great majority of Past Presidents (95 percent) reported overall that being President was a positive experience which had changed them for the better. They reported that the experience of leadership often led to increased confidence and enhanced self-awareness. Three Past Presidents highlighted the fact that they were shy, and that the experience of being President had helped them to be more assertive, outgoing and confident. (The word *confidence* appears more frequently than any other term in the data.)

Only one respondent out of 21 reported a negative personal effect. He or she wrote that the experience of being TESOL President "made me cynical for one thing—cynical about trying to do the right thing in the face of so many personal agendas."

Procedural/Organizational Issues

Not surprisingly, several respondents said the experience of being TESOL President had led to enhanced procedural and organizational skills. These included how to run meetings tightly and effectively, how to manage complexity, and how to deal with conflicting issues. Many respondents mentioned that, while they brought organizational and managerial skills to the position, the presidency enabled them to hone and refine those skills.

Interpersonal/Communication Skills

Several Past Presidents referred to the fact that their term as President enabled them to develop their interpersonal skills. Some said that they learned to be less critical of those whose opinions diverged from theirs, to be more indirect, to see that "leadership is all about people and that people skills are vital for effective leadership" and that leadership necessarily involved teamwork. The experience also led some to be more assertive. As one respondent reported, "[I have become more] assertive and clear about roles and responsibilities. I am now quite blunt in saying 'no' to suggestions or silly requests."

Communication skills that were enhanced by the presidential experience included presentation skills, the ability to listen, and problem-solving skills. Exposure to diverse audiences, particularly international audiences, enhanced communication skills and led to a great appreciation of diversity and complexity. For instance, one Past President noted, "I learned how much more complex international organizations are to manage/direct than those that are national or local."

Many of the personal and/or professional changes Past Presidents identified in themselves as a result of their TESOL leadership show that they learned or developed many of the essential soft and technical skills on-the-job. This finding can be seen as problematic if it is viewed as a deficiency of these leaders. On the other hand, this learning and development could be considered normal, and could even be seen as a benefit of taking on leadership responsibilities.

Task 15.3

Think of someone whom you see as a good leader. List five characteristics of that person. After you have listed those characteristics, discuss with a colleague why they are characteristics of a good leader. Compare the characteristics that you listed with the strengths identified by the TESOL Past Presidents whose comments are cited in this chapter.

Analysis of the Quantitative Data

The final part of the questionnaire consisted of four items asking the respondents to indicate the extent to which they agreed or disagreed with each statement, using a Likert-scale format. The Past Presidents responded using a scale on which 1 represented "strongly disagree" and 7 represented "strongly agree." In this analysis, we treated the Likert scale data as interval data, so we could calculate means and standard deviations.

The aim of these quantified analyses was to see what sorts of divergence and convergence there were in the Past Presidents' responses to these four statements. There are, of course, debates about whether rating scale data should be treated as ordinal or interval. Following Hatch and Lazaraton (1991), we used a relative long (seven-point) scale to generate interval-like data (see also Turner, 1993; Busch, 1993). In addition, the Past Presidents were asked to "assume equal intervals between the numeric values" so that we could justifiably assert that we had created equal intervals between scale points. The results are shown in Table 15.1.

From these results we can see that people reported that they gained new knowledge (Item 11) and skills (Item 12), or developed existing skills (Item 12). We can also infer that for the most part, the experience of serving as TESOL President was generally positive (Item 13). It is interesting to note that on Item 14, the statement about running for the office of President again, one person provided a rating of 1, indicating strong disagreement with the desirability of serving as President. However, 12 respondents gave ratings of seven, indicating strong agreement with this statement.

Discussion

We began this investigation with three questions, which were informed by Freeman's (1989) discussion of awareness, attitude, knowledge, and skills. The patterns that emerged in the responses pertinent to each of them will be addressed briefly here.

Table 15.1 Leadership Questionnaire: Likert-scale Item Data

Item	Mean	S D	N
11. By serving as TESOL President, I acquired new knowledge.	6	1.45	20
12. By serving as TESOL President, I acquired new skills and/or developed existing skills.	6	1.12	21
13. Overall, serving as TESOL President was a positive experience.	6.3	.73	21
14. Knowing what I know now, if I had the chance to be TESOL President again (not for a second term, but for a first term), I would choose to run for office again.	5.9	1.73	20

The first question was, "Does the experience of being TESOL President change the people who hold the office?" According to these self-report data, we can confidently say yes: Most of these respondents did experience changes in many areas. (Only one person out of 21 said he or she had not changed.)

The second question asked, "If so, how?" The answer to this question is that, with some variability, most of the Past Presidents reported changes in their skills, knowledge, attitudes, and awareness. Although one person did report that he or she was "basically the same person" before and after being TESOL President, all the other respondents provided answers to the various open-ended items about change. In fact, some wrote copious comments about their reflections. It may be that self-reflection is important in leadership development, just as it is in professional development for teachers. Perhaps completing this questionnaire served as a reflective experience for the Past Presidents who responded.

The third question asked how the Past Presidents view the experience of serving as TESOL President after the fact. For the vast majority of the 21 respondents, the experience was quite positive. As shown in Table 15.1, the responses to the statement, "Knowing what I know now, if I had the chance to be TESOL President again (not for a second term, but for a first term), I would choose to run for office again" were very positive. The mean response for this item was 5.9 on a seven-point scale. The standard deviation (1.73) is the largest reported for the four Likert-scale items. However, as noted above, although one person rated this item with a 1 (the strongest possible disagreement), 12 respondents gave it 7, indicating the strongest possible agreement.

The fact that some of the changes Past Presidents reported were acquired "on-the-job" suggests that there may be a place for more formal mentoring and training in leadership skills. While TESOL has embarked on a program for leadership training for future TESOL leaders (not only future presidents), many of the skills emphasized are technical in nature. It may be useful, therefore, for TESOL to invest in training in the soft skills of emotional intelligence as well (see especially Chapter 5 by Murray and Christison).

Of course, these findings are based on data derived from only half of a very small population. Relatively few people (40 in all at the time of this writing) have served as President of TESOL. Of the 36 living Past Presidents, only 21 (58 percent) responded to this questionnaire. It may be useful to learn about whether (and if so, how) the experience of holding other leadership roles has influenced other individuals in our profession.

Empirical research on leadership (Murphy, 1996) influenced Murray (this volume, Chapter 1), who writes: "Leadership can be defined and measured as a form of intelligence, but it is an intelligence that is only activated through experiences, and then only if the person learns from those experiences . . . So then leadership is essentially learning." It appears from our data that many of the TESOL Past Presidents who responded to our questionnaire did indeed learn from their experiences.

We close this chapter with a quote that seems to characterize the learning-from-challenges which many of our respondents experienced:

> As people . . . recall two or three of the most important learning experiences in their lives, . . . they will never tell you of courses taken or degrees obtained, but of brushes with death, of crises encountered, of new and unexpected challenges and confrontations. They will tell you, in other words, of times when the continuity ran out on them, when they had no past experience to fall back on, no rules or handbook. They survived, however, and came back stronger and more adaptable in mind and heart.
>
> (Handy, 1990, p. 11)

Notes

1   "TESOL" is the acronym for "Teachers of English to Speakers of other Languages Inc." This is an international professional association with over 14,000 members worldwide. (For information, visit www.tesol.org)
2   TESOL's Leadership Mentoring Award is a program for developing leaders within the association. Its purpose is to encourage non-native speakers of English, persons of color, and teachers in primary and secondary schools to engage in leadership activities in the association.
3   The TESOL association is governed by an all-volunteer Board of Directors elected by the membership. The board creates policy, which is then enacted by the paid professional staff, including the Executive Director and the Central Office staff members.

References

Bailey, K.M. (2002). What I learned from being TESOL president. In J. Edge (Ed.), *Continuing professional development: Some of our perspectives* (pp. 32–38). Whitstable: IATEFL.

Busch, M. (1993). Using Likert scales in L2 research: A researcher comments. *TESOL Quarterly, 27* (4), 736–739.

Cooper, R.K., & Sawaf, A. (1997). *Executive EQ: Emotional intelligence in leadership organizations.* New York: Grosset/Putnam.

Dörnyei, Z. (2003). *Questionnaires in second language research: Construction, administration, and processing.* Mahwah, NJ: Lawrence Erlbaum Associates.

Freeman, D. (1989). Teacher training, development and decision making: A model of teaching and related strategies for language teacher education. *TESOL Quarterly, 23* (1), 27–45.

Gibb, J. (2004). Generic skills in vocational education and training: Research readings. Retrieved January 22, 2007, from http://www.ncver.edu.au/research/proj/nr2200.pdf

Goleman, D. (1998). *Working with emotional intelligence.* London: Bloomsbury.

Handy, C.B. (1990). *The age of unreason.* Cambridge, MA: Harvard Business School Press.

Hatch, E., & Lazaraton, A. (1991). *The research manual: Design and statistics for applied linguistics.* New York: Newbury House.

Murphy, E.C. (1996). *Leadership IQ.* New York: John Wiley and Sons, Inc.

Norman, D.A. (1993). *Things that make us smart: Defending human attributes in the age of machine.* Reading, Mass: Addison-Wesley.

Turner, D. (2002). Employability skills development in the United Kingdom. Retrieved January 21, 2007, from http://www.ncver.edu.au/research/proj/nr 1004.pdf

Turner, J. (1993). Another researcher comments. *TESOL Quarterly, 27* (4), 736–739.

Appendix 15.1

Leadership Questionnaire for TESOL Past Presidents

Dear Past Presidents,

We are writing a chapter for a book edited by MaryAnn Christison and Denise E. Murray about what we learn by being leaders. We are asking TESOL's past presidents to respond to the following questions. Doing so takes about 15 to 20 minutes. We would really appreciate your help in responding to this brief questionnaire. Thank you!

Kathi Bailey and David Nunan

===

1. Your name (to be kept confidential in the report):

2. Years you were TESOL President:

3. Who was the TESOL President immediately before you?

4. Who was the TESOL President immediately after you?

5. What would be three **strengths** you had as you entered the role of TESOL President? That is, at the beginning of your term, in terms of your experience, training, and/or personal attributes, what were three positive characteristics you brought to the job?

6. What would be three **gaps or deficiencies** you felt you had as you entered the role of TESOL President? That is, at the beginning of your term, what were three areas of your experience, training, and/or personal attributes that might have worried you about carrying out the role of TESOL President

7. Please describe the **one (or two) most significant challenge(s) TESOL was facing**, as an organization (not as the profession at large) when you became president? Please write a paragraph or so for each challenge you choose to describe.

8. Please list the three most important things you learned as TESOL President. Please think in terms of **actual knowledge or/or skills** you gained.

9. Were there any ways that being TESOL President changed you in terms of your **attitude(s) and/or awareness**? If so, please describe them in a paragraph.

10. Given your answers to the questions above, how did the experience of being TESOL President change you **as a leader and a person**, if at all? Please write a paragraph or two.

Please respond to the following Likert scale items. Assume equal intervals between the numeric values. I = Strongly disagree and 7 = strongly agree. (You may eliminate all the numbers except your choice, underline your choice, bold your choice, etc.—whatever procedure makes it easy for you to reply.)

11. By serving as TESOL President, I acquired new knowledge.

    Strongly Disagree   I   2   3   4   5   6   7   Strongly Agree

12. By serving as TESOL President, I acquired new skills and/or developed existing skills.

    Strongly Disagree   I   2   3   4   5   6   7   Strongly Agree

13. Over all, serving as TESOL President was a positive experience.

    Strongly Disagree   I   2   3   4   5   6   7   Strongly Agree

14. Knowing what I know now, if I had the chance to be TESOL President again (not for a second term, but for a first term), I would choose to run for office again.

    Strongly Disagree   I   2   3   4   5   6   7   Strongly Agree

15. Please make any other comments you would like to make. Thank you!

Chapter 16

Developing Servant-Leadership Skills Through Cooperative Development

Juliet Padernal

Introduction

I come from an academic culture where class visits by supervisors are generally welcomed; however, many of these visits are also threatening and dreaded occasions. Dreaded and threatening because these visits are associated with evaluation —and evaluation implies some form of rating or ranking of performance either of an individual teacher or the organization as a whole or both. Most teachers, if not all, become very tense and nervous in these situations. While this is perhaps a normal reaction when we know that somebody influential is observing and evaluating our performance, it is so pervasive that it is not healthy and thwarts professional development.

Another dimension to this negative attitude toward traditional supervisory activities is that they seem to be rushed, superficial, and perfunctory. It leaves the teacher with a feeling of no involvement, maybe dissatisfaction, or maybe a feeling of "I wish there's more that I could do!"

When I was a schoolgirl, I grew up sensing this tension and nervousness whenever there were visitors from the education department in the provincial district where my school belongs. Now that I am a teacher educator myself, I find that the atmosphere has changed very little, if at all. This negative attitude toward supervisory visits has been so ingrained in the culture that it is difficult to excise. It is ironic because the term "super-visory" carries with it a note of guidance and nurturance. Supervisory visits should not be threatening situations but should be welcome opportunities for professional growth. The negative associations attached to this academic activity have obscured its general aim of improving instruction. Even if some department heads do try to find time to give positive, supportive feedback to the faculty, these perceptions remain.

What, then, can academic administrators such as department heads do to greatly minimize, if not totally eliminate, these pervading negative thoughts and feelings towards supervisory visits that have great potential for professional benefit? How can academic heads whose responsibilities include faculty supervision and evaluation deepen and expand the processes of accountability? How can teachers be empowered for their own professional growth? What tools or strategies are available?

What is Peer Coaching?

In this chapter, I describe a supervisory activity that I have tried practicing called peer coaching, which I used as the basis for peer review. I find these professional development activities rewarding not only for my colleagues but also for me. They are facilitative of my aspirations to practice servant-leadership. According to Nelson (1996, n.p.) "Servant leadership is about a group of people mutually submitting to each other for the purpose of achieving something they could not achieve alone." Larry Spears, CEO of the Greenleaf Center for Servant-Leadership (quoted in Chase, 2005, n.p.) provides a summary of the basic position of servant-leadership: '[It] seeks to involve others in decision making, is strongly based in ethical and caring behavior, and . . . enhances the personal growth of workers while improving the caring [atmosphere] and quality of organizational life.' Nelson strongly posits that first and foremost, the type of motivation a leader has is what makes one a servant-leader, not temperament, strength, or energy. The motivation of the servant-leader is to "unleash the potential of the [group members] and primarily benefit the organization."

Peer coaching as a professional development activity is truly servant-leadership. In peer coaching, educators "consult with one another, to discuss and share teaching practices, to observe one another's classrooms, to promote collegiality and support, and to help ensure quality teaching for all students" (Association for Supervision and Curriculum Development, electronic version, n.d.). Edge (1992, 2002) calls such strategies "cooperative development"—personal professional growth through cooperation with colleagues in order to become a better teacher.

My opportunity to practice peer coaching and peer review came upon me quite suddenly, when I became chair of the English and Literature Department of Silliman University in the Philippines. Although a peer coaching and peer review program has yet to be established and institutionalized in my workplace, I wanted to try these strategies out for myself as a way to encourage professional development among the teachers. One need not be a department head or an academic staff supervisor to engage in peer coaching. It only requires usually two teachers (sometimes three) coming together, sharing in conversations, and reflecting on and refining their practices. In this way they learn and grow together in a non-threatening, non-evaluative environment that fosters a relationship built on confidentiality and trust (Gottesman, 2000; Rogers and Threatt, 2000). However, as department head I also have to exercise my evaluative responsibilities for the improvement of instruction. How can I do this in a non-threatening atmosphere? I have to couple peer coaching with peer review, an effective way of ensuring quality teaching and helping teachers improve (Hutchins, 1994; American Federation of Teachers and National Education Association, 1998).

In this chapter, I will describe peer coaching as a form of peer review as an example of what Edge (2002) calls cooperative development. These concepts all imply that individual teachers can have power over their own professional growth by understanding better their own experiences and judgments and enriching them with the understandings and experiences of others through cooperation (Edge, 1992, 2002).

My Experience with Peer Coaching

My own experience with peer coaching and peer review is not very extensive although I intend to pursue the practice. Nevertheless, I have already seen positive results with the colleagues I tried these strategies out with in my own department. To introduce the idea, I informed my colleagues that when I do classroom observations, I was not going primarily as an evaluator but as a peer or as a mentor. Then I shared what I had learned about peer coaching and peer review work and presented the observation procedure I adapted using the peer coaching principles. I have roughly categorized the department faculty into three priority groups: the young and new teachers with temporary status (first priority); the not so new with regular status but who need assistance based on performance evaluation (second priority); and the teachers with a track record of quality teaching (third priority).

Let me describe the procedure I followed. The activity is divided into three phases: Pre-observation, during-observation, and post-observation.

Pre-observation

So far, I have worked with colleagues from the first two categories, but with more from the first. Before I go to observe a class, I invite the teacher to have a pre-observation conference with me. I sit down with the teacher and ask what aspects of his/her teaching he/she would like to improve. These could be on questioning techniques or patterns, "stage demeanor" (e.g. eye contact, voice modulation, movement round the classroom), or classroom management matters, among other things. I also ask how he/she feels about classroom observations/visits by academic heads or even a co-teacher. Invariably, the answer is that it makes them nervous, or they feel threatened or intimidated. I then tell my colleague that I understand exactly what he/she means because I have experienced it myself. Afterwards, I review the procedure with the teacher and reiterate that I am not there primarily to evaluate—not to make judgments and rate his/her performance—but to observe and note down my observations that we are going to discuss in the post-observation conference.

During-observation

As much as possible, I walk with the teacher to the room and stay from start to the end of the class. I sit at the back inconspicuously so as not to disturb the students. Also I ask the teacher not to introduce me to the class for the same reason. In my notebook, I jot down as much as I can hear, see, or sense, focusing on the delivery aspect we have identified previously. I have to take great care not to write anything judgmental or any notes that contain the word "should."

Post-observation

The post-observation conversation is usually done as soon after the observation as possible. I usually start with the "feeling" by asking my colleague how he/she felt about my presence in his/her class. Then I invite him/her to go over my observation notes together. Although this exchange is supposed to be non-judgmental, I suppose appreciating the obvious good points won't do the procedure any harm. I mention this on the premise that peer coaching is a non-evaluative or non-judgmental activity, but the word "appreciation" connotes a judgment—of the positive kind, however.

I have to be very careful about the items that need improvement as identified by the teacher and that the teacher would like to talk about. I must respect my colleague's choice of what to talk about even if during the observation, I saw something that I thought really needed to be addressed immediately. I also have to be careful how to say a comment or a question so that the conversation encourages my colleague to reflect on and analyze the teaching-learning event and come to helpful realizations him/herself. I have to take extra care not to point out an "error" or offer a solution straight away! I mustn't say, "This is what you did; you should have . . . " Or "This is what you said; you shouldn't have . . . " I have to take extra care not to impose my own standards and values on my colleague. To do this, I need to listen intently yet actively; I have to help my colleague articulate his/her reasons for doing something in a particular way. I have to let my colleague know that I want to hear his/her ideas and will value them.

In practicing peer coaching, I employ facilitative questioning—open-ended questions that encourage the speaker to say more. In the process of listening and facilitative questioning, I also exercise empathy. I try to understand the teacher's views about teaching and learning, the specific learning situation, and the student composition of the class. Through my conversation with the teacher, I try to enter his/her world and walk in his/her shoes. Again, I have to be sincere and honest in my interaction with the teacher, and be aware that in listening and empathizing, I don't do it to understand the teacher and gain insight into his/her world so that I can bring him/her round to my own way of doing things. On the contrary, I have to let my colleague know that I understand his/her problems and difficulties and how these encumbrances are affecting his/her life—his/her beliefs and aspirations as a teacher.

I would have liked to enrich this article with a recorded conversation from my peer coaching attempts with colleagues whose classes I had the privilege of observing, but unfortunately I have not recorded them. However, below is some "cooperative development data"[1] that I'm using with the kind and encouraging permission from the author, Julian Edge to illustrate a peer coaching interaction (Table 16.1). I have annotated it according to Edge's (1992, 2002) cooperative development terms of Exploration (attending, reflecting, focusing); Discovery (thematizing, challenging, disclosing); and Action (goal-setting, trialling, planning). Not all of these speech acts are represented in this short discourse data; nonetheless, it serves its illustrative purpose.

Table 16.1 Peer Coaching Interaction

Text		Annotations
Speaker	Okay, talking about feeling annoyed and frustrated, I face a problem lately with giving instructions in class. For some reason, the children just don't seem to take any notice. I try to carry out the lesson in English as much as possible, and then when it comes to the, let's say, homework, comes to the point of telling them what to do for homework . . .	*Good opening for exploration* *Reflecting* *Focusing*
Understander (Listener)	Just to get this straight, you mean the Junior classes?	*Indicates Attending*
Speaker	Yes, the problem is worse with A Preliminary and B Preliminary, the first classes.	*Reflecting* *Focusing*
Understander	The first classes, yes, and you've got a problem because they don't get the instructions . . .	*Focusing*
Speaker	Yes, it seems that they don't understand what is said, or they don't listen to what is said—I can't decide what is what.	*Towards Discovery*
Understander	And you say that you speak English to them?	*Attending; Focusing*
Speaker	Ah, yes, I try, as much as possible, I could say, to speak in English, though lately, to save time, I suppose, I explain their homework in Greek. But even in Greek, if I say, 'Chapter 35,' as soon as I say that, someone says, "Chapter 34?" Or "I didn't hear that, say again!"	*Reflecting* *Focusing*
Understander	You mean there is a problem here with the class . . .	*Discovery: Challenging*
Speaker	Yes, they just don't . . . however I say it.	*Discovery*
Understander	You mean in Greek? Even in Greek?	*Focusing*
Speaker	Yes, even in Greek, they don't, they don't follow. There's something I'm not doing right here, I think. I find this such a waste of time and I end up shouting, "Can't you understand? Listen!"	*Discovery: Disclosing* *Not easy to admit own fault or inadequacy*
Understander	So, you think it is you who is to blame?	*(Clarifying)*

Table 16.1 Continued

Text		Annotations
Speaker	Well, funnily enough, we have another teacher and I wanted to watch, to observe her, and at the end of the lesson she explained in Greek very clearly what the homework was, and from my position at the back of the class I saw the same thing. Immediate she said it, the children said, "What have we got?"	Disclosing Seeing someone else in the same boat gives a feeling of "I'm not alone in this." And having admitted own part in the problem— feeling of catharsis
Understander	Did this give you any thoughts? I mean, did it make you think of any other ways to do that?	Challenging
Speaker	Mmm, maybe it's a question of classroom management really, that we need to establish some rules, perhaps: "Right! Now we're going to give the homework instructions, everybody must pay attention!" Mmmm, or perhaps if I could write it on the board and say, "This is what you have to do." And they could, they could follow, they could write it down, they could copy it down, yes, maybe that's a good idea, to stop the confusion caused by the oral explanation of the instructions.	Thematizing—positive turn action

Planning |
| Understander | So, you think the confusion is caused by the oral explanation of the instructions? | Challenging: clarifying |
| Speaker | Eh, it certainly is a part, a major part, yeah, I think it is. I think that's right. I need to try it. I do write on the board sometimes, but I'm not consistent. Mmm. Maybe that's the problem, then, I am not consistent about it and they don't know what to expect. Mmm, that could be a discovery there! (laughs) | Planning

Reflecting; Disclosing |
| Understander | You mean, every time, the same thing . . . | Challenging: Clarifying |
| Speaker | Yes. OK. So, five minutes before the end of each lesson, they know, "Now the teacher is going to tell us the homework so I must pay careful attention." Maybe that's the way they see it. And maybe I could ask how they do it at their regular school, and see if there's anything I could learn from that situation. | Planning

Visualizing

Planning (leading to Goal-setting and Trialling) |

Where do Servant-Leadership Skills, Practice and Development and Cooperative Development Through Peer Coaching and Peer Review Meet and Journey Together?

Now we are returning to the concept of servant-leadership. My aim in this next section is to provide a more in-depth framework of how peer coaching and peer review are excellent examples of servant-leadership in action. As I see it, personal professional development through collegial cooperation is a very firm ground for servant-leadership development.

I have noted that the underlying principles of servant-leadership are highly in sync with Covey's (2004) seven habits (see Chapter 2, this volume for a discussion of Covey's work) that emphasize personal development to obtain effectiveness in an organization. Similarly, Edge (2002) in the course of his work on cooperative development found that the principles governing teacher-to-teacher, pair work mode are also applicable to group work and development that, in turn, support individual development. Furthermore, such positive group dynamics greatly increases workplace collegiality that has great potential for both individual and organizational development.

Spears (in Barbuto, Jr. & Wheeler, 2002; Hampton House 2003) considers the following features to be the core of servant-leadership: listening, empathy, healing, awareness, persuasion, conceptualization, foresight, stewardship, commitment to the growth of people, and building community. Barbuto, Jr. and Wheeler added a further characteristic of willingness to sacrifice self-interest for the benefit of the group.

From my point of view, the commonalities of principles between cooperative development and servant-leadership lie in *listening, empathy, stewardship*, and *commitment to the growth of people*. I strongly suspect, however, that given more detailed examination, intersections and parallels may also be found in the other principles, since by and in themselves, servant-leadership principles or characteristics are all inter-related. Listening with respect and empathizing with sincerity and honesty can be seen directly in the cooperative development interactions in the transcript above. I also illustrated these strategies when I described the peer coaching activity I have used with my colleagues. But as an aspiring servant-leader, I would like to identify, particularly from the pre-observation and post-observation conversations, some movement toward stewardship and commitment to growth.

From the perspective of servant-leadership, stewardship refers to the "desire [of the leader] to prepare the organization to contribute to the greater good of society" (Barbuto, Jr. & Wheeler, 2002; Hampton House, 2003, p. A-15). (see also Anderson's Chapter 7 on leading from behind). To determine if we have stewardship potential as a servant-leader, Barbuto, Jr. and Wheeler invite us to ask ourselves whether people believe that we are preparing the organization to make a positive difference in the world. To gauge if somehow I have some germ of stewardship in me, I personalize the question: Am I making a positive difference within the sphere of my work for the good of the Department, the College, and the University? And since an organization, big or small, is made up of individuals, I then ask myself: Am I able to touch lives such that I contribute to the honing of the skills and the development of these individuals?

The non-threatening and non-evaluative conversation between me and my colleagues in peer coaching as a cooperative development activity is a highly conducive environment for stewardship. I believe I am exercising stewardship when I listen, and listen with respect and understanding, to my colleague articulating his/her thoughts and feelings about any of the items I have noted in my observation notebook. I believe I am touching lives when I try to empathize with sincerity and honesty, and in so doing encourage my colleague to reflect on and analyze his/her teaching practice. To paraphrase the ancient philosopher: Reflection and analysis make life worth living. Reflection and analysis enable the teacher to see what needs improving and what action to take. This enabling process, I believe, keeps the teacher from mediocrity and stagnation. And when the individual is enabled or empowered, then the organization to which he/she belongs will also be empowered. Let me call this the *building block principle*. Edge in fact uses cooperative development as the framework of empowerment, that is, trying to move forward based on one's own understanding.

Moreover, I believe that in cooperative development as in peer coaching and peer review, I am manifesting and acting on my commitment as an aspiring servant-leader to help my colleagues develop and grow professionally, personally, and spiritually. Again, the peer coaching interactions are invaluable. Through this channel, I can convey my belief that this person has something to offer beyond his/her tangible contributions. I can convey that I care about this person's developmental needs, and that I will actively find ways—within the power inherent to my position as department head—to meet these needs.

I have to be careful, however, that as a peer and mentor, I honor the confidentiality and trust on which peer coaching is built. This foundational principle sits well with the spirit of servant-leadership in which the "desire to make a difference for other people . . . and to pursue opportunities to impact others' lives—never for their own gain" (Barbuto Jr. & Wheeler, 2002, p. A-15). My motivation, as an aspiring servant-leader, in helping colleagues develop and grow through cooperative development should be to serve the interest of the other person, not self-acclamation. Thus, I must keep sensitive matters that may arise from peer coaching interactions confidential. In addition, I must not crow about what or how I have helped a colleague particularly in the context of cooperative development. Doing so would be the quickest way to destroy trust and confidence in the partnership.

In my experience with peer coaching and peer review (albeit not yet extensive), I have already seen affirmative and encouraging results among my colleagues with whom I have worked. I gathered this not only from my own observation but also from their feedback about the activity. And so, despite the main constraints of time, we try to fit peer coaching into our schedules.

At Silliman University, there is a system of evaluating faculty performance using a four-pronged evaluation instrument: Student, Peer, Self, and Superior (direct head or supervisor). In this measuring tool, performance is rated on a scale of 1–5, in which 1 means Poor and 5 is Excellent. In my view, apart from student evaluation, cooperative development activities can greatly facilitate performance evaluation by Self, Peer, and Superior. Insights gained from the interactions add substance, credibility, and reliability to the evaluation results. The superficiality and perfunctoriness that tend to be associated with filling out an evaluation form that has to be done once a year are surely reduced. This is the peer review benefit of peer coaching, of cooperative development.

Finally, I hope that in the bigger context of my academic culture where teachers are threatened and intimidated by supervisory visits, teachers and administrators alike will be open to the possibilities and will be supportive of cooperative development activities such as peer coaching and peer review.

For an aspiring servant-leader like myself, to see my colleagues, whose lives I have somehow touched, experiencing positive changes because they have been empowered in their teaching practice would be enough reward and reinforcement to pursue servant-leadership through cooperative development.

Note

1   These data demonstrate peer coaching in action to help the reader understand the principles I try to follow in my peer coaching.

References

American Federation of Teachers and National Education Association (1998). *Peer assistance and peer review: An AFT/NEA handbook.* Washington, DC: AFT & NEA.

Association for Supervision and Curriculum Development. (n.d.). *Peer coaching.* Retrieved June 2, 2007 from: http://webserver3.ascd.org/ossd/peercoaching.html

Barbuto, J.E. Jr., & Wheeler, D.W. (2002). Becoming a servant leader: Do you have what it takes? Retrieved June 2, 2007 from http://www.ianrpubs.unl.edu/epublic/live/g1481/build/g1481.pdf

Chase, M. (2005). Brief overview of servant-leadership. Retrieved June 2, 2007 from: http://old.quincy.edu/academics/genassem/info.php/15

Covey, S.R. (2004). *The seven habits of highly effective people: Restoring the character ethic.* New York: Free Press.

Edge, J. (1992). *Cooperative development: Professional self-development through cooperation with colleagues.* Harlow: Longman.

Edge, J. (2002). *Continuing cooperative development: A discourse framework for individuals as colleagues.* Ann Arbor, MI: University of Michigan Press.

Gottesman, B. (2000). *Peer coaching for educators.* Lanham, MD: Scarecrow Press.

Hampton House, Butler University (2003). *10 principles of servant-leadership* (electronic version). N.P.: Author. (Date accessed: April 18, 2005).

Hutchins, P. (1994). Peer review of teaching: New roles for faculty, *AAHE Bulletin, 47* (3), 3–7.

Nelson, A. E. (1996). Servant leadership and a servant leader versus a servant leader. From *Leading your ministry.* Retrieved June 2, 2007 from: http://www.teal.org.uk/Trainingbox/Servant%20Leadership.pdf

Rogers, R.K., & Threatt, D. (2000). Peer assistance and peer review. *Thrust for Educational Leadership, 29*(3), 14–16.

Index